QUEEN OF THE
BREMEN

The Autobiography of Marlies Adams DiFante

Written with Ann Marie DiFante

QUEEN OF THE
BREMEN

*The True Story of an American Child Trapped
in Germany during World War II*

iUniverse, Inc.
Bloomington

Queen of Bremen

The True Story of an American Child Trapped in Germany during World War II

iUniverse books may be ordered through booksellers or by contacting:

iUniverse
1663 Liberty Drive
Bloomington, IN 47403
www.iuniverse.com
1-800-Authors (1-800-288-4677)

Because of the dynamic nature of the Internet, any Web addresses or links contained in this book may have changed since publication and may no longer be valid. The views expressed in this work are solely those of the author and do not necessarily reflect the views of the publisher, and the publisher hereby disclaims any responsibility for them.

ISBN: 978-1-4502-5129-7 (sc)
ISBN 978-1-4502-4968-3 (e)
ISBN: 978-1-4502-4967-6 (hc)

Printed in the United States of America

iUniverse rev. date: 2/6/2012

Affectionately dedicated to my children:
Kathy, Tony, David, and Tommy.

I hope you'll learn that no matter how bad things become, there's always light at the end of the tunnel. As long as you have faith in God, respect, and love for each other, you can make it—no matter what.

I have been extremely fortunate to be blessed with all the good things life has to offer. I had the best brothers, the kindest parents, a remarkable extended family, and of course good friends.

I married a wonderful man and together we've created our own beautiful family. I would gladly give up anything in my possession to keep them safe, and for all of this, I thank God for the blessings he has bestowed upon me and my family.

—Marlies Adams DiFante

Contents

Introduction

In the spring of 1939, a letter arrived from Germany stating that Opa, my grandfather, was terminally ill. He had already undergone two operations for stomach cancer, and his doctor said there was nothing more he could do. Opa was slowly dying, carrying Mama deep into the depths of sorrow. Unbeknownst to me, she was pregnant at the time with my baby brother and had become physically ill, which compounded her troubled thoughts that she might never again see her father.

It had been seven years since she gazed into the eyes, felt the tender touch, or heard words of wisdom from the family she yearned for day after day. Attempting to be true to the young family she had created in America, she was deeply torn between the two. She had grown to love the husband she was committed to, although she silently resented him for taking her an ocean away from the kinship she pined.

The doctor informed Papa that the illness plaguing Mama was depression, primarily due to homesickness, and if she didn't return to her homeland, we could lose both her and the baby. Knowing his beloved wife needed closure with her father before cancer devoured him, Papa faced an impossible situation.

Hitler had come into power; Germany was in dire straits; and yet the decision was made to leave New York and head overseas to free Mama and the baby from danger. Little did we know that what was intended to be a three-month stay would turn into seven years of living hell. With Poland coming under attack, World War II began, and all ports and borders were closed, prohibiting our family from leaving the Nazi-controlled country. The atrocities and prejudices we endured are forever burned into my memory.

1
Papa

My story begins with John Adams, born in 1892. He was one of seven siblings, but only ever spoke of two brothers; Nick and Peter and an older sister called Lena. The family lived in a small farmhouse in Oberemmel, a quaint village in the Rhineland of Germany. The land surrounding the house consisted mostly of vineyards, and the grapes produced supplied a meager income for their large family. As the children grew older, they helped work the vineyard out of necessity. It was a big job. Their mother, Anna, needed a great deal of assistance tending to the small plot of earth as she found herself sadly married to a cruel man who refused to lend his support and, more important, a helping hand.

Rather, her husband's efforts were focused in a much different place. He was the proprietor of the local tavern, and as the owner-operator, he led a two-bit, raunchy lifestyle in which his alcoholism flourished. Virtually any time of the day or night, he could be found at the bar where whatever profits his wife earned from her tiny vineyard were quickly swallowed in support of his drinking habit, leaving the family deficient in more ways than one.

The children were subjected to constant beatings as they grew and often witnessed their softhearted mother enduring the same abuse. As time passed, their father frequently reeked of booze and became increasingly violent. As a result of his cold-heartedness, self-indulgence, and lack of affection for his family, the children had no respect for him or his way of life.

Violence and fear became part of young John's life, and the simplicity of childhood slowly dissipated with every beating he sustained. As he came of age, John began to recognize how sorrowful and lonely his mother had become. He desperately yearned to ease his mother's pain. Trying to make light of the situation or telling jokes from time to time were only temporary distractions; her smile would quickly fade.

Standing five feet and eleven inches and weighing 150 pounds, John's thin build and chiseled face were a reflection of his youth and, despite a nonexistent childhood, he grew up to be a decent, hardworking, and handsome young man. Attempting to make a better way of life for himself, he finished school and attended a university where he studied the processing and planting of grapes. It was a business he knew well: the wine business.

During his course of study, he was called to serve in World War I as a non-commissioned officer in the cavalry. He instructed Turkish troops in warfare and was wounded twice in action, including once when he was shot in the head. While recuperating from that excruciating injury, he received word that his brother Peter had also been wounded in the war. However, the injuries that Peter sustained were life-threatening, and he never recovered.

The loss of Peter was devastating to John. The special bond built during their childhood and shared into their adult years had come to an end. He felt as though he had not only lost his brother, but his best friend. Peter, unfortunately, had felt the brunt of the abuse, and John had taken it upon himself to provide guidance and affection while protecting him from their father's heavy hand. The two had shared their hopes, dreams, and their innermost thoughts, and now there was a void he could never fill. Although he loved his other siblings, his relationships with them were never close. In fact, his ties to the others slowly faded over the coming years, and the relationship he shared with Lena would end many years later violently and abruptly, in a fit of rage.

Recovering from his injuries and heartbroken over the loss of Peter, John had no choice but to move on with his life. After the war ended, having filled him with knowledge and life experience, he found a position working as a teacher in a government-owned vineyard. The school was located in the town of Aachen Hausen, on the Rhine River; a place he would always feel was one of the loveliest parts of the district.

John was charged with overseeing a class of fifty students, and he enjoyed his work tremendously. The pay was sufficient, but due to inflation, the German mark was of little value; every bit of what he earned was spent during the coming week. After paying room and board and purchasing his necessities, he was left with nothing at the end of the month. The inability to save money was discouraging for John and most of the men he worked with. Some of his co-workers spoke of opportunities and high-paying jobs in the United States. They talked about the demand for workers and teachers with their knowledge and expertise. Night after night, their conversations turned to the land of opportunity.

John listened intently to the stories of how a man could become rich by knowing how to teach others his trade. During one such conversation, he uttered a few words that would change the course of his life. "I have an uncle who lives in the States, and I am going to contact him to obtain a visa." He had made up his mind to dare to dream. His friends secretly wished they could conjure the same courage, but with envy, they wished him luck. In 1923, with the financial help of his uncle, he packed what little belongings he had, bid farewell to his family, boarded an ocean liner, and departed Germany, bound for America and what was sure to be a better way of life.

In America

After days of traveling to the mysterious foreign land, John moved in with his uncle in Oregon and found a position at the Mission of the Divine Worth, a catholic school where he continued working for two years teaching wine making. During that time, he taught many of the students to speak German and in return they taught him English. Between the young priests and nuns at the mission and listening to play-by-play baseball on the radio, he was a quick study of the language and became a big fan of America's favorite pastime. John was happy in Oregon for a short while, but the novelty soon wore away. Besides, his uncle turned out to be as hardened and cruel as his father.

Even though he worked long hours to repay his debt for the trip across the ocean, it seemed the amount he owed decreased ever so slowly, and with no room in the main house, he was forced to take up residence in the barn. It was not exactly or even remotely close to how he imagined his new-found life to be. When he dared to dream, his visions never included sleeping in anyone's barn. He was willing to pay his dues, but in the back of his mind, he knew change was imminent.

Priding himself on being a man that always kept his word, he remained living under the less-than-stellar conditions until every dime he owed was paid in full. Afterwards, John saved his earnings and began making plans. Although he appreciated what his uncle had done for him, he decided to leave Oregon and the sooner the better.

His new destination: New York. He traveled to the Upstate area where he found a position working at Saint Michael's Mission on Conesus Lake. The mission, better known as the Bishop's Farm, was run-down and in desperate need of repair. His job was to bring the vineyards back to order, so the grapes used to make communion wine for Sunday mass could be produced. It was a dream come true, and the break he had been working diligently toward.

He was living in the land of opportunity and although the pay was not as much as he had expected, John was proud to be making a difference. His experience and knowledge brought the once depleted vineyards back to life. The harvest of grapes that year was tremendous and his hard work appreciated. John's innovative techniques revitalized the land that had been forgotten.

Continuing to teach the priests, together they cultivated the land he grew to love. John also focused his attention on a much grander goal. In 1929, he reached that goal as he received his citizenship papers, becoming an official United States citizen. His smile stretched across his face, exuberant. This was what he had dreamt of, what they had all dreamt of six years earlier back at the government-owned vineyard in Aachen Hausen.

By the following year, he had saved enough money to travel back to Germany to visit his mother, who was finally beginning to succumb to years of abuse. He was proud to return home and share the stories of his experiences as a new American with his old friends and family. He had been home for a few weeks, visiting his ailing mother, when some friends introduced him to the most beautiful woman he had ever laid eyes upon. Elisabeth Hans was soft-spoken and petite with dark hair and blue eyes. In one glorious instant, he fell deeply in love and immediately summed her up as gentle and caring, the kind of woman he must get to know.

She was working as a seamstress, and she was a master of her trade. She had many customers and kept extremely busy. Nevertheless, the two made time to get acquainted. Every moment they spent apart, he dreamt of their next rendezvous. He could think of little else.

Elisabeth was smitten with him as well, and they truly enjoyed each other's company. After dating a few times, she invited him to her hometown of Kell, near the city of Trier, to meet her family. The trip to her lovely village, nearing the border of Luxemburg, gave them ample opportunity to get to know one another. John was delighted to go and meet the family he had heard so much about.

Anxious to see Elisabeth and meet her new beau, her parents, five brothers, and five sisters gathered to greet them at the family home. Being warm and hospitable, they welcomed John one by one, making him feel a part of their family, something he had longed for. As the day wore on, his mind wandered; he pictured a family of his own that loved and respected one another and imagined how wonderful life would be with Elisabeth by his side. All he had to do was ask for her hand in marriage. He was one question and one answer away from true happiness.

After spending a fair amount of time growing closer to Elisabeth and her family on the farm, and realizing that his trip was nearing its end, John believed the perfect moment had arrived. Nervously, he turned to her and proposed. "I love you Elisabeth. Will you marry me? I promise to make a beautiful life for us in America."

As far as she was concerned, the question came out of nowhere. She responded nervously, "I barely know you, and you want me to cross an ocean to live in a strange land? No. I'm sorry, John, but I can't do that."

Devastated, he approached her father, hoping that he'd agree with the proposal and change his daughter's mind. However, to John's dismay, Herr Hans responded in kind.

"No. John, I won't try to change her mind. I wouldn't let any of my daughters cross that ocean and travel so far away, especially not Elisabeth."

Feeling completely dejected, he asked her, "If you won't be my wife, could I at least write to you when I return to America?" She agreed, believing no harm could come of it. Upon returning home, he immediately began his correspondence. He wrote from his heart, hoping to touch hers an ocean away.

As the letters arrived, Elisabeth was overwhelmed. His handwriting was impeccable, and she was amazed by how intelligent and thoughtful he was. Even though she had turned down his marriage proposal, deep down she missed him and waited patiently for his letters to arrive.

Days turned into weeks, weeks into months, and as time slowly passed, John had all but given up on a life with Elisabeth. With his mother only days from death, he knew he would most likely never return to Germany.

John's mother, however, knew in her heart how much John loved Elisabeth. She also knew, as a mother, that she should do everything possible to bring the two of them together. She sent a telegram to Elisabeth asking her to please come visit her, as she had something of extreme importance to discuss. Elisabeth responded, telling her that she would come as soon as possible. Upon her arrival, at first sight, she realized how very ill John's mother was.

Mrs. Adams spoke bluntly: "I have a very serious question to ask you, and I hope that you will give me the right answer. I'm not going to get well, and I'm asking you as a last dying wish, to please agree to marry my son. He's a good man, and he'll be kind and gentle to you. I'm positive that you will learn to love him as much as I do. He is alone in America, but with you, he'd be complete. And that would be all I could hope for."

Elisabeth sheepishly replied, "I'm sorry but I can't do that. John seems like a wonderful man, and I love the letters he sends, but he's still a stranger to me. I cannot cross an ocean and marry a man I barely know." His mother began sobbing. When Elisabeth saw the tears on the face of a dying mother, pleading with her, she couldn't bear it. "Please don't cry. I'm sorry." She tried to explain the situation but failed to make her understand.

In that moment, Elisabeth reached out and touched the dying woman's hands. With tears swelling in her eyes, she promised to marry John. A smile crept across Mrs. Adam's face, and she blessed Elisabeth as she held her tightly. She wept, "Now I can die in peace, thank you my daughter." Two days after the promise was made, John's mother passed away. She was finally at peace and free from her sorrow-filled existence.

Elisabeth left Oberemel and returned home feeling burdened with the promise she'd made. Before she knew it, six months had passed, and still she couldn't bring herself to forget the words she had spoken. Night after night, she'd lay awake in bed thinking of her promise to a dying mother, yet how could she bring herself to leave her beloved family and move so far away? "I would die of homesickness. I just couldn't master this," she thought to herself. "But how could I break my promise? I gave her my word."

Elisabeth tried to put the conversation out of her mind, but the words taunted her every waking moment, and returned at night to haunt her dreams. Unable to untangle her inner turmoil, she sought her father's opinion and came to a decision. As much as he hated the idea, he felt that being a person of your word was non-negotiable. Promises were not meant to be broken. In fact, they couldn't be broken when made to someone on her deathbed. Agreeing with her father, and truly believing she'd remain in a desperate plight if she didn't tell John what had occurred, she sat down and wrote the letter that would alter the only existence she had ever known.

After receiving the long, detailed letter, John could not believe the words before his eyes. He learned of his mother's request, and in keeping with the promise, she went on to write that if it was still his wish, that she would indeed marry him. John was shocked and overjoyed. He immediately replied that he would return to Germany and marry Elisabeth.

Upon John's arrival, plans were swiftly made for an impromptu wedding. It was a bittersweet moment for Elisabeth as they prepared to become husband and wife. The marriage ceremony was scheduled to be held in Kell on July 26, 1932, with Elisabeth declaiming, "It is the will of God that I should marry this man."

The wedding day was as beautiful as any little girl dreams of. It seemed as though the whole town gathered to attend the mass. The sun was shining and John was beaming. His dreams had come true, and all of his prayers had been answered. The most beautiful woman he had ever crossed paths with was moments away from being his bride.

The church was decorated with the most fragrant flowers. As a surprise to John and Elisabeth, Mr. Hector, the organist had gathered flowers from all of the homes in town, from which the people contributed gladly. They were pure white, and looked like little white stars all in bloom. Her youngest sister, Ida, took her role as flower girl with great earnestness. She was only five years old and the quintessential vision of beauty. She wore a lovely white, long-sleeved frock, ankle socks with patent leather shoes, and a charming white bow in her hair. She carried a bundle of fragrant, white flowers nearly half her size.

In Germany during the thirties, it was tradition for the bride and all the attendants other than the flower girl to wear black. Elisabeth followed tradition to a T, wearing a floor-length, black gown with white trim at the scoop of the neck. Her jet-black hair was pulled back tightly and adorned with a gorgeous, white, flowing veil, trimmed with lace that trailed far behind her as she glided like an angel across the floor.

John was also dressed exquisitely in his dark suit and high-collared, button-down, white shirt and top hat, the only difference from the other men in attendance was that John was not wearing a necktie, making him stand out.

Elisabeth's mother and father also wore black and, perhaps in their minds, it signified their mourning the loss of their precious child who in a matter of weeks would leave them indefinitely. Regardless, Elisabeth's mother looked beautiful in her long flowing black dress, and her father exuded an aura of dignity. Wearing a fabulous top hat that must have been eight inches tall, he was smartly dressed in a bright white, high-collared shirt and dark necktie. Maintaining his composure under a perfectly tailored suit, he stood proudly next to his daughter as the organist filled the air with the most jubilant tones.

Elisabeth began her march down the aisle. John waited patiently at the end, his heart overflowing with love for his beautiful bride. At the end of the journey, she faced him, and the ceremony began.

The choir sang a high mass, and the first-grade children read a touching poem for the couple at the altar. John was amazed at what was happening, at how his bride was loved not only by her family, but by all the townsfolk. His eyes clouded with tears while the two exchanged their wedding vows.

A beautiful reception followed the wedding. Family photographs were taken, good food and wine consumed, and for the first time in public, Mr. and Mrs. John Adams were introduced. It was a wonderful chance for everyone to get together and enjoy each other's company. A good time was had by all, and afterwards, the couple thanked everyone, including Mr. Hector, the organist. John handed him five silver coins, saying, "This is for all you've done to make our day so special, and I thank you."

In the weeks that followed, Elisabeth spent time tying up her affairs and visiting all whom she'd miss once she departed for America. With an uncertain future, she truly didn't know if she'd ever return home, so she tried to make the most of her remaining days. Adding to the family's despair, another daughter would also soon be lost to the convent. Elisabeth's sister Rose had chosen to dedicate her life to the Lord, and would depart a couple days before Elisabeth.

On September 3, a little more than a month after the wedding, a dismayed Elisabeth and a jubilant John prepared to board an ocean liner, as newlyweds bound for the United States. Elisabeth's father, sister Clara, and brothers Peter and Bernard saw them off at the dock. They held her close, all crying bitter tears. They couldn't imagine a loved one traveling to a strange country, and each wondered if they'd ever see one another again.

One by one, they said their goodbyes. Her father was last. Brokenhearted and somewhat regretting the decision he had helped her make, he hugged her closely as they both wept. She was gasping for air, trying to catch her breath, and wiping her tear-filled eyes, when softly he whispered, "God bless you always, and I will say a prayer for you every day. You will always be on my mind and in my heart, as I don't know how I will ever learn to endure this loss. I have many children, but losing one, especially you, is unbearable."

Heartbroken Elisabeth kissed her father, turned away with her head down and boarded the ship, secretly hoping someone would yell, "Stop! Don't go! Please, Elisabeth, don't go." But no one did.

The trip to the United States was supposed to take seven days, but on the third morning, a storm of colossal magnitude struck, and as the waves rolled under the ocean liner, Elisabeth became violently seasick. The wind and waves crashed over the rails for two solid days and nights. It was a treacherous storm the likes of which she had never experienced. Being confined to their cabin was a fate not nearly as awful as watching passengers grip railings and doorways, anything to keep them from being hurled overboard. People were lying everywhere, covered with vomit, unable to make it to a lavatory. Terrified, with no land in sight, she didn't think that they'd ever arrive safely, but miraculously the waters calmed, and on the *ninth* day, they anchored in New York City Harbor.

She had heard about America, but never imagined that it could be as vast as it was. Beyond the Statue of Liberty and Ellis Island, the buildings went as far as her tear-filled eyes could see. It couldn't have been any more different from her tiny village of Kell. The hustle and bustle of the big city was overwhelming, and she was glad to finally board their train and leave the commotion.

From Manhattan, their train traveled Upstate, to the smaller city of Rochester, New York. It was a long ride and Elisabeth had plenty of time to think about what she had just done. It was finally sinking in that she was not just a married woman, but one married to a man she barely knew. On top of all that, she was without her loving family whom she had grown accustomed to having near her side. Elisabeth had never felt the pain of loneliness as she did at that moment.

The newlyweds' journey reached its end when they arrived back on the Bishop's farm and moved into the little white farmhouse John had rented. After unpacking and settling-in the best she could, Elisabeth needed to keep busy, so while her husband worked the vineyards, she did all the cooking for the thirty priests who resided in the main house.

She enjoyed the priests very much and was grateful to them for sponsoring her trip to the United States, so she eagerly sought their approval. It was a big responsibility, monopolizing most of her time. Regardless, she remained homesick and yearned for the family she left behind. There were no women for companionship or conversation, compounded by the fact she didn't speak English. She tried to learn, and John feverishly tutored her, but it didn't happen over night. In the meantime, she continued to feel disconnected and lonely.

Fortunately, her family was concerned about her well-being and curious about America, so letters from home were delivered nearly on a daily basis. Not a single week passed without at least four or five letters from Germany. Her sisters, brothers, friends, cousins, and especially her parents wrote. Their words kept her going. They told her of the happenings that occurred during the weeks that passed, and for a brief moment, she'd feel at home again. Laughing while sharing their experiences became the highlight of her day.

As John prayed for a solution to ease his young bride's turmoil, God must have been listening, because her loneliness subsided when they were blessed with a baby boy born in the spring of 1933. They named him Peter Philip, and the love she bestowed upon him was immeasurable. His mere presence filled the void within her and gave her comfort. He was everything she needed, the greatest gift she could have received. She thanked God every day for her beautiful baby boy.

Taking care of her newborn was paramount; she tended to his every need, never regretting the crying or the sleepless nights, but it became difficult for her to maintain her other responsibilities. Ultimately, her job on the Bishop's Farm became too much; cooking for thirty priests and taking care of her household was overwhelming. John recognized that she was struggling and began looking for new employment for himself and a new home for his family. One of the priests on the farm knew how homesick Elisabeth had become and offered John a solution. He told him about a town called Naples, also in upstate New York that reminded him of the small villages in Germany. He suggested she might feel more at ease in a place that felt more like home. Additionally, he mentioned that Widmer Wine

Cellars in Naples was hiring, and John was perfectly suited for a position there.

It so happened that while John was attending university in Germany, where he'd learned about cultivating grapes, he met a gentleman named William Widmer, the son of the owner of the very wine cellar of which his friend was speaking. John traveled to the winery and spoke with the Widmers.

William indeed recalled John from Germany and offered him employment, along with the opportunity to rent a small white house on West Avenue. The countryside was breathtaking—rows of vineyards gracefully lined the beautiful hills surrounding the town in every direction. The area reminded John of his hometown, and he felt sure it would give Elisabeth a small piece of the home she'd left so far behind.

The Family Grows in Naples

Naples was a closely-knit community where the people knew and looked out for each other. German was the primary language spoken amongst the first generation immigrants who made up the majority of the small town. They also brought with them the values and traditions of their homeland, making Naples the perfect place for the young couple to raise their new baby.

John's instincts were correct. After making the move to Naples, his wife blossomed, it was indeed a little bit of home. Making friends easily and communicating with the villagers in her native tongue, she came alive, and for the first time since she arrived in America, she finally felt at ease.

Though their little house was humble, with squeaky doors, cracking floors, chipping paint, and general repairs needed throughout, it suited them perfectly. It had a wide front porch with four pillars supporting the roof overhead. The large widows were decorated with shudders that matched both the screen door and the lattice that wrapped around the bottom of the porch. Two steps down, the sidewalk was completely surrounded with plush grass for the baby to romp on, while Elisabeth, watched from a rocking chair with a comfy handmade pillow, surrounded by the many plants and flowers she had randomly placed in clay pots.

Upon settling in, she purchased a sewing machine and began sewing for her newly found friends and neighbors. Her work was uncompromising: whether repairing old clothes or making new ones, it didn't matter. She could study an item and duplicate it effortlessly without using a pattern. She used precise measurements, so when the item was complete, it fit perfectly. She became quite popular with the ladies in town looking for the perfect outfit.

Word quickly spread, and soon just about everyone in town was asking for her services. Although she sewed to earn money, she also sewed for poor families, who often weren't charged anything. If she noticed someone in town with a hole in their clothing, she'd ask them to bring her the item. If they replied they couldn't afford to have the garment fixed, she'd smile and say, "That's okay. I'll fix it, and you can pay me some other time."

Certainly, Elisabeth still yearned for her family, but she seemed happy to be in Naples. The quaint little town and the people who lived there gave her a taste of home. Simple conversations with neighbors who had also left their families behind gave her the strength she desperately needed to carry on in America.

The following spring, 1934, John and Elisabeth had their first and only daughter. They named me Maria Elisabeth Adams. My full name was often pronounced quickly as one word, Mariaelize, and then shortened to Marlies. Thankfully, my family life was much different from that in which my father had been born into. Our home was filled with love, affection, and gentleness from the very beginning.

Mama was building a family and couldn't have been happier— though from time to time she still had obstacles to deal with, like my tummy not agreeing with breast milk. Luckily, she realized that the one thing I could tolerate was goats' milk, so they purchased a goat from one of the farmers on Rhine Street.

Our goat had long, brown and white hair, floppy ears, brown eyes, and a short nubby tail. Mama milked her daily so I'd have proper nourishment, which made everyone happy … except the goat.

She had been moved out of her comfort zone and was terrified of the train that turned around on the railroad tracks behind our house. The rumbling that increased as the train moved closer, along with the shrill of the whistle, sent her into a frenzy. To alleviate her fears, my parents always made sure that her stall door was open, so she could run into the shed as the train approached, and find shelter.

However, one Sunday morning while rushing to get to church, they forgot to open the stall door. When we returned from mass, our next-door neighbor, Mr. Blier, rushed over yelling, "John, if you'd like your goat back, she happens to be in my dining room!" Our poor goat had nowhere to run. She had become so petrified with the sounding of the whistle that she broke loose from her rope, ran across the yard, and jumped through the Bliers' window, landing smack in front of their dining room table. Miraculously, she wasn't hurt beyond a few scratches.

Needless to say, the Bliers were shocked and not too happy. Papa replied, "I don't know what to do with that goat. Marlies doesn't need the milk any longer, and I just don't know how to get rid of her."

That night, Mr. Blier and Papa concocted a plan to take our goat past the railroad tracks and deposit her over a fence into Mrs. Bowles's back yard, and so they did. The next day an ad appeared in the evening paper stating that someone had lost a goat, and would they please come and claim it. If no one answered her ad, she was going to give it to one of the farmers up on the hill. Papa and Mr. Blier were happy to get rid of her, and likewise, I'm sure our goat was happy to be as far away from the locomotive as possible.

As we grew older, my brother, Peter, and I had become best friends. He was a joy to be with and there wasn't one minute that I thought I could spend without him. Unlike our poor father, we enjoyed every pleasure that childhood had to offer. Every single day, we played to the point of exhaustion. Our childhood had a beautiful beginning with everything we needed to be happy and healthy. We even had a mutt named Moxy who spent most of his time chasing us in circles. Wherever we went, he was never far behind. We also had the cuddliest black kitten whose favorite spot was perched on our shoulders purring in our ears. Because of her color, we naturally, but not too creatively, called her Blacky.

Occasionally, Papa took time out of his busy workday to take us for walks into town. If we were lucky, and he had a few extra pennies, a piece of rock candy was never out of the question. Mama also made time to take us for walks into the beautiful hills that surrounded our town. She taught us about many different plants and birds, making the time we spent together in the hills a wonderful learning experience.

Life in Naples was wonderful. It was a town that we couldn't help but love living in. There were friendly, beautiful people, and we had such fun each day. Since my brother couldn't say Marlies, he called me Dee-Dee. Dee-Dee in German means something very small. I couldn't say Peter, so I called him, Booby, meaning, little boy. Instead of Marlies and Peter, we were known to everyone in town as Dee-Dee and Booby, everyone that is except Papa, he called me Marushka. Why, I have no idea. If he wasn't calling me Marushka, I was Snooks. I think it was his way of showing me affection. Even though he was strict, I knew he loved me immensely. He had a special place in his heart for both of us, but for some reason I think I was a bit more special to him.

Peter, likewise, was very close to Mama, and although I knew she loved me, she loved him a bit more. It didn't bother me—he *was* special. Peter was neat, obedient, and never got into trouble. While he could always keep his clothes nice and clean, I was just the opposite. Finding a mound of dirt to play on, or a mud puddle to stomp in even on the driest of days was what I lived for. If I didn't have dirt on my face or on my clothes and shoes, I didn't have fun that day. Not Peter; he was always impeccable. He would come to the dinner table with the same clean clothes he had put on that morning.

Peter was extremely cautious when it came to germs, and nothing could change his mind. If anyone picked up his glass and took a drink, it would be the last time he drank from it. If you tried to eat from his fork, or pick from his plate, then he'd go hungry that night. When we went to other people's homes, the same rules applied, and then some. If they offered him some type of snack, he politely refused. He wouldn't accept anything, from anyone. Occasionally, I admit I was guilty of indulging in his share from time to time. Why not? But I never took advantage of Peter's issues with cleanliness or poked fun at my brother. I loved him too much.

As a young girl, the world was my teacher and I always had to know why things were. I will never forget my first encounter with a woman who appeared different from me. One afternoon while grocery shopping at the Red and White store, Peter and I were in awe of a young, black woman standing behind us in the checkout line. I kept staring at her and asked in German, "Mama, why is that woman all black?"

She replied, "God made her that way because he loved the color. Just as God makes the sky and sunsets different colors; we have dogs and cats and cows that are different colors; and God made people different as well. He made some people black, some people white, some people yellow, and some people reddish, but he made them all because he liked each color. That doesn't mean that he likes one more than another. He loves everyone and everything equally."

Since we had spoken only in German, Mama explained to the woman what I had asked and what she had said in reply. The lady went into her shopping cart and took out a package of cookies handing one each to Peter and me. I took mine and thanked her, but of course, Peter refused his. The woman looked a little upset, but Mama explained how Peter didn't take anything from anyone; it was just the way he was.

I asked what she had told the woman and Mama translated. After which I told her that I was quite hungry and sure that I could eat two cookies, if she wanted to get rid of the other. Mama again interpreted, and the woman was nice enough to hand me the other cookie, and I again thanked her. She gave me such a nice warm smile, and I returned it. Peter continued to stare, but she gave him a smile just the same.

Christmas in Our German American home

Christmas was approaching, and our Christmases were quite different from the traditional American celebration. As children, we never knew the fat man with a white beard and red suit. We knew

Saint Nick the Bishop. In Germany, when Christmas arrived, no one came down the chimney. Our Saint Nick was dressed like a Bishop wearing a big hat. Walking with a huge staff, he came to the front door, bringing with him an angel and a little guy named Knecht Ruprecht, a servant carrying a pouch on his back filled with sticks.

It was customary for parents to sneak a slip of paper outside the door with all of the sins their children had committed throughout the year. The angel would read the list to determine if we were worthy of receiving anything special. Every year I was amazed at how many sins we had committed that we didn't think anyone knew about, but somehow, Saint Nick knew.

If our sins outweighed our good deeds, instead of getting a gift, we'd get a stick. Needless to say, around Christmastime I worked on trying to be a little better. Despite everything, we always got a little something for Christmas, and I can't remember ever receiving a stick. Every year we'd cross our fingers just the same.

One Christmas in particular, Saint Nick came to our home and brought Peter a little red wagon and brought me a doll. She was a replica of the Dionne quintuplets that were born in Canada the same year I was. I loved my beautiful little doll; she meant the world to me. I never got mad at her even if her clothes became soiled from playing with me. She drank from a small bottle and wet her pants exactly the way a baby sister would. Mama made diapers for her, and gave me a small tub, so on Mondays when she washed our clothes, I could wash my baby doll's. Papa made me my own little clothesline and carved clothespins from the trees in our yard so I could hang her diapers on the line just like Mama did.

Peter enjoyed his wagon, and we found dozens of uses for it. Sometimes we tied our dog, Moxy, to the front with a long rope, and he'd pull us down the sidewalk for what seemed like miles as our fingers clutched the sides of the wagon, hanging on for dear life while the breeze gently blew through our hair. When Peter was tired of playing, he loved to help out. With the addition of his new wagon, he felt as important to Papa as ever. With the red Radio Flyer at his side, he'd pull weeds until the load maxed out. Taking it around to the back of the house for disposal gave him a real sense of accomplishment and made the job just a little easier on Papa.

That summer, I played for countless hours with my doll in the sandbox Papa made for us. Built off the ground so water wouldn't seep in from the bottom, it was the perfect size—roughly three feet by four feet—with each corner containing a built-in seat to sit on and play with our buckets, shovels, and sifters. He built it in front of the house where they could sit on the front porch and watch over us as we played. It must have given him great pleasure to see his children actually being children—quite the opposite of his stolen childhood.

Even though I told my doll never to suck her thumb, *my* thumb had become a problem where Mama was concerned. I had long braids and enjoyed taking hold of the right one, putting it under my nose, rubbing it, while sucking my thumb. Nine times out of ten, the braid unraveled, and there I'd be with one braid nicely done and the other hanging loose like a ragamuffin's. Mama tried everything to get me to stop, but nothing seemed to work, so she finally gave up and let me outgrow the bad habit on my own.

At the time, I believed the only problems Mama ever had were with me, but I was wrong. It seemed she often had a look of sadness on her face, and it wasn't because I sucked my thumb or got dirty from time to time. It was because she was homesick. She missed her family desperately. She had been in America for seven years without ever having gone home to visit the ones she loved and missed so much. Letters continued arriving from Germany, and every time we found one in the mailbox, we'd run into the house with it. She'd drop everything to sit and read to us.

Never having met our family in Germany, we listened intently about the events of their lives and, little by little, we began to learn who they were and how much they loved us. In our minds it was like having a pretend family, since they lived so far away and never came to visit. Christmas, Easter, Mother's Day, and birthday's were always just the four of us, and that hurt Mama deeply. Living an ocean away, the only way she could touch them was through the pictures sent along with their words. She did her best to hide her sadness, but we knew from the tears she wiped from her cheeks while looking at their pictures that she missed them more than we, as children, could imagine.

Those letters, pictures, and most importantly the stories that Mama told, over and over again were what we all held dear, especially Mama. She would light up as she reminisced. I asked her time and time again to tell me about the adventures they lived in Germany, and that's how I became quite an expert on Mama and Papa's past.

With Mama not feeling well, we tried to be good kids and help around the house as much as we could. We had good guidance, as Papa was extremely strict and didn't allow anything to go on in our home that he didn't approve of. He made us obey him at his first command. There was no such thing as repeating rules or directions, and he never did. We learned from early on that every command whether picking up toys or getting ready for bed was to be carried out without hesitation. We knew the rules, and if we didn't obey, we received some painful swats on our back ends as reminders.

When it came time for supper, we immediately sat down at the table. If we were outside, we were never farther away than the sound of Papa's whistle. He'd stand at the door and whistle once; that meant no matter what we were doing, we had to drop it at once and get into the house. If we were too slow, he'd close the door, and there'd be no supper. After going to bed hungry once or twice, we learned to listen for that whistle and respond really quick.

There were rules to be followed at the dinner table too. Once mealtime commenced, we couldn't utter one word until the meal was finished. Mama and Papa were the only ones allowed to speak. He demanded silence from the rest of us. Mama made sure that we had enough food on our plate, and she'd ask us if we wanted more when we ran low, eliminating any reason for us to talk.

One evening, Mama invited our priest over for dinner, setting a separate table for Peter and me to have our supper. The priest remarked, "Your children don't say anything, I haven't heard a word from them throughout the entire meal."

"They know that they are not supposed to talk during mealtime," Mama answered.

"They're not sitting at the same table, but I don't even hear them talking to each other," remarked the priest.

She proudly answered, "No, they've learned not to do that."

The priest was quite amazed to think that two small children could be so obedient. As the evening wrapped up, he rubbed our heads and smiled as he left our home.

Back in those days, children respected their elders, and Peter and I were no different. Fighting, arguing, and creating loud noises were not permitted in our home. Our parents abided by these rules too and never argued in front of us. If something needed to be discussed, it would be; if they didn't agree on the solution, they waited and discussed it later. I never heard them arguing, ever.

It was no secret that Papa was quite a bit older than Mama—he was forty years old when he married her at twenty-six. But age didn't make any difference and, unlike his father, Papa never abused Mama verbally or in any other way. They were very close and extremely happy. He loved her with every ounce of his being; she was without a doubt the essence of his world. She too had become enamored, reciprocating his love just as he had prayed, and that's all that mattered. We felt their love, and Peter and I were without a care in the world. We were typical kids who enjoyed walking, laughing, and playing with our friends there on West Avenue in Naples.

2
Modern Life in the Great Depression

The depression hit everyone hard, making it difficult for most to save money and leaving them wondering what they'd do if an emergency occurred. But Papa worked hard to make sure we always had what we needed to live, and his labor paid off. By no means were we well-to-do, but we were finally in the position to purchase an automobile, which was necessary to get him back and forth to work. It made life easier and gave Papa the opportunity to spend more time with us, rather than wasting so many hours walking everywhere.

An old Ford Model T was his car of choice. He used it to take us to church on Sundays and to pick up groceries in town. He'd also take the car up to Rhine Street when he worked the vineyards on top of the hill. We loved riding in Papa's car and felt so proud waving to neighbors and friends as we rolled by.

It also gave Papa, who was an avid hunter, a way to explore fields and woods that he would otherwise never have been able to hunt. He routinely came home with rabbit, pheasant, and whatever else was in season at the time. Mama would clean, skin, and cook the fresh game so we had delicious meals to enjoy for dinner. One thing about Mama, she could make anything taste good.

Even though we were able to buy the car, those were tough times for my folks, and like most people around, they used what they had to get by. Mama and Papa taught us to be frugal. They planted a garden and diligently took care of it. As immigrants, hoeing, weeding, and watering so fruit, vegetables, and herbs could be canned or preserved in some other way was simply second nature.

After the grape harvest, Mama went through the vineyards and collected all of the unpicked grapes from the vines. She used them to make grape pies and fresh juice so we always had something healthy to drink. Papa also grew elderberries in the garden and, mixing them with the grapes Mama collected, he'd make wine. He always claimed that there was nothing better than homemade elderberry-grape wine.

Mama was also a fabulous baker, baking the most delectable German *kuchen*, otherwise known as special coffee cakes. When she did, the aroma filled the air, and it was like a piece of heaven as our mouths watered with anticipation of how delicious they'd taste. Saturday was baking day, so every Sunday morning we had a variety of fresh goodies. Friends came from all over to visit; sometimes they had a fresh cup of coffee and a piece of kuchen, and sometimes they were served a nice glass of wine. Regardless, we loved having the company, and Mama enjoyed socializing with everyone who stopped by.

The ladies who stopped were always intrigued by Mama's self-sufficiency. She kept us afloat, making all our clothes herself. People always commented that ours were the most beautiful, little outfits in town. Peter's and mine usually matched. Two of these, one pure white and the other navy blue, looked like little sailor suits. The tops had big collars, just like in the navy. The white one had navy blue trim, tie, and cuffs; and the navy one was just the opposite, with white trim, tie, and cuffs. Mine had a pleated skirt, and Peter's had long, white pants.

We were always dressed the same and received compliments whenever we went out. We also had pink and green outfits. Mama made a flowered shirt for Peter with a pair of green pants, and I had a flowered skirt with a plain, green top. We were proud of our beautiful garments, and Mama was proud to see us wearing them.

She also made all of Papa's clothes. He never again purchased clothing from a store after they were married. She made his pants, shirts, suits, and whatever else he had to wear. All of his clothes were perfectly tailored. Each year, Naples had a contest for the best-dressed couple. Our friends always encouraged Mama and Papa to enter; they believed they were shoe-ins to win. As it turned out, they were right—two years in a row, our parents were voted the winners, and deservedly so; they always looked sharp.

Mama also cut our hair whenever we needed it.. We never went to the barbershop or salon. She took care of everything for us. I had beautiful long hair, usually kept in braids, and only needed a trim once in awhile. We looked good and felt good, because she made it possible.

It seemed as though everyone knew each other in Naples, and we were all making good friends. Mama's closest friend was Mrs. Widmer, the wife of Papa's employer. When someone didn't know any better, they thought the two women were sisters, because of their uncanny resemblance.

With Mama's family so far away, developing friendships was of the utmost importance to her. There were a number of people that held a special place in her heart. Living across the street from the church, the Hartmans became very close friends, as did the Wamps, the Whileys, and the Bliers.

The widow across the street, Mrs. Wetherlow was another story. She was a crotchety old woman in her seventies who didn't much like anyone. The townspeople reciprocated the feeling. She never had a smile on her face and didn't appreciate visitors in her house or on her property. She simply preferred being left alone. Her husband had passed on some years before, and her home was in desperate need of repair. There was one exception however: Papa helped her from time to time and I think she took a liking to him, because every Wednesday she brought us a homemade, warm, apple pie.

Mama thought the pies were delicious and asked, "Mrs. Wetherlow, would you be so kind as to show me how you make those pies? I'm good at baking kuchen, but I've never made a pie. Would you please show me how to do so?"

Mrs. Wetherlow looked at Mama and, in her throaty voice, replied, "No, I will not. I'm not showing anybody how to do anything." Disappointed, Mama figured she'd have to find another way.

The following Wednesday morning, Mama left us children next door with Mrs. Blier and, with a couple jars of homemade jelly in hand, she went to visit Mrs. Wetherlow. Mama knocked, and Mrs. Wetherlow opened the main door, looked through the screen, and barked, "What do you want?" Mama requested, "Would you please let me in to have a cup of coffee with you?"

Amazed that someone would bring her something and knowing she couldn't very well send her away, she agreed. "Come on in; I'm just starting to make my pies." Mama handed her the jars of jelly and sat down at the kitchen table. Mrs. Wetherlow noted, as she placed the jars on the table, "The only reason you came here is to learn how to make pie."

Feeling somewhat awkward, Mama admitted, "Yes, Mrs. Wetherlow, that's why I came—to bring you some jelly and learn how to make those pies."

Irritated, Mrs. Wetherlow said, "I will give you one hint." Mama listened tentatively as she revealed her great secret. "When you take it out of the oven, always place a kettle cover or a plate on top of the crust while you let it cool. That way, the crust won't bubble, and the apples will stay close to the top."

Mama was elated. She thanked her for the advice, went home, and immediately began baking. That day, she learned how to bake the greatest pies I have ever eaten. Even Mrs. Wetherlow said they were almost as good as hers, and that made Mama proud. She always tried to learn something from everyone she met and always did her best to make a friend. As time went on, I thanked God for all the knowledge she picked up along the way.

A number of weeks had passed when Papa stopped by Mrs. Wetherlow's house to borrow one of the many tools her husband had acquired. She had told him if he ever needed to borrow anything, he was welcome to, so he often took her up on the invitation.

Papa rhythmically rapped on her front door but received no answer. Looking through the glass, he could see Mrs. Wetherlow at the top of the stairs, wobbling back and forth with a glass of wine in her hand. Everyone knew she had a drinking problem, but no one ever discussed it.

Leaning over, she saw Papa and waved, losing her footing and bouncing all the way down the stairs on her behind. When she reached the bottom, her body lay among the large rug that dressed the entrance as she held her empty wine glass high. He laughed so hard tears filled his eyes as he opened the door to let himself in to help her.

"Mrs. Wetherlow, I'm sorry for laughing. Are you all right?"

"Yes, I'm fine," she snapped in a nasty voice, "now help me get out of here!"

Papa, still laughing, helped her into a chair, making sure she wasn't hurt before he left. Aside from her pride, nothing was damaged. When he returned home, he laughed so hard he was nearly unable to tell us what happened. He laughed for hours, stopping only when he realized that he had forgotten the tool he originally went to borrow.

I don't think that I had before, or would ever again see Papa laugh that hard, and even though my parents tried, that was the last time Mrs. Wetherlow ever spoke to either of them or brought us one of her delicious pies. She was embarrassed and we knew it, so they kept an eye on her and left her alone. Thank goodness Mama learned the secrets of baking her delicious apple pies prior to being disowned as a friend!

Even though we were poor and often had to borrow items from our neighbors, my parents never took anything from anyone that didn't belong to them. One day, after cashing Papa's paycheck, Mama realized she'd received ten dollars more than she was owed. Immediately, she returned to the bank to give back the extra money. The teller, who only spoke English, was having a difficult time understanding Mama's request to return the money. Nevertheless, Mama kept trying and never became upset or walked away with the money. Thankfully, a woman that spoke both German and English entered the bank and explained what Mama was trying to communicate. The teller understood and fervently thanked both Mama and the lady who translated.

During the exchange, the owner of the bank overheard the conversation. He approached Mama, "Your honesty and your consideration to this young lady who works here is greatly appreciated. Therefore, your family will have access to any money you need to borrow in the future, with no questions asked." My parents were well respected in town and from that day on maintained a standing, open account with the bank.

A Trip to the Old Country

Things couldn't have been going better for our family when, in the spring of 1939, another letter arrived from Germany. This one was different. Opa, my grandfather, was very ill. He had undergone two serious operations to treat stomach cancer, and the doctors said there was nothing more they could do. His odds of survival were very much against him. Opa was dying, and Mama was devastated. To further complicate matters, Mama was again pregnant and had become physically ill herself. She loved her father desperately, and it broke her heart to think that she might never again see him.

She reached a point where she couldn't keep any food in her stomach, vomiting all the time, not only in the morning. When Papa took her for medical attention, the doctor determined that her illness was due to homesickness and depression. The doctor explained, "I have no cure for it, and I have no medication for her. The only thing you can do to help, John, is take your wife home. Take her back to Germany. If you don't and this sickness continues, you may lose both her and your unborn child."

Normally, it might have been a harmless idea. But things were not normal during that time and Germany was in a state of tumult. Hitler had come into power and the German people were becoming increasingly frightened of him and of war, at least Mama's family was. Letters from home indicated the country was in dire straits, and Opa's concerns were clearly reflected in the letters he wrote. Statements such as, "What have we done by electing this man?"

and "The First World War was devastating. Do we have to go into something as serious as that again?"

Papa knew in his heart that Mama had to go back to Germany and struggled with the difficult decision. He feared for the safety of their family and discussed his concerns with her. She was also concerned, of course, and agreed to try to overcome her homesickness. Unfortunately, with each passing day she became increasingly ill, forcing the decision to leave the safety of Naples, our hometown and head overseas.

The plan was that we'd all leave for Germany on August 1st for a three-month vacation. Mama would have ample time to spend with her family and seek the closure she needed to accept the inevitable death of Opa. While we were there, the baby would be born, allowing for a safe delivery for both, and we'd return to our home in the United States afterwards.

However, during that time Papa was rethinking his career as a wine maker. His salary at Widmer's wasn't increasing and with a new baby on the way, he desperately wanted to make a better life for us. He decided to contact his uncle in Oregon again. The two settled their differences and Papa updated him about our situation. He inquired about the employment opportunities out west and explained his quest for better working conditions and higher pay. His uncle responded that jobs out west were plentiful and that he'd make sure something would be available upon our return. Additionally, we could send our belongings and some of our furniture ahead, and he'd store it until our return.

In an effort to avoid having to ship too much, we auctioned the bulk of our belongings, which also provided us the cash we needed for four round-trip tickets overseas. The arrangements were made, and we shipped many of our belongings, including Mama's sewing machine, our beds and bedding, the kitchen table, couches, and more. All of this was placed on a train and sent to Oregon to be put in storage until we returned. Peter had finished his kindergarten year, and I was supposed to begin in September, so Mama contacted the school to inform them that we wouldn't be registering for the fall.

The time came to say our good-byes to the people of Naples, the very close friends that we had been privileged to know. Our neighbor Mrs. Wrongy was willing to take care of little Moxy, promising to send him to us once we were established in Oregon. Our cat, Blacky, went to Rhine Street to stay with our close friends the Baaders, who had a large barn with lots of room for him to romp. It broke my heart to say good-bye to those two, but I knew it wasn't forever, and I was thrilled about our upcoming adventure.

Our suitcases and the large trunk Mama brought from Germany were packed, leaving us with nothing to do but head for the train station and begin our journey to a land thousands of miles away. We took linens and essentials necessary for the trip, nothing more and nothing less. Of course, these essentials included my doll and Peter's wagon! There was no way we'd leave the comfort of our little village for three months without our most prize possessions.

Traveling wasn't going to be much of a problem for our parents. Papa could communicate beautifully, having learned to speak, read, and write English fluently—if you didn't know any better, you'd swear he was born in America. Mama had more of a problem. She finally had learned to speak English nicely, but with a very heavy accent, and although she could read it, she never learned how to write anything but German.

Peter and I had worked hard to communicate with the Americans. Peter was fortunate enough to have had a teacher who spoke English and German and made great efforts to help him learn the English language. It took less than six months before he also spoke fluently. Consequently, he had done very well in kindergarten.

He came home from school each day and spoke with me in English, and I learned as well. But I understood the language long before I could speak it, instinctively almost always answering in German. However, not wanting to be left out of anything, it wasn't long before I was able to jabber right along with the others.

On the first leg of our journey—heading for New York City—we made our way through Rochester. It was amazing how large the city was compared to our quaint town of Naples, and until then, the small city of Canandaigua had been the largest place I'd ever visited.

The trip was fascinating, seeing all of the magnificent buildings and the busy streets with automobiles and people everywhere. Everyone seemed to have something to do and somewhere to go, but then so did we. We were on a mission, a mission to make our mother well again.

Once in Rochester, we boarded a train, and I was thrilled. I ran back and forth across the aisles with my face pressed up against the windows trying to take in everything at once. I was filled with wonderment and my imagination was running wild thinking of all our trip had in store.

After many hours of traveling, we neared our final destination. We were heading for the seaport and, upon our arrival, we saw the monstrous ocean liners that appeared to mesh with the crystal blue sky. Mama pointed out the *SS Bremen,* "There she is." It was gargantuan, the largest thing I had ever seen. I couldn't believe my eyes, she was longer than three football fields, and the two stacks on top were each bigger than our farmhouse. There was row upon row of tiny windows where the 2,200 passengers would see the world from a whole new vantage point.

With a bit of time to spare before having to board, we saw the Statue of Liberty, and Mama explained that she was the lady who welcomed everyone into her country and made them feel at home. "She's a fine lady and she smiles at all of the people from foreign lands who wish to visit or settle in America." Mama continued, "The only people actually belonging to America are the Indians, all others have come from somewhere else. That's exactly how she welcomed me, and now, she's smiling on you children and wishing you a safe trip. And she'll welcome us back when we return."

They promised me the *Bremen* would float when they hoisted the anchor and the ropes were untied to set her free. I surely didn't see how that was possible, but I trusted Mama. And she told us that in six, short days we'd arrive safely in Germany. Since we were leaving the first of August, the weather on the ocean was expected to be fairly calm, and we weren't to encounter any storms. Not being a fan of the unforgiving water and completely unable to swim, I truly hoped they were right.

We waved good-bye to the statue and as we pulled out of New York Harbor, the huge buildings that graced the skyline and the fine lady became smaller and smaller, until they completely vanished from sight, leaving nothing but calm blue water as far as my eyes could see.

The ship was elegant, and we all shared a lovely room. There were some very interesting people on board and, luckily, many children our age. The people were all traveling to see friends and relatives or returning to Germany after being on business trips or vacations.

Many of the folks on board were talking about the political happenings in Germany and some were concerned about us taking such a trip at that time. My parents explained the situation and the severity of the circumstances behind their rationale.

Crossing the Atlantic on the Bremen

The trip across the ocean was amazing. As we stood on the bow of the ship, I saw nothing but water for as far as my eyes could see. But while looking for land, we saw different kinds of fish. We saw swordfish and dolphins that jumped high into the sky with the beauty and grace of ballerinas. But there were also sharks. Many sharks, especially when the ship's employees threw mealtime garbage overboard. Mama warned us that the sharks were deadly, and just as quickly, our attention turned to the whales that we encountered. They looked like islands in the middle of the ocean, and we could see water squirting out of them with great force. They were never really close to the ship, but we saw schools of them from a distance. I couldn't believe that a living creature could be so massive. I watched them play in amazement.

Our trip was exciting and we had a wonderful time. People were friendly, and we played lots of games like soccer and hide-and-seek with the other children, with so much room to run and explore. Most kids spoke different languages, but we communicated superbly with makeshift sign language and hand signals.

Even though we couldn't afford any of the on-board luxuries, we also had fun strolling around window-shopping at different shops and salons. Spending so much time with Papa was like a dream come true, since he was usually busy working somewhere. Most of our time had been spent with Mama, but this trip was different. He would tell us nice stories, and for the first time in a long time, we spent real, quality time together.

Two days before we docked in Germany, an evening was set aside especially for children. A show for the parents and all the guests on-board was being coordinated, and Peter and I were included in the festivities. It was a competition, and the children who had the best performance would be declared the talent-show winners.

The two champions, one boy and one girl, would be crowned King and Queen of the *Bremen,* and we were sure we didn't stand a chance of winning. We weren't used to being at the center of attention, and we were both riddled with nervousness, but Mama had faith and said that it would be nice for us to get up there and recite the "Our Father," first in English and then in German. She said it would be our performance, but it would also serve as a prayer for everyone on the ship. Peter and I agreed.

We were appropriately dressed in our coordinated sailor suits, and we got up on the stage and proceeded to say the "Our Father" just as she had instructed us:

Our Father who art in heaven,
Hallowed be thy name.
Thy kingdom come. Thy will be done
On earth as it is in heaven
Give us this day our daily bread.
And forgive us our trespasses,
As we forgive those who trespass against us.
And lead us not into temptation, but deliver us from evil:
For thine is the kingdom, and the power, and the glory,
Forever. Amen

To my sheer disbelief, immediately upon saying "Amen," we received a standing ovation, and after the judging, were crowned King and Queen of the *Bremen.* They gave us each a crown to wear and took our pictures behind the huge life preserver with *SS Bremen* printed on it. For the first and only time in my life, I was truly a queen, and I felt great! My reign lasted only two days, but those two days meant the world to me, and I was sure it was a sign of good things to come. We were winners, and we were proud. Not only were we proud of ourselves. Mama and Papa were beaming with pride too.

As promised, on the sixth day, our ship pulled into port and docked in Bremerhaven, Germany. We didn't need to worry about our trunk, the ship's crewmen would make sure that it was loaded onto the train and delivered to our next stop. We simply grabbed our carry-on items and stood in line, waiting our turns to walk down the wooden planks and eagerly embrace the next leg of our voyage.

As we departed the *Bremen,* and walked along Mama's familiar streets, she asked a question that surprised us all. "I feel very hungry, John, could we stop and get something to eat?" Papa smiled, amazed by her request, since she'd been unable to keep anything in her stomach our entire voyage. She had lost a lot of weight, and he was concerned, so we immediately found a restaurant, and Mama ate the first meal that actually stayed in her stomach in weeks. Papa began thinking that perhaps the doctor was right.

Once she stepped foot on her own soil and was in close proximity to her family, it seemed to have made all the difference. We children were thrilled and thankful; she seemed healthier and happier than she had in a long while. As we began our journey, we were all excited that it would not only shine a light on Mama's past, revealing the reasons she yearned to return, but also unleash what was in store for us and our future.

After we finished our meal and left the restaurant, we walked along the wide sidewalks. I was in awe of the beautiful, block buildings with large awnings and wrought-iron railings. There were potted flowers and well-groomed trees in all directions, and everything was lovely.

Papa hailed a taxi that drove us to the depot, and we boarded yet another train, which took us to Trier, the city closest to Mama's hometown. Trier was in western Germany, bordering Luxembourg. It was going to be a long ride, but we looked forward to reaching our destination and finally meeting the beautiful family we had heard so much about. To pass the time, we talked and listened to stories while the fast train forged on.

The "Laws" of Beauty

Germany had a beautifully maintained countryside. It wasn't like traveling from Naples to Rochester, where there were no villages until nearing the city. In Germany, as we traveled a short distance, we'd see a lovely village, travel a little farther, and see another. It was an exciting trip for us. We noticed the beautiful fields and many trees. It was delightfully charming and with each passing mile, I began to understand why Mama longed to return. As we traveled through some of the smaller villages, we noticed that there were no broken-down houses, boarded-up buildings, or junkyards.

Those were sights that I had seen along the railroad tracks as we traveled from Rochester to New York City. I recalled many broken-down areas on that trip, but not here. It seemed that everything was in order. Small villages were decorated with flower boxes, and it seemed as though people were trying to out do each other with flowers both inside and outside their homes. Everything was well taken care of and beauteous. I said something about it to Mama and she said that it was the law in Germany.

"You have to take care of your property," she said. "As a matter of a fact, on Saturdays people have to sweep their property from one side to the other and halfway into the street to make sure that everything is kept tidy. In addition, no littering is permitted. You will learn this while you are here, if people don't take care of their property, someone from the village or the city will come and take care of it for you and send you a bill."

That's why everything looked wonderful. If a building needed repair, it would have to be repaired immediately. If someone accidentally broke a window, it had to be fixed within the next day. You either had to have someone come and fix it or do it yourself, but you weren't allowed to let it remain broken.

Another thing we noticed during our stop in Bremerhaven was that all the store owners had beautiful displays. The windows were shiny and clean, and every shopkeeper took great pride in the shop's presentation. If it happened to be a dress shop, there were nice mannequins in the window, and you could see the items for sale. Messy storefronts were unacceptable. There weren't any advertisements pasted on the windows or any other kind of paper showing. If proprietors didn't abide by the laws, their business could be—and would be—closed down.

It hadn't been that way in Rochester. While passing through, we took a short ride before our train left and saw many dilapidated buildings and businesses with dirty windows and old rocking chairs and other broken-down items adorning them. There were plants everywhere that needed watering as they withered away, and trash blew freely throughout the streets. Our short ride yielded only deterioration of what I imagined was once a beautiful, thriving metropolis. I felt sadness for the buildings that no one seemed to care for.

3
Mama's Village

We received word that our train was pulling into the station in Trier. As we evacuated with our belongings, Mama realized her entire family had come to greet us. They had all taken time out to welcome her home after so many years. Most important, Opa was standing there, and she thanked God for another chance to spend time with the father she adored.

Even Uncle Johann had made the trip. He was Opa's youngest brother and a member of the family from the day that Oma and Opa married. When Johann was three years old, he developed a high fever, leaving him mentally disabled. The fever caused developmental problems with both his motor skills and his ability to talk. Over time, he improved his speech and began walking again, but his ability to think never evolved. For the remainder of his life, Uncle Johann had the mentality of a small child. He had a difficult time understanding most things, but Mama said he was an extremely hard worker with a heart of gold.

When Opa met his bride-to-be, he introduced her to Johann and told her about his family and the problems that they had. Opa's parents had passed away and, being the eldest, he decided that he would take responsibility for his brother. When he asked her to marry him, it was on the condition that she accept Johann living with them. Oma willingly and happily accepted his offer, and from the day they were married, Johann lived there too. He was already an adult, but he was a gentle, childlike man, and she considered him her son, and he called her "Mother." She loved him unconditionally, and he immediately became a permanent member of their family.

There was something special about him, and I couldn't help but love him from the first moment we met. As our family stepped off of the train, he was the first of many to run up and grab Mama and hold her tight. The tears ran down his face, as he cried, "Oh Elisabeth, I'm so very happy to have you back, I am so happy to have you back!"

It was the most beautiful reunion. I couldn't believe all of those people. There were ten brothers and sisters, Oma, Opa, and Johann. It was a surreal moment for all of us and the most uplifting remedy for Mama. She blossomed with joy, and happiness was written all over her face. There was an abundance of tears, kisses, hugs, and smiles, and I was in awe of how beautiful each one appeared. My uncles were handsome, and my aunts were each a vision of loveliness. They all resembled Mama, but Oma stood out. She was a mesmerizing, petite lady, and she so gladly received Peter and I. She hugged me tight as she said, "Oh, Marlies, I'm so happy to finally meet you! Now, let's go home."

Again our trunk was transferred, and we boarded another train in Trier that took us to Kell, Mama's farming village. I was really beginning to feel like a world-class traveler. After all, it was my fourth train trip within six days! With all the commotion of my new-found relatives, I strangely had time to notice that there was no fruit trees along the way. Mama explained that fruit was difficult to grow for some reason, but other crops grew fine. Potatoes, corn, grains, and barley were plentiful in Kell. It was a charming little town, and I instantly felt at home.

When we stepped off of the train, we met many people from the village that had come to welcome Mama home. There were women she had gone to school with, neighbors, and good friends. It seemed like we were back in Naples. Everyone was friendly, and they all knew each other. Cheers, waves, and friendly smiles and greetings were handed out everywhere we went—Mama was really perking up.

Our suitcases and belongings were picked up and placed on the wagon, which was drawn by two cows. As we all loaded ourselves on the wagon, Uncle Matthew jumped into the driver seat. He immediately became the recipient of my Favorite Uncle Award. I was only five, but I fell in love with him the first time I saw him. He was handsome, rugged, and personable. And he resembled Opa to a T. I was caught completely off guard when he asked, "If you'd like to drive the wagon, you come right up here and sit with me." Of course, I wasn't going to miss that opportunity! So I climbed up as quickly as I could and took hold of the reins. Holding those leather straps in my little hands, filled me with importance.

In the small villages of Germany, they didn't use horses for farm work—at least not in Kell where they were innovative, yet poor. Everything was done with cows. They were used for travel, milk, plowing, and working in the fields. Wealthy farmers used horses for sport and travel. However, our family was definitely not wealthy, and the cows were efficient, in the long run saving them money. The only problem I could see with this form of travel was that it was taking too long. No matter how many times I yelled "Giddy up," those cows just didn't move any faster. They went along at their own rate of speed. But I was getting hungry; not to mention that I couldn't wait to see all the animals Uncle Matthew had told me so much about along the way.

The Family in the Farmhouse in Kell

After a long ride, the wagon finally rolled to a stop in front of the large, corner lot. The white, two-story house, accented with green shutters, was nestled quietly along the hill that graced the back yard. It was almost as I had imagined. The large, green flower boxes hanging beneath each window were filled and fully in bloom, adding to the warm, inviting feel.

My eyes gleamed with excitement as my attention was drawn to the big, white barn attached to the left side of the house and facing the road. I quickly eyed the situation: Attached to the left of the barn and extending back toward the road was a covered walkway. At the end of the walkway were two smaller buildings, with an outhouse to the right. Looking back at the two large doors that faced me, I thought to myself, *This must be where the animals are kept.* Wasting no more time finding out, I climbed off the wagon and ran across the cobblestone-covered courtyard, determined to find the entrance.

"Slow down Marlies. Wait for us!" As Oma and Mama caught up, I waited at the tall, barn doors.

"Is this it?" I asked, while taking in the fresh smell of hay and pulling on the handles.

"Yes, this is it, Marlies." Oma said, and as she began to open the door, I quickly scurried under her arm.

"Oh, look Mama!" I counted out loud, "One, two, three, four, and the two pulling the wagon, makes six. Six cows!" I continued my exploration. "What's in here?" As I jumped up and down trying to peek over the mysterious waist-high wall.

"Oh wait until you see her," Oma said. She lifted me from behind, and I perched my arms on top of the wall and peered into the pen.

"Oh my, she's huge! How can she see where she's going? Her ears cover her eyes."

"She manages to bump into just about everything, Marlies, but Mama Sow can always find her food." Oma gave me a kiss on the cheek and set me back on the ground, and I was off again.

After seeing the rest of the animals, Mama said it was time to go inside, so I counted the cows one more time. "Good-bye everybody!" I yelled into the barn, before the door closed in front of me. I was determined to become best friends with all of them.

When they finally dragged me out of the yard and into the main house, I was struck by the most tantalizing aromas. Inhaling through my nose, I closed my eyes and could only imagine what all the combinations could be, making my stomach rumble just a tad. I pushed back my thoughts of food and started to do a little more exploring inside. The first thing I noticed was how large the downstairs portion of the home was. "Wow! Mama, this room is so big."

"This is the great room," she told me.

The sun poured in through several large windows, illuminating the hardwood floors and white walls, which were filled with knickknacks, religious pictures, and family photographs, each having its own story to tell.

One of the windows faced the flower garden that Oma had planted. Mama told me how much Oma loved flowers and how she always had them growing in her gardens. "See, Marlies, when Oma sits in the great room, she can look outside and be proud of all her hard work." Being much smaller than Oma, I looked out from the comfort of her chair but could only see the blue sky. Pulling myself out of the soft cushion, I went to the window. The flowers were magnificent, and I could only hope to someday have a garden as beautiful as hers. Also within the great room was a comfy couch and several overstuffed chairs, providing plenty of room for everyone to sit. A wonderful potbelly stove added to the warm, cozy feeling.

The next thing that caught my attention was a big, round, wooden table that I suddenly realized was the source of the wonderful aromas—which by that point had become impossible to ignore. I walked to the table with my nose in the air and climbed into the closest chair to get a better look. My eyes opened wide as I looked around the tabletop in disbelief. I couldn't believe all of the food that had been prepared for us, and as I glanced back into the great room, a feeling of togetherness filled my heart. It wasn't like it was the first time we had been there; it was like we'd been there all along and that we truly belonged.

As I sat there thinking, Mama walked over and explained that Opa had made the table by hand, and that the removable top rested on half a rain barrel. Inside the barrel were Oma's mixing utensils and the flour used to make her delicious homemade sourdough bread. After removing the tabletop, Oma mixed the dough inside the rain barrel. When the dough was ready, she'd replace the tabletop and form the dough into round circles, placing them into large baskets to rise. I poked my head under the table and looked at the barrel. Although it was interesting, what was on top quickly became my topic of discussion. "Mama, is all this food homemade for us?" Mama just smiled.

Finally, I heard the word I had been waiting for. "Dinner!" Oma cried, in a loud voice. With the whole family gathered, I looked around the table and tried to count everyone. There was Aunt Ida, Aunt Clara, Aunt Rose, Aunt Mary, and her three children—Carly was five, Marlies was six, and Yosefa was four. It was great not only to have aunts and uncles, but now we also had cousins our own age to play with, and we were ecstatic.

Continuing with my counting, also at the table were Oma, Opa, Mama, Papa, Peter, Uncle Johann, Uncle Peter, Uncle Bernard, Uncle Nick, and my favorite uncle, Matthew, who was nicknamed "Metz." That made seventeen people total, eighteen, counting me.

Opa said grace and we began our meal. The food was delicious, and I had not seen Mama eat or laugh that much in a long time. Even though it was my first time meeting all of them, I felt at home, and I knew I was going to like it in Kell.

After dinner, I had a chance to do a little more exploring, and the first place I headed was back into the barn, with my newly found cousins. There was a huge wall dividing the barn into two sections. On one side they kept the animals, and on the other the food for the cows. There was hay and straw up above in the hayloft, and underneath, along with the many farm tools, were two big wagons that were used to work the fields and a trough with a huge knife, where Uncle Johann put hay, straw, and sweet beets to chop into pieces prior to feeding the mixture to the cows. Adjacent to the main barn, were smaller areas that needed checking out. One was a workshop that Opa used for blacksmithing, and next to that was an area for woodworking and a large, open area where the wagons could be kept and repaired as well.

Items were repaired out in the open; however, the tools were kept in enclosed areas. Off to the side was a chicken coop full of cackling chickens, and next to that was the outhouse, which the thought of using didn't completely thrill me. Who knew what creepy, crawly trespassers might take up residence, and what if I had to go in the middle of the night? I decided to worry about that when the time came. Behind the outhouse was an area that was blocked off for the manure pile, and in the middle of everything, a center courtyard completely paved with cobblestones.

Dusk had set in, and once again, I was summoned to the main house, so I took it upon myself to check things out there as well. Quickly sizing up the situation, I noticed that on the other side of the great-room wall, was a huge area enclosed with glass doors and shelves that led into the large L-shaped kitchen. A monstrous wood stove, topped with eight burners, sat to the right of the entrance.

They had a sink with an attached pump that drew water from their well into the house, and near that stood a freestanding closet; I couldn't help myself, so I opened it just to see what was inside. It contained Oma's kettles, dishes, cooking utensils, glasses, and so on—nothing that I'd be interested in.

I continued on. In the far corner was a machine that piqued my curiosity for a moment. "Mama, what's this?" She told me they used the machine for canning vegetables and meats, and that I should leave it alone. "All right, Mama, I will." Mama looked back at me again, as I looked at her. I knew she meant business, so I decided to go look for other things to do.

Next to the stove was a door. "What's this door for, Aunt Clara?"

"That's the chimney room, Marlies. Would you like me show you?"

"Yes, please."

She opened the door, and I walked in, but all I saw were bricks and a big bathtub. She told me to look up, and to my amazement, I could see the sky. "What does it do?" I asked. As she explained, she pointed to the large steel door that hid an oven that Opa had built, solely of brick.

To use the oven, Opa took large bundles of brush gathered from the forest and threw them inside. He lit them on fire and closed the door. Once the brush burned to ash, it was scraped into a pan that hung on the wall to be disposed of later. In the meantime, the bricks retained enough heat to bake twelve to sixteen loaves of homemade sourdough simultaneously, and in a short time, all the loaves were piping hot and ready to eat. I wanted to see how it worked at that very moment, however, my aunt pushed back my request until the following afternoon.

Since there wasn't a toilet in the house, we had to use the outhouse to relieve ourselves, and the chimney room was used for bathing. There was a great big tub, and I imagined that in the summertime it would be great to take baths, but in the winter snow would fall right through the chimney, cutting bath time real short.

I was learning more and more about Opa and how amazing and innovative a person he was, as I continued to travel proudly throughout their home. The back of the house was built directly against a hill, and to the right of the kitchen was another large door. "What's in here, Oma? Can I open it and see?"

"Sure you can, Marlies."

As I opened the door, a cold rush of air passed by. "I can't see anything."

"Pull the chain on the wall."

I reached up and gave a quick yank on the chain that dangled next to the door. A single bulb hung in the center of the ceiling illuminating the entire room. "Wow! What's this, Oma?" "That's my refrigerator, Marlies. Opa built it for me." She said proudly.

The entire room was hand-carved out of the hill and reinforced with two-by-fours and beams. It had paneling, a wood floor, and huge shelves where Oma kept anything that she wanted to preserve. There were eggs, milk, canned goods, vegetables, and a butter churn to make creamy homemade butter. Even during hot summer months the room was naturally air-conditioned and everything inside remained fresh.

I wanted to see my room, so we retreated back through the kitchen and through the great room and headed upstairs. The first small bedroom belonged to Uncle Matthew, next to that was a door that led to a string of others, most of which were not being used, as many of the children had grown up and moved on.

The hallway contained rooms on both sides, and at the end, a door that led into my grandparents' bedroom. Off of their room was another small bedroom that was used as a nursery in the past, but currently, Aunt Clara was using it. She was a doctor who worked many long hours and was exhausted at the end of her day, needing a quiet place to rest. Next to her room was a door that led to the attic, but I was primarily interested in myself, and inquired. "Where's my room, Oma?"

"Come, I'll show you." We walked back down the hall, and she opened the first door on the left next to my Uncle Matthew's room. "This will be your room, Marlies." I was delighted to be next door to Uncle Matthew, and I couldn't have wished for a better location. That was the layout of my grandparents' beautiful home, and I was thrilled as I uncovered every square inch of the place.

The "Laws" of the Family: Listening, Rising Early, and Keeping Busy

Our first evening was exciting, with multiple discussions going. Everyone was thrilled that Mama was home, especially Opa. He had feared that he'd never lay eyes on her again, so he was relieved beyond words to have her back home and to meet us, his grandchildren. Everyone respected Opa and listened intently as he conversed. What I found most amazing was that when someone spoke, everyone listened. It wasn't a group of people all talking over each other at once with a lot of confusion, and I finally understood why Papa was so insistent on us children listening when they spoke.

In my grandparents' house, the elder people had the right to talk first, while the younger listened, but everyone took a turn. As I sat next to Mama, listening intently to the conversations, my mind began to wander. I wondered what tomorrow would bring, and I couldn't wait to visit my new friends in the barn.

Mama sensed I was tired and said it was time to turn in. As I knelt beside my bed, I gave thanks for everything and everyone I had experienced throughout the day. After my prayers, Mama tucked me in as I slipped my legs under the huge, down pillow that stretched across the bottom of the bed. She gave me a kiss on the forehead and told me she loved me. "I love you too, Mama." As she smiled at me, the way only a mother does, I could clearly see that although it was only our first day in Kell, she had already improved 100 percent.

In my grandparents' home, early rising was the key to success. Uncle Matthew told me that if I was awake before he left, that I could ride the wagon down to the fields and help work the brake. Needless to say, I was up and at 'em before anyone else and ready to go. Uncle Matthew laughed as I knocked on his door at four o'clock in the morning and in a quiet voice I asked, "Are you up yet?"

We went downstairs and started our day with breakfast, and before leaving for the fields, the rest of the house was up and busy. The livestock needed to be fed, and there was work to be done in the fields. Harvesting had begun, and that meant getting to it early. The women were already in the stalls, feeding and milking the cows. They were all busy at work, and the sun hadn't even risen.

Oma needed small, splinters of kindling for starting the fires in both her stoves, which meant that someone had to prepare it. There was cleaning and sewing that had to be done, socks that needed mending, butter that had to be churned, and plenty of eggs to gather—some of which went to market, and some that was kept for the family. Everyone was buzzing in different directions; it was always busy on the farm.

I learned on my first day working in the fields that everyone stopped working at noon for lunch and at six o'clock for dinner. The interesting thing was the cows, much like Pavlov's dogs, instinctively stopped what they were doing the second the noon church bells rang. Even if you needed to go two feet farther to finish what you were doing, they wouldn't move an inch. They knew it was time to be released for lunchtime grazing, while everyone else ate too.

The main meal was at twelve o'clock noon and consisted of meat and potatoes and often soup, followed with a rest period of forty-five minutes to an hour. During the rest period, everyone sat quietly and discussed what needed to be done, and then it was back to the fields, and the jobs that needed completion.

The bells rang again at six o'clock, and the cows waited to be hooked up to the wagon for the trip home. They became accustomed to listening for those bells, and they instinctively knew their way home. Like everyone else, they were tired and looked forward to dinner and a good night's sleep. I certainly related to how they felt; working in the fields all day was exhausting!

The wagons had huge beds with high, spindled sides, so a great deal of hay could be stacked in them. On the back of the wagon was a huge chunk of wood with a screw on it. When the screw was turned, the wood pressed against the wagon wheel acting as a brake. As promised, Uncle Matthew taught me how to work the brake, and I thought it was great. He told me that when approaching a hill, someone had to jump off the wagon to work the brake. The next hill was approaching fast, and I was ready. As we started down the hill, I turned the big screw, slowing the large load so the cows could safely make it down the hill, without the wagon running into their legs. It was a big job, but I did it and was proud to be helping.

After returning from the fields, we were all tired and hungry, but the cows needed to be taken care of first. I stood in awe, as I watched Oma milk the cows. "While you're here, I'm going to teach you how to do this. Would you like to learn, Marlies?"

"Yes I would Oma. Can you teach me tonight?"

"Sure I will, and as long as you and Peter stay with us, I'll have jobs for you both. Now let's start by learning how to brush the cows. We don't allow the cows to have manure or dirt on them, so they must always be brushed when they come home from the fields."

While we learned how to brush the cows, Johann and my uncles put clean straw down in the barn, so the cows would never lie in manure or dirt. Keeping the stalls clean also kept the pesky flies out. Oma milked the cows, and the warm milk was brought into the kitchen. For the first time, Peter and I tasted fresh milk directly from udder to glass. It tasted great, unlike anything I had ever tasted before.

My grandparents were considered poor farmers, and having such a large family, they taught everyone early on to pitch in and help with the workload. Whether it was farm work, taking care of the house, or taking care of each other, the children all had jobs to do, and it was very important to keep busy. That was one rule Oma always insisted on, because as long as you're busy, you can't get into trouble. They were all used to pitching in and doing what had to be done to survive. In addition to the work they did on the farm, most had some type of profession that they studied as well.

The Family and German Law

Uncle Joseph had become a master carpenter, and in Germany, that was quite a feat. While learning how to do carpentry work, he started out with "rough work" like framing the outside of a home. From there, he proceeded to "finish work"; next came cabinet making, and finally small things such as jewelry boxes, rocking chairs, children's toys, and other difficult items.

When young students went to trade school, they went through different stages that required passing tests. Upon graduating from the different training sessions, they received licensing that gave them the right to set up shop. Simply doing some woodwork, setting up shop, and claiming to be an experienced carpenter was unacceptable. Like it or not, the training process had to be completed.

Those requirements were not only for carpenters, they were for all professions. Seamstresses like Mama and Aunt Mary had to start out learning how to do small things, and then how to use a pattern, before moving on to the fine sewing of things like ball gowns, suits, and so on. They had to go through all of the stages to become licensed in order to call themselves a seamstress. Likewise for Uncle Peter, who was a tailor for men's clothing.

Uncle Bernard wanted to be a businessman and have his own store. He took business courses and obtained a degree to learn all there was to know about business, including how to take care of his books, how to take care of the people that worked for him, how to set up payroll, what deductions to take, how to prepare his taxes, and so on.

Uncle Nick decided he'd remain a farmer. He didn't attend trade school, because he had learned the necessary skills at home. It was assumed that his intentions were to stay with my grandparents and help them on their farm, because they needed him. Although Uncle Johann was a hard worker and extremely valuable to them, it was a blessing that Uncle Nick was staying as well.

Aunt Rose went into the convent and became a nun in order to serve the Lord. She was living in the city of Trier with the Saint Joseph's Order, which was similar to the Carmelites. They were extremely strict, and she was only allowed to come home for two weeks every three years. Luckily, she happened to be home when we arrived. She only had a couple of days left before returning to the convent, and it would be another three years before the family saw her again, but she was thankful to have been able to see Mama, even if only for a short while.

Aunt Mary, a housewife was taking care of her family in Kell. They also had farmland and she also sewed at home for extra income. Their home was in walking distance of Oma and Opa's house.

Aunt Ann was also a housewife, she had never gone on to pursue any other trade; she simply wanted to pursue one of life's most challenging positions, that of wife and mother. She lived in Idelsbach with her husband and their children, but she too was there to welcome us upon our arrival. I felt connected to Aunt Ann and my cousins

Leeny, Carly, and Yosefa right away. We got along just fine. My Aunt Clara had gone on to become a doctor, and Aunt Ida, Uncle Peter, and Uncle Bernard were all too young to do anything besides pitch in on the farm and help around the house.

Before becoming a carpenter, at seventeen, Uncle Joseph had become a member of the Hindenburg's guard. It was an elite group of soldiers chosen with one major prerequisite: they had to look as if they were cut from the same fabric. They had to be a certain height, a certain weight, and their head sizes had to be exactly the same; they had dark hair and their facial features were similar. Their arm lengths, leg lengths, and shoe sizes all had to be the same, so that when they bought shoes and clothes, they only bought one size. Joseph was one of the chosen few, and it was an honor for my grandparents … prior to Hitler becoming chancellor of Germany.

It was exciting to learn about my extended family, to sit alongside Oma in the great room after the long day's work, and to listen to all of them as they discussed current events. The topics were much more than chitchat, often hair-raising and profound beyond my comprehension. The discussions about war and Hitler and what he was doing became very prominent in our home.

Back row L-R, Uncle Peter, Uncle Matthew, Aunt Rose, Uncle Nick, Uncle Joseph, Aunt Mary, Uncle Bernard. Sitting/Front Row L-R, Aunt Clara, Oma, Aunt Ida, Aunt Ann, Opa, Mama.

Prior to the rise of Hitler and the National Socialist German Worker's Party (the Nazis), Germany spent nearly fifteen years enduring constant instability under the Weimar Republic. The government had split into dozens of factions that were unwilling to reach a consensus on anything. The economy was suffering, and with the weakening of the Weimar Republic, communism and fascism were emerging. Adolph Hitler, leader of the fascist Nazi Party, skillfully manipulated the population into electing him chancellor and leader of Germany, known as the fuehrer.

The majority of Germans blamed the government for the slump they were enduring and welcomed the changes that Hitler proposed. He challenged the status quo while regenerating a long-lost feeling of nationalism, promising economic prosperity and restoration of power. Opa, however, saw through the smokescreen of propaganda, claiming, "Hitler's trying to make us believe that he has done some good for Germany, but I have a feeling he's driven by evil."

They were quite serious when they spoke about politics, and Opa made it a point to express to his children that he wanted them to have absolutely no connection with Hitler. He believed that becoming a member of Hitler's organization marked the end of a religious upbringing. He was reverent and serious about his children being strict Catholics and remembering that God always comes first. He built a home on faith, filled with Bibles, rosaries, and crucifixes. Opa would have gladly sacrificed anything in his possession, before he'd ever abandon his faith.

It was paramount that the entire family promised that they'd never consider becoming associated with Hitler or any of the Nazi organizations, and that they'd always remain devout Catholics. As much as Opa despised Hitler, statements against him were forbidden by law, because Germany did not share the same freedoms as the United States like freedom of speech.

What was discussed in my grandparent's living room was to remain only with family members. When a friend or neighbor came calling, those discussions ceased. If others unwittingly brought it up, my grandparents, aunts, and uncles sat and listened, but never added to the conversation, and certainly never said anything derogatory regarding Hitler's reign.

An underlying fear of the oppressive regime quietly spread through Germany, as most began to realize the less said the better. Anything could irrevocably come back to haunt them as an uncertain fear began crawling in. Even as children, we noticed it. There was something frightening going on, and we could feel it in the air.

Amid the trials and tribulations of everyday life in Kell, we carried on the best we knew how, and as far as I was concerned, things were going splendidly, until the first of September when a news report was announced over the radio, stating Hitler had declared war on Poland. The Allied Forces did not look favorably upon the invasion, and in turn declared war on Germany. The news was especially upsetting to the people in our village, and Oma was exceedingly concerned. "With war breaking out, all of my sons will be drafted to fight." A numbing sensation overcame her as she pictured in her mind, the beautiful faces of her five boys. Making matters worse, two days later another report came over the radio indicating that all visitors in Germany had to return to Bremerhaven and board the awaiting ocean liners heading back to their original destinations.

They were all being immediately evacuated and that of course included us. Saddened, we had only been there one month, feeling cheated out of the remaining two months of our vacation, but with the sudden notice, we had no choice but to leave. We had played, laughed, and learned a great deal; it was difficult to say good-bye to our family and to the friends we had already made in town.

Our priest at church announced that our visit had been cut short and that we'd been ordered to leave, so friends and neighbors came to bid farewell as we packed our belongings. Before climbing on the wagon for the long ride down the dusty road, I tearfully said so-long to each and every one of my furry friends in the barn. I wondered if they would miss me as much as I'd miss them, but as I tried to be strong, I told them not to worry, because Oma would surely take care of them.

Once again, Uncle Matthew let me drive the wagon as we headed for the train, which we boarded in Trier. My uncles Peter, Bernard,

Joseph and Matthew, Oma, Opa, and Aunt Clara came to accompany us to the *Bremen*. As much as I loved that ship, I wasn't happy about having to board it again so soon. Feeling deprived of spending time on the farm, it was a quiet ride to the port.

Upon arriving at Bremerhaven, Mama was asked to visit the doctor due to her pregnancy, while the rest of us were checked to make sure we were up to date on our vaccinations. A nurse came out of the doctor's office and called Papa in. A short while later he came out and told my uncles and grandfather that Mama couldn't leave. The doctor had examined her, determined that she was seven months pregnant, and refused to give her permission to board the ship. Due to overcrowding, there wouldn't be a facility to take care of her in the event that the baby should decide to arrive early.

They had given Papa permission to take himself and us children aboard the ship, but Mama couldn't leave until after the baby was born. The very thought of him leaving without her was preposterous. He was fully devoted to her and was determined to keep his family together through thick and thin, through good times and bad. From the day she graciously said, "I do," he made a promise before God to remain by her side for better or worse. She was his reason for waking up each morning, and there was no way he was going to leave her there alone, so with simplicity, he proclaimed, "If she can't go, then we can't go. We'll just have to wait until the baby's born."

Although the doctor was sympathetic, he proceeded to warn Papa, "Mr. Adams, take great heed, since Hitler has ordered everyone to leave now, I hope you still have that opportunity in two or three months." The doctor's words exacerbated the circumstances. Regardless, without Mama, there was no way we'd board that ship, so we began our journey back to Kell. Opa and the others were thrilled that we were staying, so they hastily boarded us on the train and we returned right back to where we'd come from.

Of course, Peter and I were overflowing with joy, but Papa, although he tried to hide it, had taken great pains with his decision. He pondered the predicament his loved ones could face, and with war breaking out, his concerns might prove to be justified. After all, Papa had already served in one war, and was fully aware of the severity of this situation and what the future could possibly bring.

We arrived back in Kell, and Opa sat with Papa and Uncle Joseph to discuss what we'd do if we couldn't leave after the baby was born. Uncle Joseph spoke up, "I think it might be a good time for you to start looking for employment. I could help you with that with my connections in Rüsselsheim. I worked there in the Opel factory, and I'll see if I can secure some type of work for you—as a security precaution." He added, "You should also look for a decent place to live. I don't feel comfortable about your being able to leave in two months, so let's make arrangements just in case." Papa agreed, and after the rest of us were safely back at the farm, the two of them immediately left for Rüsselsheim, a town not far from Frankfurt.

In the meantime, although we missed Papa, Peter and I continued to act like normal five and six-year-olds, and one afternoon, while outside playing with my cousins, I fell and scraped my elbow. It bled a little bit, but I wiped it off and continued playing. I should have gone in to have Mama check it out; however, playing took precedence, so I stayed outside.

By nightfall, after a full day of whimsical games with my comrades, I was filthy and it was due time for a bath. As Mama scrubbed me clean, she noticed the injury to my arm, which by then had become swollen and infected, so she called for Aunt Clara to come and examine it. They immediately applied disinfectant, which hurt more than the scrape itself, and bandaged the wound before putting me to bed.

The next morning when I woke, I had developed a high fever and my arm had swollen a considerable amount. Mama couldn't get my dress sleeve over the swelling, and Aunt Clara was worried. She said, "Elisabeth, we have to take her to the hospital in Trier and have her examined. I really don't like the way it looks."

Mama bundled me up and in the cool, crisp morning air, we made our way to the train station, purchased our tickets, boarded the train, and headed to the hospital to visit Doctor Ments. He took one look at my arm, and realizing that Mama was pregnant he began yelling that I had *Wundrose* [or Erysipelas, cellulitis] a contagious disease, in my arm and that Mama shouldn't be anywhere near me.

They whisked me into an isolated ward with a huge window running from floor to ceiling. Chairs lined up outside where visitors could sit and peer in, but they couldn't enter. My fears were intensifying. I didn't understand why they couldn't come hold me and give me the assurance I desperately sought, but Mama and Aunt Clara sat outside the window never taking their eyes off of me, which provided comfort on some level. After the examination, the doctor spoke frankly to Mama and told her surgery wouldn't save my arm; he suggested his only recourse was amputation. In the days before antibiotics, staph infections such as cellulitis were deadly, and extreme measures had to be taken to survive them.

In order to save my life, amputation provided a fifty-fifty chance for survival, but he couldn't give her any better odds than that. Mama became extremely agitated, but Dr. Ments continued, informing her that he needed permission from both parents to go ahead with the procedure.

They contacted Papa via telephone, to notify him regarding the severity of the decision at hand. Feeling he had no other alternative, he replied, "I don't want anything to happen to my beautiful daughter, and a fifty-fifty chance is better than nothing—you'd better go ahead with the amputation."

Mama, however, with her eyes squinted, her breathing labored, repudiated. "You will not remove her arm! A war has started in this country, and we are Americans. God forbid what would happen to her if something should happen to us? How could she provide for herself as a young amputee? I will not give you permission to amputate!"

Disconcerted, the doctor warned her she was committing me to death. "Mrs. Adams, please; you need to understand, I cannot save her life without the amputation. Even with it, I'm not positive she'll survive." With total conviction, she answered, "In that case, I'm going to leave it in God's hands and let him decide if he wants my daughter now or later. Giving me a fifty-fifty chance for survival is not giving me enough. I won't let you do it."

Hurriedly, she left the area in search of the nuns downstairs. It was a Saint Joseph's Catholic hospital, and it was the order that her sister belonged to, so Mama asked them to start a Novena for my recovery. They readily agreed, and Mama dashed home to speak to our priest. He immediately agreed to have the townspeople pray for my survival.

While Mama was out rallying spiritual support, the doctor went ahead and performed an operation. He decided that as long as she wouldn't allow an amputation, he'd at least do the best that he could and operate. He thought maybe there'd be some chance … though there was little hope of survival … but he had to do what he thought was best … However, during the operation, complications arose, and I slipped into a coma. Mama came every day to visit, but the doctor continued shaking his head, claiming that I'd likely never regain consciousness.

"Mrs. Adams, I did all that I could."

He wanted to have a clear conscience, but all the while, she knew what he was thinking. He thought that she was a horrible woman. How could any mother refuse the very surgery that could possibly save her child's life? Mama, however, had faith and hoped that God would see me through. And then, while praying day and night, to the doctor's total shock, on the sixth day, for no reason he could fathom, my fever broke, and I was on my way to recovery. When I woke, I thought it was the next day, not realizing that an entire week had lapsed.

Mama was greatful beyond words. Her baby wasn't going to die, and the weight of the world had been lifted from her shoulders. She hurried down to the chapel to thank God and the sisters; then headed off to visit the townspeople in Kell and thanked them for their continuous prayers. She was so thankful that I was getting better and relieved that she wouldn't have to live with having made the wrong decision—if there had indeed been a different outcome.

The day after my fever broke, an announcement was made that all civilians who were not in critical condition must be discharged to other hospitals or sent home, because that hospital was needed for wounded soldiers.

The doctor knew Aunt Clara was also a doctor, and believed I no longer needed hospitalization, as long as she would tend to me, so rather than transport me to an alternate location, Mama took me home to the farm where Aunt Clara indeed took very good care of me, slowly nursing me back to health. The ordeal had left me weak and unable to walk, but it gave me an opportunity to get to know Uncle Matthew better as he carried me upstairs to my bedroom when I needed to rest, and back downstairs to be with the family.

In the evening hours, he spent quality time telling stories and reading to me in the dimly lit great room where the sounds and smells of the fire crackled nearby. I idolized him and thought he was the finest, grandest person I had ever met. He exuded an aura of dignity, and I was pleased to have been in his company while regaining my strength.

Of course, I missed my father, but he was in the city with no opportunity to come back, and Uncle Matthew was doing a wonderful job helping take care of me. At least Papa's absence hadn't been in vain: he was able to find a job and an apartment for us in Rüsselsheim. It seemed as though everything we needed was falling into place, to get us through the next couple of months until the baby arrived.

My recovery was coming along nicely on the farm when Mama received a dreadful telegram. There was no longer a way out of the Nazi-controlled country. All borders and ports had been ordered closed. We were officially confined, with no answer as to how long. Although Mama tried to protect me and Peter from the severity of the situation, our fears still continued to rise, and we felt we must be the only foreigners residing in the entire country during the tumultuous times.

4
Rüsselsheim

Thank God Papa had gone to Rüsselsheim to secure our future. Without delay, Mama notified him of the telegram, and until we could officially move into our apartment, he'd stay there with Uncle Joseph and his wife, Hanna. She was also expecting a baby the same time as Mama, and what should have been the best of times were now soured with uncertainty.

It was seven or eight weeks until the baby was due and that was cutting it close. Opa was still quite ill, and on top of everything else, Mama's brothers were being drafted into the German army. They'd all be leaving to fight the war, which was difficult for everyone. Opa had forbidden his children from having any connection to Hitler, but when the army called, they had no choice but to go. Horrible thoughts began flooding through our minds as we pondered what was to become of our newly reunited family.

As I struggled to regain my health, my family treated me with compassion. And since Opa was also incapacitated, he understood how I felt. We spent a lot of time together as I learned a wealth of knowledge from him. Besides being sick, he'd raised eleven children—he understood illness inside and out and knew exactly what to do to make me feel comfortable and loved. Opa was not recovering, but I did finally feel better, even though my hand and arm still looked grotesque, swollen to the size of a stovepipe. The doctor had made an incision at least four inches long above my elbow. That wound, in combination with the swelling, made it impossible to bend my arm. I couldn't wait for it to shrink back to normal. By the time we made plans to move to Rüsselsheim, mostly it had.

Before we left, Mama had an opportunity to go back to the city and speak with Dr. Ments. She wanted to thank him for all he had done for me, but his response surprised her.

"There was nothing we did that saved your daughter's life. Mrs. Adams, I envy you and your faith. Your strong belief is something I've never had. It is truly a wonderful gift." He told her he believed there was a greater force working than just the knowledge of the nurses and doctors there. He was kind, apologizing for the way he treated her when she first came in. He said, "I was concerned about the contagion; with your pregnancy, you were in enormous danger."

He shook her hand and gave her a hug, and wished nothing but the best for me. She saw another side of him, a side that was understanding and compassionate, a side where he tried to understand the situation in terms other than scientific.

We did the best we could to tie up our loose ends in Kell, as we made plans to leave for Rüsselsheim; as it was time we reunited with Papa. Once again, Mama was filled with sadness and fear, saying a good-bye to her parents. She was moving to a strange city and starting over while her delivery was so close at hand. It seemed as though there were so many problems. She worried about her brothers going into the service, hoping that they would all remain safe. Opa was steadily deteriorating, and the good-byes to her friends and family were painstaking. No matter how many times she had to do so, it never became easier. We gathered our things together, and Oma packed an extra large trunk of essentials for us to take along.

She placed heavy blankets and huge, down, comforters called *federdecke* inside. Different from the American down quilt, these were as thick as—if not thicker than—regular head pillows, but these covered us from our feet to our chest, keeping us toasty. There were numerous skeins of yarn for us to take along, because even while pregnant, Mama could sit and knit sweaters, hats, and scarves for us children. At least we'd stay warm when the unforgiving winter months were upon us. Oma also sent along an assortment of seeds, a couple of sacks of flour, a ham, and other items we'd find useful. She was worried; she had a sense that times were changing, and things for us were going to be difficult at best.

Papa informed us that our apartment was furnished. It came complete with dishes, silverware, beds, a couch, and lots of odds and ends. The only thing Mama was truly concerned about was how she could obtain a sewing machine. "If nothing else, I could help my husband by continuing my sewing. Maybe this way we could make a fresh beginning." She had been using one that belonged to Oma, but she couldn't take hers away. Aunt Mary had one, but she often used it, so Mama prayed that she would find one in Rüsselsheim. Papa's plan was to meet us in the city of Mainz, which was the closest city to Rüsselsheim. From there, he'd help us find the way to our new home safely.

When we arrived in Mainz, we had a two-hour layover before we could get to Rüsselsheim by train. Just as he promised, Papa was already waiting for us, sadly though, we could immediately see that he wasn't himself. Something was wrong.

He said he'd been stung by an insect on his forehead. His entire face was swollen and he was running a high fever. Mama looked frightened as she held her wrist to his forehead. We dropped our bags at the depot and hurried to a nearby hospital. The doctor examined him, and oddly enough, he had *Gesichtrose*, a similar illness to the one I had just recovered from, only not as deadly.

Since surgery wasn't an option, the infection was left to heal itself. Therefore, the doctor wouldn't release him, and Papa was quarantined to the hospital for a period of weeks. Mama had to go to Rüsselsheim alone with Peter and me. We'd have to set up housekeeping ourselves, and Papa would probably not be with her when it came time to deliver the baby. It seemed as if we were drowning in a sea of problems. One after the other they piled up and weighed us down.

We left Papa for Rüsselsheim after an emotional farewell. After all, we had just reunited with him, and now we had to part again!

Thankfully, Uncle Joseph met us at the train station. It was a huge relief to see a familiar face, not to mention, his help with our baggage, which would have been difficult for a pregnant woman with two young children. Uncle Joseph took us to his house where he helped with paperwork that needed to be filled out. Mama had to send the signed forms to Mainz, so Papa would receive the medical benefits he needed while being hospitalized.

There was socialized healthcare in Germany, and thankfully, his recovery wouldn't cost us financially as he was nursed back to health. We spent a few days with Uncle Joseph and then he made arrangements for a vehicle to bring our trunks to our new apartment, which was located approximately five miles outside of Rüsselsheim. Our apartment was on the first floor of a four-family unit.

When we arrived in our new village, we had to report to Nazi headquarters, where they issued us ration cards that were used for everything we might need: shoes, clothing, fuel, and especially food. Ration cards were not free; they had to be purchased. In addition, there were limitations to what could be purchased, and by whom— thus "ration" cards.

With Papa not working, an extremely heavy burden was placed on our very pregnant mother. There were times when she seemed so debilitated and weary, yet she pushed on with her inexhaustible work ethic. She sought work with desperation, knowing it was her only way of achieving enough money to purchase our rations.

The ration cards we received were very sparse—half what German citizens received. That meant that our rations lacked eggs, milk, sugar, and fats of any kind. All we were allotted for the week were two small pats of butter (the same size restaurants serve with rolls), three loaves of bread, a very meager amount of potatoes, three pounds of pork, and quite a bit of oatmeal. The only seasoning we were allowed was salt. Our fuel rations were practically nonexistent, and Mama wondered how we were going to survive the winter without any coal. Because we were able to get wood, the first thing we did was take Peter's little red wagon into the forest, located just past the large apple orchard on the other side of the farmland next to our apartment.

With the forest being so close, we gathered brush and small sticks for firewood. It was our only hope of surviving the winter without coal. Likewise, if someone threw out old furniture or wooden items that were no longer needed, we could pick them up at the curb and bring them home in the wagon. That little red wagon proved to be a big help time and time again.

Uncle Joseph had helped us settle into the apartment, but after he left, we realized that every time we had to travel into the city, it meant walking five miles each way—five long miles for Papa to walk to work, for us to walk to school, and for all of us to attend church.

There was only one Catholic Church in the city that was still open, but they were fortunate to have two priests. It was never an option to miss church, and when Peter and I started our first communion classes, it meant another weekly walk. At first, the walk was fun, but as the winter drew closer, the distance seemed farther and farther, making the walk nothing more than a dreadful inconvenience.

As the first, beautiful snowflakes fell to the ground, we hoped they'd melt before accumulating into banks we'd have to trudge through. And although the ice gleamed on the road below us, we ran with our hands inside our coats, trying to keep them from freezing as the water had. Mama dressed us as warmly as she could, nonetheless some days were so bitter cold that the wind chewed through us, and we felt as though our extremities would snap off with the slightest movement.

We began to settle into the apartment that would remain ours for an undetermined amount time. We had two bedrooms, a kitchen–living room combination, and our own bath. As much as I loved the farm, it was a luxury not having to go outside in the dark, chilly evening air to use the outhouse!

As we entered the front hallway, there were two stairways. One led into the basement, and one led upstairs into the apartment above us. The basement was divided into two sections: one section for the people who were living upstairs and one for us. Peter and I had to share not only a bedroom, but also the double bed. We were still small though, and we didn't mind.

Mama was concerned about finding a crib for the new baby, and once again, Uncle Joseph came to our rescue. He had many friends and was able to obtain a used one for us, which was a huge relief for Mama. Additionally, Aunt Hanna had an offer for us. She said, "I have a sewing machine at home, Elisabeth, but I don't know how to use it! You are welcome to have it if you like."

Mama was so appreciative you would have thought someone had given her a million dollars. It was only a crib and a sewing machine, but to her, it was everything she could possibly ask for.

Another mixed blessing arrived when Uncle Joseph found out that he too had been drafted. He thought since he would no longer need his bicycle that Papa could use it to ride into the city for work. "I know it's not much, but it's better than having to walk." So he rode it over one Sunday, and Mama gratefully accepted it. Still, we were all sad, it meant he would be joining the army.

Those items helped to get us going, and then everything started to fall into place. Mama went back–and-forth whenever she could to see Papa in Mainz. But he was more concerned about our welfare than his own, since he wasn't contributing financially. Mama alleviated some of his concerns when she assured him that she had begun soliciting sewing jobs, so we could buy the rations we were allotted. Thankfully, Papa's job was secure; when he was released from the hospital, it would be waiting for him.

We prayed he'd get well soon because we needed all of the help we could get and were frightened of being alone. Sure enough, it was only three weeks after we arrived in Rüsselsheim that Mama went into labor. When I found out that we were going to have another baby, I became filled with joy. Since I thought that Mama had ordered the baby, the least I could do was go around the neighborhood asking people if they had any dresses for my new baby sister.

People looked at me strangely and wondered where I got the idea that I was going to have a baby sister. I told them I just knew it had to be, and if they had any dresses, we sure could use them. They usually smiled and politely turned me away, but I didn't give up. I forged on, determined to collect clothes for my new baby sister.

Somehow, Mama knew it wouldn't be long, so she sent for a midwife who lived nearby to come and assist her delivery. The two of them were in the bedroom for what seemed a lifetime, while we waited. I felt bad for Mama. Until that moment, I thought babies came from the stork. I sat outside the door listening, and the noises that came from that room were bloodcurdling and enough to curl my toes. Then suddenly, the lady came out with a little bundle and asked, "Marlies, would you like to hold the new baby?" I was so excited, I yelled, "Yes, oh yes, I would love to hold the baby!"

A New Baby in the House

She helped me get proper hold of the tiny infant, while I proclaimed, "She's the most beautiful baby sister I have ever seen!" The lady corrected me, "Oh, no, you have made a mistake, it's not your baby sister, it's your baby *brother.*"

Feeling scorned, I told her, "In that case, you can take him right back where he came from. I don't want him!" I was not about to share my precious brother Peter. If I had to share him with anyone, a sister I could handle, but a brother was a big threat. Two boys would always have more fun together than a brother and a sister could, and I didn't want to share Peter with anyone. I loved him, and he was my closest friend. I depended on him for so much, and I was not about to be pushed aside by another brother. After telling the midwife that I didn't want him, I ran into my room and cried. I cried and cried and cried some more, feeling ever so bad for myself.

The lady came up and told me that there was no way to send him back. I would have to get used to the fact that we had a baby boy living in our home. It took me a long time before I realized he wasn't going anywhere. I didn't know what I was going to do, so I asked Peter repeatedly, "When he gets bigger, are you still going to love me as much as you do now? Am I still going to be in first place with you?" I was so concerned that someone else would win his heart.

But Peter calmed my nerves when he replied, "Can you imagine how long it will take before that little guy can walk and talk? He'll never catch up to us, and you never have to worry. You and I will always be this close." What a relief it was to hear those words!

As Mama struggled to take care of a newborn and the two of us, finally, Papa was released from the hospital; however, he was told that he couldn't even think of going to work for at least two more weeks. So while some semblance of normalcy returned for us with his return, everything was different for him. He not only needed to get used to a new place to hang his hat and a new place to earn a living, his wife's devotion was split amongst the rest of us—including a brand new baby. In addition, it was that much more difficult because we were literally poverty-stricken. Mama's sewing brought in a little, and we were able to swing the rent and manage to buy our rations for food, but Papa couldn't wait to get back to work, to bring home a paycheck, and regain his dignity through supporting his family.

Our new baby was born October 28, 1939, and thankfully, we were allotted extra rations for the additional mouth to feed. The baby would get milk for one year, and we'd manage the best we could. We walked into the city together to register him at the town hall, planning to name him John Joseph, but the Nazis informed us we couldn't give him *two* religious names. We had to give him a German name instead. Papa chose a very popular German name for him: Siegfried. Siegfried was a legendary character, powerful and strong. A kind man, he could be compared to Robin Hood. So, they named our new little brother Siegfried John, while having no choice.

Two weeks after our Siegfried was born, Aunt Hanna gave birth to her own baby boy and they were going to name him Joseph Michael, and again the authorities told Uncle Joseph two religious names were not allowed, so they also named their baby Siegfried. There was Siegfried John and Siegfried Joseph, which became quite confusing when they came to visit. We ended up calling our baby Siegfried and Aunt Hanna's baby *Little* Siegfried.

Uncle Joseph was sent away just two weeks after the birth, leaving Aunt Hanna alone in the city. She found an elderly lady who'd watch the baby for her while she worked during the day, and then she'd spend time with him during the evening. Many times she brought him to visit us, and Mama would keep him for a few days while Aunt

Hanna worked. This meant we had *two* babies, which was hard on Mama, but it helped knowing he was well-taken care of. It wasn't that the old lady wasn't taking good care of him, but Little Siegfried wasn't thriving the way our Siegfried was.

That was until just before Christmas, when our little guy developed whooping cough because there wasn't enough fuel to keep him warm. The house was always cold, especially at night. Often we couldn't sleep in our beds it was so cold. We brought our bedding and pillows from the bedrooms and placed them around the kitchen stove for warmth.

We had running water and a toilet, but with very little heat, it was taking its toll on our precious baby. We couldn't chance taking him into the city; it was too cold to walk that far. Soon enough Mama found a doctor willing to treat him at home. For a long time, things were serious with the baby, but he finally came around and pulled out of his illness. Nothing tore at my heartstrings more than that sick baby, and we were truly relieved when Siegfried was back to normal. Even though I didn't welcome him at first, I prayed so hard for his recovery because he was just a helpless little guy.

The holidays were around the corner, and the walk into the city increasingly difficult. Five miles was a long way in the bitter cold, making the walks to school tough. But we were tougher, and everyone else managed, so we would too. Papa and Siegfried were both feeling better, and I, of course, was all well. Things didn't look too bad.

As Christmas neared, we were told we weren't allowed to go into the forest to cut down trees of any kind, so our first Christmas in Germany was without a tree to decorate. We had a small manger, and Mama read Christmas stories as we celebrated the holiday in the most modest of ways. Buying presents was out of the question, but Mama made a new dress for my doll and a stuffed teddy bear for Siegfried. Papa obtained red paint from the Opel factory where he worked, and he gave Peter's little red wagon a shiny new paint job.

Our meal was sparse as well: there were no cookies, candy, or baked goods of any kind. Mama could make soup out of anything, and it was always pleasing to the palate, so we started with that.

The soup was followed by meat and baked potatoes with no butter. However, butter for our potatoes was hardly of great importance to us. We were all healthy, that's what mattered. And together we shared the holiday spirit with love and devotion, and for that, the greatest gift of all, we were thankful.

Though our family was content, worrying about how dismal our holiday could be, Oma sent us a package. What a surprise to find that Opa had taken the time to carve beautiful wooden tops for us. We couldn't wait for spring to arrive so we could take them outside to play with. They were three inches tall, and we wound them tight with string. The string had a stick on the end to flip it, and as it unwound, the centrifugal force spun the top rapidly. We took the string with the stick and whipped the tops so they'd keep going for long periods of time. They actually sailed through the air, spinning all the while.

Those were fun toys, which was a good thing, because other than my doll and Peter's red wagon, the tops were our only toys. We tried to use them in the house, without much success because our kitchen wasn't big enough, but nonetheless, we had a wonderful Christmas. It was sparse in material items, but we were together to celebrate the birth of Jesus, and to us, that was the true meaning, the spirit of Christmas.

Holidays or not, Peter and I had jobs around the house. One was bringing the wood up from the cellar. It was Peter's turn one day and mine the next. We brought the scraps of wood so Mama could cook and wash clothes. Since Peter was afraid of the dark, he always found some excuse to ask me to go with him when it was his turn. Of course, I loved him, and darkness didn't bother me, so I'd help him. But when it was my turn, I'd go alone—the wood was heavy and dirty, but a little dirt never stopped me from doing anything!

Whenever Peter did a favor for me of any kind, he always wanted me to pay him back by taking his turn at gathering the wood. Of course, I readily agreed and retrieved the wood sometimes two, three, or four nights in a row. There were also little chores we had to do to help around the house, like dusting, taking care of our toys, and clearing the dishes off the table after a meal.

Our first winter was tough, but we managed to make it through, feeling tremendous relief as spring gracefully eased into our lives. Gentle raindrops replaced falling snowflakes as the ice melted away. This meant we wouldn't have to sleep huddled around the stove in the kitchen any longer!

Spring in the Air and with it, Hope

The sky was filled with birds singing the most glorious songs. Crimson, mustard, and lavender perennials slowly peaked upward through the soil, and as spring fever hit, we happily helped Mama plant a garden to grow fresh vegetables. We planted all the different seeds Oma had sent along. There were beans, carrots, sweet potatoes, white potatoes, beets, cauliflower, broccoli, peas, parsley, and more. We planted everything, hoping the weather would hold out so our garden would provide for us next year.

Facing another winter without those vegetables could be devastating. It was vital that our garden prospered, and I could see the desperation in Mama's eyes. It was almost an obsession with her, the way she tended to that small plot of land behind our house. She hoed the soil, strategically placed the seeds, and constantly cared for them, making sure they were always sufficiently watered and free of weeds. As the tiny seeds sprouted, she was relieved and greatly comforted.

A friend from the Opel factory gave Papa two rabbits. He brought them home and built a pen for them behind the house. He told us that if times got tough and we didn't have any meat, we could butcher the rabbits and use them for a meal. I fell in love with those cuddly rabbits with the cutest, little twitching noses. I couldn't imagine ever being hungry enough to eat them.

We were still having to walk the five miles every day, of course, even at our young ages. Whether a hot summer afternoon or a frigid winter morning made no difference, we had to get to where we were going, no questions asked.

During the summer, we kicked stones around and played games to pass the time during our walks. Per Mama's orders, we went barefoot most of the time. She told us to only use our shoes when need be, in order to preserve them for the next long winter. She was always looking and planning ahead, purchasing our shoe's two sizes too big. Although that took some getting used to, the extra space left plenty of room for several pairs of Mama's hand made socks, which had kept our feet warm as we walked our way through the long winter months. But now, we kicked them off and toughened our feet up like the rest of our resolve.

5

Starving under Nazi Rule

It was 1940, a new year, and there were many changes. In a country that had never allowed posters or anything but curtains to hang in windows, all of a sudden they were displaying signs that read, JEWS GET OUT OF GERMANY. Peter and I noticed the signs while going to school or to the city, and we asked Mama what they meant. She had no answer other than, "I don't understand this. I just don't know what it means, but it seems like something very frightening."

We had already made friends with the Steins, a Jewish family that lived in our neighborhood. Mrs. Stein often visited while Mama sewed for her. She was a lovely lady from a lovely family, and we didn't understand why anyone would tell people like them to get out of Germany. Besides, the ports were all closed, how could they leave anyway?

We noticed that men everywhere were being drafted. From seventeen to eighty years old, as long as they could walk and carry a weapon, they were called to serve. The only fellows eluding the draft were those who had farming obligations. The large farms that required a farmhand were permitted to have someone remain on to do the job. If a man was ill, but able to work the land, they could also remain home because the government had an interest in making sure the crops were well tended.

The Steins were also concerned. They owned a hardware store and a vehicle and were quite well-to-do. In other businesses, the wives were asked to take over while the men were drafted; however, Mr. Stein hadn't received a draft notice. He wondered when they'd call on him and when his wife would have to go into the city and take care of the business.

Mama spoke to them about the signs. They told her they too were unaware as to what was going on, but many of their Jewish friends who owned businesses in Germany were offered double their value if they'd evacuate and go elsewhere. They were told they could go to France, Switzerland, England, or wherever they wanted, as long as they left Germany. Mama thought those offers seemed too good to be true. "Who on earth would pay anyone, Jewish or not, double what their property is worth?"

It seemed as though the Nazis were trying to rid the country of Jews, and we were concerned about the Steins. We asked them what they were going to do and what was going to happen, but they said they didn't know. Mr. Stein wondered how he could have lived in Germany for so many years and not be drafted like everyone around him. Soon after that discussion, a report came over the radio announcing that no Jewish men would be drafted. With that announcement, Mr. Stein's wait ended, and he was forced to make remarkably challenging decisions.

Until Papa was called into Nazi headquarters, he too was wondering if they were going to draft him. Fortunately, he was told that there was no way that he'd be permitted to serve in the German army, since he had become an American citizen. He was pleased with that decision, telling us, "How could I possibly fight in another war? Even if I could, I don't know if the United States will eventually be involved, and I certainly could never fight against soldiers who are now my people."

With Papa not getting drafted, the Nazis started taunting him and Mama quite severely. They started making Mama walk the five miles into the city, sometimes two and three times a week to bring her papers, including, all of our birth certificates, our citizenship papers, our *Bremen* tickets for our return to the States, and whatever other information we had with us that they might find pertinent.

She repeatedly brought the paperwork to Nazi headquarters. They'd go through it, read it, and send her back home, but not before telling her that our rations were much more than we should be allotted. That's when they began cutting them back.

Our three loaves of bread remained the same, but our meat was cut to two pounds per week. And it was no longer pork; it was downgraded to horsemeat. Our fuel rations were cut completely, meaning we couldn't get any wood for heat or cooking. Our rations for soap products shared the same fate, being cut completely. We had nothing for washing clothes or bathing.

Mama stood aghast, silently wondering, "How are we going to survive with no fuel? Winter will soon come again, and things will be worse than last year." Her eyes widened, her breathing was labored, all while she began to quiver, but she knew she had to contain herself, she couldn't let them see her contempt. Slowly but surely, they were trying to beat us down, but Mama had resolve. It only meant that we had to find our resources elsewhere, and she was determined not to let the Nazis bring peril upon us.

In addition to our deteriorating rations, the Nazis informed us that we were no longer permitted to speak English. It was completely forbidden. That way, they'd know exactly what was being said at all times. The walls in our apartment were paper-thin, and the people living above and beside us could hear every word spoken. Since they were members of the Nazi party, we did as directed and spoke German, even in the privacy of our own home.

Many people joined the Nazi party, but many others didn't. We never knew for sure who belonged, but their superior attitudes and better ration cards usually gave them away. They received greater quantities and quality of food and fuel, and as the Nazi party sowed dissension, the commandment, "Thou shalt love thy neighbor as thyself," was increasingly more difficult to obey and uphold. Not knowing who might turn you in and what they might turn you in for, made paranoia a justifiable and common state of mind.

Mama asked, "Why are the Nazis watching everything we're doing?" But neither she nor Papa could fathom.

Papa was told he couldn't leave the city, but if an emergency arose and he needed to break away, he had to report to them and let them know exactly where he was going. Additionally, he could only be gone for the day, returning by nightfall. Even if he had to go to Mainz for medical checkups, he had to inform SS headquarters of his whereabouts. The restrictions were not set up for Mama or us children, but they were strictly enforced for Papa.

For whatever reason, Mama had never followed through with the process of becoming an American citizen, but because she had married an American and had children with him, she lost her German citizenship. Never having officially applied to become an American, she had no citizenship at all, and was considered a woman without a country.

Even though she technically didn't have a country to claim, she wasn't as restricted as Papa was. My parents were both born and bred in Germany; their families still resided there; and Papa had fought in the First World War. He had been wounded as a soldier, and everyone had a great deal of respect and admiration for German soldiers—past or present. Fighting for one's country made a difference.

In Germany, sending letters or gifts to German soldiers never required postage, and neither did soldiers' mail require postage. When a soldier came home for a vacation or furlough, they didn't have to pay train fare or bills in restaurants as long as they wore a German uniform. Those benefits didn't apply to the SS or the Gestapo. Even though they wore uniforms, they were not considered soldiers. SS stood for *Schutzstaffel,* or guard corps, which eventually evolved as Hitler's elite troops, and Gestapo was an abbreviation for *Geheime Staatspolizei* or secret state police.

Since English was forbidden, and the SS and Gestapo seemed to lurk everywhere, it didn't take long before Peter and I forgot the language we had tried so hard to master. Nevertheless, our parents obeyed whatever they were told, just as we obeyed everything we were told. We didn't understand why, but we sensed the severity of Papa's request and didn't dare oppose it.

One evening, the Steins returned for a brief, farewell visit. Mr. Stein had decided to sell his property and leave the country with his family. Mama was worried. She asked, "Where will you go, and what will you do?"

Her concerns didn't matter. They had made up their minds to travel across the border. "Since it's near in distance, we're going to France. Even though they're an enemy of Germany, we've been given permission to evacuate. But we need to leave immediately while we still can." They already had relatives residing in France, and they were going to live with them. They sold their store and their home and received quite a bit of money for their belongings and property. The Steins had barely bid us farewell, when a Nazi family immediately took up residence in their home. The irony was not lost on any of us.

Mama was curious. "If the Jewish people can cross borders to other countries, perhaps we could cross over to England, France, or Austria, and from there travel back to the States." Papa inquired about Mama's suggestion the next time he traveled into the city, taking a detour to Nazi headquarters.

He summoned the courage to ask for permission to leave, but was instantly denied. They wouldn't permit us to go anywhere. The borders and ports were closed indefinitely to everyone, including us. Papa removed his hat, holding it close to his chest while pointing out, "But with all due respect, the Jewish people are leaving." The Nazis exchanged smug grins, while ignoring his words; they left him standing there, as if he weren't even in their company. Papa left, feeling more perplexed than ever.

After contemplating the discussion on his brisk, bicycle ride home, the only reason for denying our family permission to leave that he could conclude was the Opel factory where he worked. In the past, the factory manufactured all kinds of products, from sewing machines to bicycles, from automobiles to home furnishings, but few knew about the existence of the underground weapons factory where Papa was employed. General Motors, an American automobile conglomerate, had acquired the factory from the Adam Opel Motor Firm in 1929, but by 1940, the German government had seized control of the premier manufacturing plant to aid their own cause: World War II.

He worked in the weapons factory, for the simple fact that it was the only work offered to him. He was employed with Russians, French, Polish, Czechoslovakian, Hungarians, and various prisoners of war. Paradoxically, the prisoners were manufacturing the very weapons that would be used against their homelands. They were making war materials, guns, all kinds of ammunition, and bombs; and they manufactured parts that were used on airplanes and tanks. One of the reasons they didn't want Papa to leave was he knew too much, and they didn't want anyone to know about the secret factory doings. It was a highly guarded military secret, so they kept close watch on us and a closer watch on him.

Although we didn't feel it much at first, the many restrictions were starting to choke us. The Gestapo repeatedly and continuously required Mama to walk to the city and read her papers. They already knew what we had and who we were, but the constant badgering and supervision was starting to affect us in important ways. Each time she met with them, they placed additional restrictions on our family and our lifestyle.

It began by cutting our rations and moved on to forbidding us from looking for wood in the forest and collecting fallen fruit from the orchards. Only German citizens were allowed to pick up the fruit, and we didn't qualify. But Peter and I often took the little red wagon and snuck into the orchard anyway to find something to eat. Many times we returned with nothing, keeping in mind the German people were also hungry. They were going into the orchards as well and had often picked them clean. Mama never allowed us to pick the fruit from the trees because to her, that was considered stealing, and she'd rather starve than steal. If it were already on the ground, it would have rotted sooner or later, making the fallen fruit fair game.

We watched the curbside to see when people threw things away. If there had been a fire in a house or junk was thrown out, we'd pick through it, searching for pieces of wood that could be used in our stove for burning. We were never too proud to pick through someone's trash if it meant the difference between having heat and a warm meal or not.

Mama continued sewing for people, and she asked them if they'd pay her with coal or wood, because unlike us, most people were still allowed coal rations. She began stockpiling in the basement, along with the items we picked up off the street. She worked for many of the farmers around the area. One had two blind sons, who couldn't go into the war, so they remained working on their farm. She made new clothes and repaired their old ones for them. In exchange, they'd give her a little grain, while occasionally, if they could spare a bit of flour or an egg or two, they would. The extra food helped keep Papa healthy, so he could continue working. Mama was worried about him because he wasn't getting the proper nutrition he needed for someone who worked as hard as he did, at his age.

With the grain she received as payment, she often made a makeshift coffee by placing it in a frying pan and shaking it over low heat until it turned golden brown. She then put it through a grinder to make it look like coffee before scooping it into a cup and adding boiling water. It was healthy and tasted pretty good too. If we didn't have grain, we gathered chamomile flowers to make tea, which was also healthy and could be used to soothe stomach cramps, while the flowers could be crushed and used to heal infections.

When there was no coffee or tea available, Mama saved the water from our cooked vegetables and put it in containers, and that's what we drank. She knew we needed the vitamins since we didn't have milk or fruit juice available, and frugality was a way of life for Mama, who had always made the most out of the least.

The majority of people in Germany had started losing so much weight that Mama had plenty of work sewing and making alterations to their clothing. This was especially true for Papa, and she prayed for a day when she'd be able to let the stitches out again, the day he'd recoup the many pounds he'd lost.

Our shoe rations were cut to one pair per year per person, and she lovingly gave hers up, knowing Papa needed them more. When weather permitted, she went barefoot just like us to preserve her shoes longer, so he'd have an extra pair in the wintertime. While enduring the long walks each day, his boots were often soaked by the time he returned home, and at least he'd have a dry pair for the next day, while the others dried out. Those were hard times, not being able to get rations for the items we desperately needed, but Mama never made a fuss; she just kept pushing forward.

Being resourceful, since we didn't have soap, she used wood ashes from the stove to wash our clothes. She placed the ashes in a linen bag, put the bag in a tub full of water on top of the stove and brought it to a rolling boil, and then placed the white clothes inside. Without exaggeration, the clothes were positively bleached clean.

When the water temperature cooled, she replaced the whites with our wool and colored clothes. Washing with wood ashes was the only way to get the clothes clean without any detergent, and afterwards she'd wring them out by hand before hanging them out to dry. As far as soap went, when we left Oma's, she'd put some lye in our trunk, but Mama made us use it sparingly. Only when absolutely necessary did we touch it, as it was used primarily to bathe the baby and keep him, his diapers, and his clothes pristine.

Our baths were taken with vinegar and water, and although it was very clean and healthy for our skin, we usually smelled sour, like a couple of tossed salads afterwards. If we weren't dirty enough to warrant taking a bath, we washed our hands and faces with weeds we collected from outside, since Mama believed the chlorophyll kept our faces and hands free of dirt—never mind that weeds were plentiful.

Being so young, it was a big job keeping us clean. As usual, I was still the bigger problem. Some things never changed, but occasionally if we were working, there were days when Peter would throw on a pair of bib overalls, a T-shirt, a hat, and a big pair of rubber boots that went high above his knees. With a rake and wheelbarrow in hand, he'd head for the garden and on occasion, he was known to return every bit as dirty as I.

We were looking forward to the long days of summer, not only because we wanted to play with our Christmas tops, but because we had received a letter from Oma saying that she would like us kids to come and stay with her when summer recess began. She needed extra help on the farm, because Opa was increasingly getting worse, making it difficult for him to do almost anything. He was in constant pain, but forcing himself to keep going, as he knew his wife needed him. As sorrowful as I was that Opa was failing, I was thrilled to have the opportunity to spend an entire summer on the farm I loved so much. To have room to run and animals to care for were a dream come true. Most important, I loved being there with my grandparents.

Just before school let out, a notice came stating children from first grade on had to learn how to knit. It was part of the new school curriculum—all students had to comply, not just females. Each class had to provide the government with a certain amount of knitted items throughout the year. They wanted the younger children to make scarves, while the older children made hats, sweaters, gloves, and socks for the government. The winter months had been taking a toll on the soldiers; and since the factories were producing war materials, they couldn't produce the necessary clothing to keep the soldiers warm and dry. Therefore, to get the job done, the government ordered students as young as six years old to take up knitting.

It seemed like it would never happen, but summer finally arrived. I had been counting the days before we boarded the train for Kell. I just knew that it was going to be a glorious vacation, and I couldn't wait to get started. We already knew the townspeople, and they knew us—making it that much more exciting. While dropping us off, Mama was only able to spend two days on the farm. She told Oma how our rations had been cut, so Oma gathered and packed two hams, some flour, potatoes, soap, and various seeds for Mama to take back with her. The farmers were still allowed rations for seeds, and that's why Oma was able to spare some.

Within a very short period of time, we were able to see how rationing had affected the farmers as well as everyone else. We found out that when a litter of pigs was born, they were required to inform the Nazis immediately as to how many piglets there were.

All of the pigs were to be raised and fed by the farmer, but when it came time for butchering, the Nazis came and gathered them, leaving only one for the farmer. The remaining pig was to be used by the people on the farm as their main food source for the entire year. If there were less than three people in the household, they weren't permitted to keep any.

If they had chickens, likewise, they had to report how many there were, so a percentage of the eggs could be given to the government. In order to kill a chicken for consumption, they had to inform the Nazis and get permission prior to doing so. Otherwise, one feather on the chicken couldn't be harmed. Additionally, when baby chicks hatched, they were to be counted and reported immediately.

The cows were counted to see how many existed on each farm. They calculated how much milk the cows could produce, allowing the farmer to keep a portion with the rest confiscated by the Nazis. Likewise with butter. The farmers were cut to nearly the same meager rations as non-farming Germans, though they produced the items themselves. Of the large amount of grain that was harvested in the country, only a small portion was converted to flour for the farmers' use. The bulk of it went to the government like everything else.

Mama was worried about what would happen when the boys came home. What food would there be to feed the soldiers? When they came home on furlough, the family rations were not increased. They'd have to eat whatever was already available, taking away from those it was intended for. Once they left, their families were that much further in the hole. Every mouth that had to be fed was cutting into what was allotted until the subsequent year. But my grandparents planned ahead for such occasions. Having an idea of what might be in store, they concealed many items before the Nazis took inventory, including the flour and butter that was in the cooler that Opa built. The lion's share of the grain and potatoes were hidden in an underground hole, where, surprisingly, they didn't spoil. Thankfully, many hidden items remained edible. Mama was pleased, because for the length of time we'd spend at our grandparents, her rations wouldn't be cut, and she'd be able to accumulate and store some necessities for winter as well.

Another Wonderful Summer at the Kell Farm

Our summer spent in Kell was wonderful, partially because Opa was still well enough to take us children for walks on Sunday mornings. He took us deep into the forest and showed us different plants and various items he used to treat sick animals and people in the village.

He had become the village veterinarian, and he'd occasionally take care of sick people too. Often people called on him, asking, "Matthew, can you help us?" Perhaps, one of their cows was having trouble giving birth, or maybe they'd eaten some type of food that didn't agree, making them blow up with gas. Opa knew how to make an incision in the cow's stomach that kept them alive, and he was always obliged to help. Everywhere we turned, there were reminders of how competent, talented, and special he was. People sought him out for his homemade remedies, and soon he had become the town healer, with very little that he couldn't do. He was invaluable for the well-being of the villagers, and they felt great sorrow as he slowly began to succumb to the cancer.

The good part for us was that he had plenty of time to tell us stories—the kind that kept us glued to our seats. The journeys he took us on far surpassed the ones we could conjure in our own young minds. He recalled a time when he was younger and hunting for turkey and wild rabbits; he'd found himself in quite a precarious situation. The forests were filled with wild pigs, and as he quietly made his way deeper into the woods, he heard a noise. Being an avid hunter, he recognized the sound and immediately climbed a small tree in the clearing, just as a wild sow exited the thick brush. With her tusks moving from side to side, she grunted loudly, warning predators as she proudly strutted with her litter of little ones trailing behind in single file. As she and her piglets passed directly under him, Opa noticed the runt had fallen considerably behind. Waiting for the right moment, he scurried down the tree and grabbed the little one who immediately began to squeal. Hoping to muffle the sound, he quickly placed it into his pocket as he climbed back to the safety of the branches above.

Hearing the commotion, Mama Sow did an immediate about-face and went absolutely wild as she headed directly for the sound of her distressed baby. Looking up, she slammed head-on into the tree, goring, biting, and attacking it again and again from every angle. As Opa made his way higher into the tree, every branch shook violently and abruptly. He began to realize that this may not have been such a good idea.

Terrified of the outcome, he lowered himself to where he could safely drop the piglet on the ground, without allowing the mother the opportunity to shake him from safety. Unfortunately, she was not satisfied with triumph; she wanted revenge. Her tirade was far from over. Irate, she remained at the bottom of the tree for over an hour, relentlessly striking what was left of the trunk. Staying high in the tree, he prayed for his life as the top began to lean, knowing all the while that if she knocked the tree down—and it seemed as though she might—she'd surely kill him for endangering her piglet. Eventually, the wild sow gave up and walked away grunting, with her brood of babies following. Opa was thankful that his life was spared, and so was I!

Being on the farm was wonderful, but it wasn't simply a vacation and a time to tell stories. We were expected to work, and with most of the men gone, things were tougher than the year prior. Before the morning sun had risen, we were on the wagons, heading out to the fields that glistened with the morning dew. There was usually a chill in the air, but it didn't last long as we began our rigorous daily chores. Hard work always had a way of warming us up.

When it came time for digging the potatoes, Aunt Ida, Aunt Clara, Uncle Johann and, on a good day, Opa dug them by hand. It was a tough job, but our part was easier; we retrieved the potatoes, placed them in baskets, and carried them to the large sacks. At the end of the day, with huge needles, they sewed the top part of the sacks closed and lifted them onto the wagon. That was the routine day after day, until the wagon was full. And then we'd take them home for the Nazis to confiscate.

When it came time to harvest the hay, that was also done by hand. Huge sickles were used to take it down piece by piece. Peter and I learned to gather the hay with pitchforks and throw it on the wagon, at least until it got too high for us to reach. At that point, Uncle Johann and Aunt Ida took over and finished filling the wagon. When it was completely full, Peter and I hopped on top for the ride back to the barn.

Once back in the barn, Peter stood on the wagon with his pitchfork, throwing the hay up to the loft, and I stood on top with mine and threw it to the back of the loft and tried to pack it. As young as we were, we were doing heavy farm work, and even though it was challenging, our help was invaluable to our grandparents that summer.

When the cows were brought home, Oma prepared the main meal. She also prepared something for later in the evening. Sometimes she'd make bread with sausage on it, but regardless of what it was, we always had a warm glass of milk. After the last drops of milk were gone, we'd go into the barn to clean the cows, clean out the manure, and wash down the stalls with buckets and brooms.

Aunt Clara and Aunt Ida always milked the cows, and Uncle Johann always fed them. They had to feed and clean the pigs as well. The chickens also had to be fed, and we had to collect their freshly laid eggs. Those were my jobs. When it was time to retire to the house, everyone took their manure-coated shoes off and washed up for the final meal of the day. Afterwards, we cleaned our shoes and often took a quick bath, before it was off to bed so we could get up early and do it all again.

From the moment my head hit the pillow, falling asleep was never a problem at Oma's house. We worked ourselves ragged throughout the day and were well deserving of a good night's sleep. That's the way our summer went, and I loved every minute of it.

Often, Aunt Mary and my cousins Yosefa, Carly, and Marlies came over to help. Unfortunately my namesake, Marlies, was not always interested in helping us. She clearly enjoyed playing more than she enjoyed working, and lingering about suited her just fine. Oma often became upset with her, and many times, she sent her home without anything to eat, because she hadn't done any work. She'd rather play with dirt balls in the fields than pick up potatoes, always claiming her back hurt.

On Sundays, other than feeding the animals, we relaxed. Occasionally after mass, Peter and I packed a lunch and took the cows, including the milking cow that never pulled machinery, into the fields for grazing. If it wasn't raining, we usually stayed in the field until late in the afternoon. As dusk fell upon us, we'd herd the cattle back to the barn for milking.

After the animals were put away and the barn was secured, we sat in the house with Oma, and she taught us how to knit. It wasn't long until I had become quite proficient in the art and proud of my accomplishments. She'd help me get started, and then I was on my own.

Before we returned to Rüsselsheim, I had learned how to make my first scarf. Since we hadn't started school yet, I didn't have to turn it into the government; I was able to keep it. So I gave it to Papa. I thought he could wear it to work; he had to walk such a long way in the cold. I was sure it would help keep him warm. He wore it with great pride once winter came. It was almost like a medal to him.

When Oma wasn't working or helping one of us, she headed for a private spot that she called her retreat. Sometimes when she became depressed over Opa's failing health or her nerves simply gave out, she needed to be alone, and she'd go there for solitude.

Many years prior, Opa had purchased this charming piece of land where berries grew. Oma had blueberries, elderberries, currant berries, as well as others. It was set up nicely, with a fence surrounding the area and a covered bench that Opa had built in case it should start to rain or when the sun was too bright or too hot. She sat in that beautifully shaded little garden of hers to reflect, pray, or do nothing at all. It was her private retreat, and she always went there alone.

To my surprise, one Sunday she invited me to go with her, which was something I never thought would happen. We chatted all the way, and when we got there, I helped her remove the weeds around the berry bushes before we picked some. We ate a few as we gathered others to take home to Opa. He loved fresh berries, and they were good for him. Most important, he could still tolerate them, unlike many of his other favorites.

We sat for hours discussing life, and my grandmother asked if there was something bothering me. I told her that the Priest was explaining to us about the Blessed Trinity and I could not understand that God could be three persons in one. "Oma, how could he be God the Father, God the Son, and God the Holy Spirit?" She explained it to me very simply by saying, "Let us pretend that God is a freshly baked apple kuchen. I will cut a small piece of the kuchen for you and we'll call it Jesus. Then I will cut a small piece for me and we'll call it the Holy Spirit. The rest of the kuchen is still God the Father." She then went on to say that, "It's almost time for dinner so we will wait until later to eat the kuchen. So lets place the pieces of the kuchen that we cut back on the platter in the same place from where they came. It then becomes the same whole kuchen as it was before we cut it." Our conversation made me happy because I was able to understand that God the Father, God the Son, Jesus and God the Holy Spirit are one, just like the kuchen. From that moment on, it became easy for me to understand the blessed trinity.

While we were there, she also told me another wonderful story. "Sometimes, there are things that we don't like doing, but we shouldn't try to avoid them; we simply need to do them anyway. Do things for a brick," she said.

"Oma, I don't understand. Why should I do things for a brick?"

"Well, when the time comes that you go to heaven, you want to make sure that you have built yourself a lovely home." She proceeded to tell me the story of a very wealthy woman who had a poor, elderly lady working for her. The wealthy woman didn't treat her servant with kindness or respect. She made many demands on her and never thanked her for anything. Even though the servant was treated poorly, she never once complained about the abuse she endured.

It so happened that the servant knew how to drive, and she chauffeured the wealthy woman around when needed. One day, they had a severe automobile accident, and both women perished. They each went to heaven, and when they got there, they met Saint

Peter, who took them for a walk and showed them all of the heavenly homes. He indicated which ones were empty and available. As they walked down the street toward a gorgeous mansion, the rich lady said, "Is that mansion available?"

Saint Peter said, "Yes it is—available and not yet occupied." They walked a bit farther, where there were even more beautiful homes. But as they continued down the street, the homes became smaller and smaller, until the last one was no larger than a shed. "Now we'll pick out a home for each of you two ladies."

The wealthy woman said, "Since I'm used to wealth, I would like to have the first house. It seems to be the stateliest and the most beautiful on the street. That is the house I prefer."

Saint Peter asked the little old lady, which one she would like to have, and she replied, "Oh, I'm just so happy to be in heaven that it doesn't matter. I'm used to not having a lot, so whatever's available is fine. In fact, if you don't mind, I will take the small one at the end of the street."

Saint Peter smiled at her and whispered, "Oh, you have it all wrong. You have things reversed, the big house at the end of the street is already your house, and that little house belongs to your former employer."

The wealthy woman was furious and bellowed, "There is no way, no possible way! What would this little, old woman be doing in that big beautiful house, while I spend my time in that chicken coop? I'm not going to live there. I won't have it!"

Saint Peter informed her, "Well that's what you've purchased."

She proceeded to argue, "I didn't purchase anything. I don't know how you can say that!" Saint Peter explained, "Well you see, up here we build homes according to the material sent to us, and since there was no material sent from you, this is all you get. This little lady here, however, sent us all of the material to build that beautiful mansion."

The women didn't understand, so Saint Peter reiterated, "Whenever you do a kind act on earth, you send us a brick or a piece of material. She sent enough to build that mansion. You, however, were so busy collecting items for yourself on earth, that you had no time to send us anything with which to build your house in heaven. The kind deeds that you did on earth were so minuscule that we had virtually nothing to work with."

Oma reminded me, "When you are here on earth, and there are things that you don't like doing, do them anyway—do them for a brick. That way, someday you'll build yourself a beautiful home in heaven."

Oma's story made such an impression on me that from then on, no matter what I did, that I didn't like doing, I did it anyway. Oma always had something good to teach, something nice to share, and she made life on the farm beautiful.

A "Real Adams"

After returning home, we entered the barn and realized that it was nearly time for the old sow to have her litter of pigs. I waited and waited for the wonderful event to occur, and all of a sudden one afternoon, Oma told me that the sow indeed had her litter.

Oma warned me not to go near her, "When she has a litter of pigs, she becomes very violent. She wouldn't hesitate to kill someone if they ventured to close to her babies." She also warned, "We can't even go near her to clean out her stall for at least a week or more."

The sow had become so nasty that they built a partition with huge planks to separate her from the area where she did her duty. Someone had to go with a long rake to pull out the old straw, so that fresh straw could be thrown in the pen.

She wanted nothing and no one near her little ones, and to prove it, she repcatedly tore the partition down. It had to be fixed several times. Oma told me when the time came for me to see the babies, she'd lift me up so I could peek into the stall. That was a major let down for me, because I wanted so badly to see them that day, and I didn't figure she could be so horrible. After all, we had always gotten along just fine.

I had gone to spend some time with Aunt Mary later that day, and I was told to be home by three o'clock in the afternoon. I was never late, because I was used to having to be home on time from the days when Papa stood outside the door whistling. Aunt Mary knew I had to be home by three, and at quarter till, she told me I had better get going. Three o'clock came, and Oma was waiting for me, but I had arrived a bit early and snuck into the barn to see the sow.

Mama Sow was my friend, and I had walked with her, lifting her enormous ears above her eyes so she didn't bump into harm's way, talking with her until she trusted me, so I didn't understand why she'd be angry with me now. I proceeded into her stall and started opening the door as she approached, grunting loudly. She appeared to be extremely agitated, so I began talking to her while petting her short bristly hair. I knew if she heard my voice, she'd understand. I told her, "I only came to see your babies. I won't hurt them. Is it all right if I come in and just peek a little bit?"

I eased my way in and slowly closed the stall door behind me. Still grunting, she moved sideways pushing me up against the wall with her massive body, which she kept between the nest of piglets and me. She proceeded to lie down, so I'd be behind her. Stretching my neck, I could barely see over her when I finally caught a glimpse. She didn't seem to mind that I was there, and as I peered over the top of her, I was fascinated to watch them come out and drink from her nipples. I was trying to count the little ones, when all of the sudden, I heard Oma calling me. And so did Mama Sow. She jumped up and headed toward the door, angry, biting at the stall, and grunting loudly. I yelled to Oma, "I'm right over here," and when she saw me, I thought she was going to have a heart attack right then and there. Aunt Clara was with her, and they'd been looking for me for quite some time when it dawned on them that I might be in the barn.

They were frantic as the sow charged the door, attempting to get at Oma, who was trying to distract her, while in one big sweeping motion, Aunt Clara proceeded to lift me right over the wall. Mama Sow was irate, and so was Oma. As she stood there, I thought for sure she was going to collapse before recouping herself and scolding me, "What on earth possessed you to go in there?"

"Oma, don't you understand? She's my friend, and she trusts me and loves me, and she would never hurt me, and she didn't." I told her how the sow let me in. Oma contained herself, realizing that she was simply relieved and thankful that the sow hadn't killed me—and that I was very much alive. She hugged me, warning, "Never, never, *ever* disobey me again! How could you possibly do that?"

Neither of them could believe that a sow as wild as theirs didn't hurt me. Aunt Clara uttered, "There must be something special about you and those animals. I don't understand how you can act the way you do around them. You crawl under the cow's legs and they don't bother you. The pigs follow you everywhere. And I can't believe this. There's just something about you and these animals."

I told her, "Aunt Clara, I love them so much, I could spend forever with the animals here on the farm. It's the most beautiful place in the world."

They took me into the house and told Opa what happened. He rubbed my head and said, "Yes, you have something special with the animals. They all love and trust you, and that must be a wonderful feeling, as very few people have that gift. When animals love someone unconditionally, there can't be any bad in them."

I figured, there might not be any bad in me, but I wondered why I wasn't like the Hans family. Every time someone referred to me, they always added, "She's a real *Adams*." That was another thing that puzzled me. We had been in Germany for over a year, and in all of that time, we had never met anyone in Papa's family. How could I possibly be so much like people I never even met?

He had informed his sister and brother that he had returned to Germany. He had told them where we were living. Every now and then, he received a letter from one or the other, but they never made any attempt to visit. Conversely, they never invited us to go see them. I suppose it didn't really matter, since Papa was forbidden to leave the city. He probably wouldn't have been able to make it to their homes and back within the same day anyway. However, he rarely mentioned them, and that seemed odd, considering how close Mama was to her family.

Since I had never met any of my Adams relatives, when someone said "you are a real Adams," I always felt insulted. I wanted so badly to be a *real Hans*. I wanted to be just like them. I loved them all so much and was so proud to be part of their family, but why did people view me as an Adams? How come they considered Peter to be more of a Hans?

Troubled by the thought, I spent much time contemplating, and finally concluded that it must be because I was stubborn, got into more things, and was less obedient. Peter was neat, clean, obedient, and hard working, while I'd rather try and get around things. I recalled times like when I went into the sow's stall and didn't obey Oma. That was something that Peter would never do, yet I did. I always attempted to push the limits doing things that I knew I wasn't supposed to. It seemed like the harder I tried, the more trouble I got into. There were many things that caused me to be different, and that must have been why they called me an Adams. But I didn't want it to be brought up or made known, nor did I appreciate it.

The Two Marlies

That summer, while we were still with Oma, I spent time with my cousin Marlies. She usually instigated problems and arguments, while she and I usually went round and round and were always into it with each other. Perhaps it was due to the fact that we were both stubborn and very close in age. I could see that Oma wasn't happy with the type of person that my cousin was turning out to be. Marlies was defiant, disobedient, and oftentimes Oma simply sent her home. While I had the occasional Adams flare-up, I wasn't generally disobedient, defiant, or lazy. I'd never dream of back-talking anyone, while for Marlies, it was common practice. She was extremely mouthy with Aunt Ida, who was also close in age to us. I considered her more like a sister than an aunt, because she was only seven years older than I.

One day, Marlies' father, who was in the service, sent home a package containing candy, among other things. Marlies came over to Oma's farm with a large piece of the chocolate and stood in front of Peter and me, taunting us. She said, "My father sent this, and it's too bad your father's not in the war and can't send presents home to you. Your father can never send you any candy, but mine sends it to me." She stood there licking it in front of us, teasing, "This tastes so good; it's such a shame that you don't have any." I imagined how that chocolate would taste, but after a while, it didn't seem so appealing to me. What really bothered me was the way that she was eating it.

"Why didn't you eat it at home? Why did you bring it here to aggravate us?" Peter stood staring, as if his tongue were following hers as she licked that chocolate up and down. I felt sorry for him, and I decided that there was no way that I was going to stand there and let her taunt Peter. I didn't care if I had any of it. I just wanted him to have some, so I ran over and knocked her down, grabbed the chocolate, and yelled, "Peter, here, quick, take it!"

I handed it to him as I held her down on the cobblestone. I sat on her, holding her beneath me with all of my might. She clawed and scratched, while trying to escape. I waited for Peter to finish eating the chocolate, and as soon as he did, I let her go. She was infuriated!

All of the sudden, I looked up and saw Aunt Clara step out from behind the barn door. Realizing she had seen what happened, I turned and told Marlies, "I'm sorry for knocking you down and taking your chocolate away. But you shouldn't have done what you did."

Aunt Clara walked over, stood before us, and instead of punishing me, she said, "I don't know what took you so long to knock her down and take that candy away. If it had been me, I would have done it long before." She told Marlies to go home immediately, and she did, blubbering all the way.

I didn't want my aunt to be disappointed in me, so I explained, "I'm sorry. I know what I did was wrong," but Aunt Clara told me I wasn't wrong, and she walked into the house.

Not long after, Aunt Mary came by, with Marlies trailing behind, demanding to know what happened. "Clara, my daughter came home crying and told me some kind of story. Now, I want to know the truth!"

After hearing what happened, Aunt Mary spun around, looked at Marlies, and bellowed, "How could you do such a thing? I sent you over here with that chocolate to share. You were to break it in half and give one to Peter and the other to Marlies. You already had your chocolate, and that piece was a gift for them! They deserved to have it because, unlike you, they never have anything special, they work hard, and they're good kids." Without taking a breath, she continued, "I thought I could trust you, and this is what you did! Well, there's more candy home, but you've had your last piece. The rest will be shared between Yosefa, Carly, Peter, and Marlies."

Even Oma was upset with Marlies, telling her not to come around for the next three days. "You're not welcome in my house. Your brother and sister can come, but trouble makers are not welcome." After being made to apologize and with her head hanging low, she turned away and headed home.

These were the things that made the family refer to me as an Adams. Peter was the type of person who could stand back, let it happen, and walk away. He never wanted turmoil, and he didn't like arguments or fighting of any type. He was always kind and gentle, and if he had something special, he'd give it away before keeping it to himself.

Aunt Mary later brought me a piece of chocolate, and I thanked her for being so nice to us. She was a beautiful, warm, and a lovely lady who always had a smile on her face. I loved her a great deal.

Pigs, and Spiders, and Mice, Oh My!

My problems with Marlies were the least of our troubles. We knew the time was nearing for the Nazis to pay us a visit, so our baby pigs had to be accounted for. When we finally had the opportunity to count them, we were amazed to find sixteen of the cutest, pink babies. When the Nazis came demanding to know how many there were, Aunt Clara told them fifteen.

In the meantime, she had taken one piglet and hidden it in a stall that Opa had built in the attic, specially designed for a piglet in hiding. It had a tin floor with a sunken bucket where the urine could be collected. Straw, food, and water were taken up and all the necessary preparations made, without the Nazis having knowledge of it. We knew that lying was wrong, but desperate times called for desperate measures.

Our tiny piglet was fed with a baby bottle and Oma made us promise we'd never tell a single soul about our secret, because if the Nazis found out, it meant imprisonment and possibly death for my grandparents. It was my job to take care of *the baby* and of course that was one job I loved. I'd make sure he was fed and the stall was clean, and on a daily basis, I opened the window to give him fresh air and walked him back and forth for exercise.

Oma had told me that in addition to food and water, animals need fresh air, sunshine and exercise, which I was determined to provide for my little pig. I spent a lot of time with the piglet, and as he started to flourish, we grew quite attached to one another. He looked forward to our visits, and so did I. Life on the farm was thrilling, and I was proud to be such a big part of our little secret. It was a lot of hard work, but the many praises made it all worthwhile.

Although I lived to take care of the animals, we still had our farm work to attend to. One afternoon we brought home a wagon of hay, and Peter was on top pitching the hay up onto the mound, when he called up to me, "Marlies, there's something on my back. It's biting me!" I went down the ladder, pulled his T-shirt up, and a big black spider fell into the hay. I was terrified of spiders and screamed, "Aaahh! You better come down and get into the house!"

Aunt Clara was home, taking care of Opa, so she looked at Peter's back, but within minutes, it became swollen and red. She applied medication to the bite, and although it was a poisonous spider, he was going to be fine. She comforted us, promising, "Yes, we do have poisonous spiders here, but don't worry, none are deadly." We went right back outside and continued pitching hay on the mound. That night, when she examined his back, it looked as if someone had beaten him with a club. His entire back was black-and-blue and very red. It looked terrible, but Aunt Clara continued to care for him, and within days, the swelling went down and the black-and-blue marks began to fade.

On the farm, along with the spiders, we also encountered other troublemakers. There were mice—and lots of 'em. All the mousetraps we had were already being used in the lower part of the house, and we couldn't purchase any new mousetraps anywhere.

Sometimes, upstairs in my bedroom, I'd hear noises, and I knew that one of those little critters had somehow gotten upstairs. I could hear them scurrying around. Luckily, I wasn't afraid of mice, and Opa had taught me how to build my own mousetrap. I used an empty thread-spool and put a cereal bowl upside down on the edge of the spool. Underneath that, I put a small piece of cheese. I'd go to bed and occasionally hear the noise of the bowl slamming onto the ground. In the morning, I'd get up and move the bowl back and forth to feel if something—or someone—was underneath. If so, I'd call the cat. Anticipating what we might find, she'd sit patiently and watch as I lifted the bowl for her to catch the mouse. My mousetrap worked wonders! After a short period of time, I no longer heard any scurrying critters. The cat did such a nice job that I set up other bowls in other rooms hoping to catch all the pesky vermin.

There was so much to learn and so much to do on the farm. It kept us busy and happy. Sadly, summer and our vacation had to come to an end, and finally we returned to Rüsselsheim. Mama came to get us and, of course, we were happy to see her, but we were not happy to leave the farm. I would have given anything to stay there throughout the year. That not being possible, we tearfully, said our sad good-byes, and wished Opa well, and headed back to the city.

6
The Rule of Fear

Things had changed drastically. It was like returning to a different world where people were all busy doing their own thing. It was hard to be friendly with them; most seemed so drawn into themselves. The intriguing kinship I'd experienced on the farm was not to be seen amongst the people of the city. They were standoffish and seemed frightened of something, but we still didn't know exactly what it was.

Upon returning to school—just as they'd promised—the first thing we were instructed on was knitting. Thanks to Oma, I had already learned. I felt very proud as some of the other children struggled just to hold the needles. Our teacher supplied us with yarn, and we had one class where we did nothing but knit. Anything we didn't finish in school, we were required to take home for completion.

Our studies were difficult, and our teachers were strict—often abusive. We had to wear a rucksack, a leather bag that we strapped to our shoulders and carried like a backpack. We used miniature blackboards to do our studies, because paper was no longer available. There were two strings attached to the sides of the blackboard: one held a dry cloth, and the other held a wet one. We used the wet one to wipe off the chalk and the other one to dry it, so we could continue with our studies. We carried our blackboards and our books in our rucksacks making it easy to carry everything, leaving our hands free to put in our pockets on wet, dreary days.

Our teacher was strict about not having smudges on our blackboards. Our work had to be neat and legible—and if there were irregularities, the teacher would erase our work, not even looking at it. They didn't want to have to ask, "Is this a nine or something else?" All letters had to be standing up perfectly straight, and one letter couldn't be any higher than the next. They also had to be the same width and have consistency, and since we were terrified of our teachers, we did our best to comply.

Education was of the utmost importance in Germany. We'd enter the school building, stand in the hallway, and line up with our classmates. The teacher checked our cloths and made sure that one was wet and one was dry. Next, we walked into the classroom, stood at attention next to our desks, and saluted Hitler. When the teacher walked into the classroom, we completed the routine by taking our books and belongings out of our rucksacks and placing them into our desks. Without a word being spoken, we folded our hands, sat at attention, eyes on the teacher, and waited for further instructions. We all understood what was required, and there were no exceptions.

If we wandered off track, we were called up front. The teachers had willow sticks, and they'd order us to hold out our hands, while they gave us a swift swat on our fingertips. What we had done or not done determined how many swats we received. The swats were always on the fingers we wrote with, which made it difficult to complete our work—the stinging pain pulsated throughout the hand.

One afternoon, I received a painful swat across mine when I dropped my chalk. It rolled across the floor and underneath the chair of the girl who sat next to me. The teacher was talking, and he told us to take down notes. It was the only piece of chalk I had, so I raised my hand for permission to pick it up. He barked, "There are no questions at this time."

I couldn't take down my notes, and I was getting nervous, so I made a hissing sound. The girl in front turned to see what was going on. I pointed to my chalk on the floor, and the teacher saw me.

The girl bent down to pick it up, just as he yelled, "Talking in this classroom is not permitted, and you know better!"

I proceeded to tell him, "My chalk has fallen, and I couldn't take the notes. That's why I tried to get her attention—to pick it up for me."

"That's no excuse!. Come up here, and hold out your hand!"

Hesitantly, I crept to the front of the room, and he swatted me across my fingertips, followed by, "Now get back to your desk, and on the way, pick up your chalk." I was able to begin taking notes, but with the burning sensation, it was difficult.

After returning home and sitting down for dinner, Papa asked how our day went at school. He always checked our hands; we had to place them on the table and turn them around. If there were any marks on our fingertips, he knew that we had done something wrong in school. There was no way to hide it. As soon as he saw the marks or redness, we'd get a solid swat from him too, and then he'd ask what happened. It hardly seemed fair to be punished twice for the same incident.

He was strict, and we got away with nothing. We grew up learning to show respect for our parents, for our elders, for teachers, for priests, for everyone. If older people walked into our home, we got up from our chairs immediately and stood there, waiting until they sat down. If there was still seating available, we could join them. When the visit was over and they left our home, I'd curtsy and Peter would nod his head and shake their hands.

That's the way we always said our goodbyes. It wasn't hard to abide by the rules, because there wasn't a choice. We couldn't bend them, and we never broke them; there was simply no reprieve. We did the best we could to live accordingly, but we certainly weren't perfect. In fact, there were many things we did that we hoped our parents wouldn't find out about. And we never told on each other.

Preparing for Another Hard Winter

After we returned to the city, we helped Mama and Papa harvest our garden, and even though we weren't supposed to, we still took trips with our wagon into the forest in search of fallen fruit and firewood. As I said, desperate times called for desperate measures, and with winter approaching, we were getting quite concerned about our outlook.

We needed to accumulate as much as we could to prepare for the upcoming frigid months. The leaves had fallen, and as they lay on the ground, the wind scattered them about. Squirrels were feverishly gathering food for winter, and we knew we must too.

Mama often took us for walks to see if we could exchange items she'd made for some type of food. It became common practice, these attempts to gather food that we wouldn't be able to obtain any other way. Many times as we walked, she would be summoned over by someone in a passing automobile. It was always the Gestapo telling her that she was again wanted for questioning at headquarters. Sometimes she'd take all of us with her, but often she took only Siegfried. She had to drop everything she was doing and walk all the way into the city, when all they wanted to do was ask her the same questions over and over again.

She was angry with them, but always careful of what she said. It started to occur to us that we had no rights to converse about anything. No one questioned why the food supply was decreasing, or why the soldiers weren't coming home on furlough. People were very reluctant to talk about anything, and fear was spreading like wildfire amongst the Germans. The Nazis even required our family, along with all the others, to take photographs of ourselves, so they would know exactly who lived where and who belonged to whom. A way to put faces to the names of the people they monitored.

Josef Goebbels, the Nazi Minister of Information spread propaganda via radio channels and newspapers, claiming we were winning here, we were winning there, and Hitler was doing a great job. However, it seemed the more they talked about our victories, the worse things became.

Many people joined the Nazi party because they sympathized with their cause; others joined for fear of being terrorized; and some simply to receive better rations. Everyone was starting to feel the pain associated with the lack of food. Mothers were concerned—especially those with many mouths to feed—and we could certainly relate, because we only had half of what they had.

We noticed that as Nazi membership increased, church attendance decreased. With each passing week, our parish was dwindling. It became apparent that there were two different types of people living in Germany: those who joined the Nazi party and those who didn't. Regardless of where people stood politically, everyone was frightened and struggled to obey the laws that were set in place.

The Hitler Youth

One morning, while sitting at my desk in school, an order came through that all children must join the Hitler *Jugend* or youth group. It was explained, and we were told to go home and inform the primary caregiver within our homes. It was a great shock for many of the mothers who didn't want to be involved with the Nazi party; however, the order had come through, and there was nothing they could do about it. All children had no choice but to join the youth group and attend meetings.

One reason Hitler enacted Hitler Youth was that he was running out of manpower to fight his war. As large numbers of his troops were captured or left for dead, members of the Hitler *Jugend* took their place. Requiring young children—ages ten and up—to attend meetings and training prepared them for future combat. He was engaged in war, not only in many parts of Europe but around the world. Even though the Italian, Romanian, and Japanese armies joined the Germans, it seemed as though he had bitten off more than he could chew, and now he needed the resources of the children. Their fathers of course were already fighting, so with no alternatives, the children had to belong. By his own admission, the Fuehrer expressed without remorse, "I can send the flower of German youth into the hell of war without the slightest Pity."

Fearing the Nazis would soon approach us, Mama became visibly troubled. She figured that if there were any connection between us as Americans and Hitler, the chances of our being able to return to the United States were nonexistent. Mama and Papa were adamant about having no connection to Hitler, but they didn't know how to explain it to us, as they feared we'd say something and get them into trouble.

When the Gestapo came to our home to finalize our membership, Mama was very clever. She questioned them, "Are you sure that Hitler wants my children? You know they're American citizens, and I'm not sure that they're the right kind of children for the Hitler *Jugend*." They pondered her question and told her they'd make a determination and let her know at a later date. Riddled with anxiety, Mama waited for their reply. Luckily, she didn't have to wait long.

Surprised by the speed of their decision, returning early the following day, the Gestapo officer indeed told Mama, "We don't want your children, and they're not permitted to join the Hitler Youth." Mama had gained a victory over them, and they didn't even realize it. Without fighting them in any way, she left the decision up to them. And then she thanked God that she had been able to spare us from joining the Hitler Youth Group, even though she couldn't spare us from the general practice of war.

At school, we learned there might be future air raids on our city. They were teaching us what the different warning whistles and sounds meant, and we often practiced what we'd do in the event that an actual bombing occurred. Initially, the sounds were frightening, but after a while, they became a way of life. After all, we had no idea what a bomb was, or what its capabilities were. We only knew that when the sounds alerted, in a calm and orderly fashion, we sought shelter in the underground bunkers; until the all-clear sound, when in an orderly fashion, we returned to our desks.

Coinciding with the teachings on war, the Hitler Youth started wearing uniforms to school on Mondays and Fridays, when they had meetings. Since Peter and I didn't have uniforms, right away, the other children began asking why. We told them that we were simply not asked to join.

It became apparent that there was superiority for those children who belonged, yet we had no answers as to why we didn't belong and no understanding of why we were different. Mama evasively told us that the Nazis simply didn't want us. It was hard for us to try to explain it, and we couldn't to tell them we were different because we were Americans, since we didn't understand what being American meant. We had lived in Germany for so long that we felt like we belonged. It didn't matter to us whether we lived in one place or another. Why should we be called something different? We spoke German, our ancestors were of German descent, but why did we have this stigma placed upon us?

We were indeed Americans, but we didn't understand the connection, so we never told anyone. However, it didn't take long for the teachers to tell them. When we entered our classroom, the teacher stood in front of the class and said, "Marlies and Peter Adams are not members of the Hitler Youth, and they are not going to be members because they are not German. They are Americans."

All of the sudden, the other children were looking at us as if we were enemies. Even though Germany was not at war with America yet, it became an enormous problem. Now, we were outsiders. We were no longer considered part of their country. Right after that, jeering, disparagement, and cruelty against us commenced. The children started calling us names. They were taunting us, telling us to get out of Germany, that we had no right to be there, and that Hitler didn't want us. From the time we left our home in the morning, they badgered us relentlessly.

After failing to befriend them, Peter and I tried to walk together and not bother with them at all. The only children that didn't initially give us a hard time were the ones in our immediate neighborhood, but that soon ended, as their parents forbade them to play with us. Peter and I began to spend all our time together alone.

Mama gave us jobs that kept us busy, and for a short while, we seemed to be fine. We took the baby for walks in the carriage, and we spent a lot of time with Mama in our own yard. But often, I sat and stared out my window at the others playing hopscotch or tag and wondered how we had gotten to this place. Mama did her best to keep our minds occupied, so the abandonment by our friends wouldn't be such a devastating blow, but it was as if we had leprosy—only worse, because with leprosy, people leave you alone. In our case, the opposite held true. Our former friends and classmates were out to get us.

Many children rode bicycles to school, but we didn't have bikes, so while we walked, the bike riders deliberately struck us in the legs, knocking us to the ground and calling us names while circling round and round, before finally riding away in boredom. It was a constant threat and a problem of great proportion as the children were feeding off of each others' hatred and nastiness. I always tried to fight back, hiding my fear, but the truth was Peter and I were extremely frightened of them and stuck very close together. We were each other's only friends, and I thank God everyday I had my brother by my side.

Air Raids and Ground Assaults

When we thought things were as bad as they could get, they got worse. Just prior to winter, in the middle of the night at approximately two o'clock, our slumber abruptly ended with a piercing shrill of the air raid siren and the sound of the baby crying. Groggy, I looked around the room, trying to get my bearings, wondering if I was dreaming, or if we were having another practice drill. It was frightful—the alarm sounded with a long wailing and then it dropped; it wailed again, followed by a long howling sound and then dropping again.

As the sirens continued, I realized that this was indeed not a dream and instantly became consumed with terror and confusion. My surroundings became distorted as tears began pooling in my eyes, not knowing what was happening. Papa scrambled into our room and ordered us to dress quickly and to get into the cellar. The cacophonous sounds were warning us to seek shelter in the basement, but we couldn't turn the lights on, so we huddled together, holding hands as we tried to make our way down the dark, cold stairway. We were terrified, but Mama didn't have time to comfort us. There was a lot to accomplish in a few brief moments.

Papa frantically grabbed our suitcases and rushed them into the cellar with us, practically out of breath. Skipping steps to get back to the top, he bolted upward to bring the trunk down, so nothing would happen to our clothing. The sewing machine was moved close to the doorway, because it was too difficult to carry up and down the stairs. We had barely gathered ourselves together when the long wailing arrested, and short wails commenced, rapidly going down and up, down and up, continuing for a period of time. Mama warned that this sound meant the bombs had been released from the aircraft.

We sat in shock, wondering what our fate would be, when all the sudden, the first one hit and official, mass destruction had begun. It sounded as if the entire world had been blown to smithereens. There was a horrifying, deafening explosion, immediately followed by a chain of others; so many in fact, we gave up counting. I thought my eardrums were going to erupt; the worst thunder couldn't compare, nor could the sound of two trains colliding head on.

As we huddled in the cellar, Mama began to pray out loud while Siegfried, terribly frightened, started screaming. He was huddled on her lap staring deep into her eyes, his face flush with fear as he sank his tiny fingernails so deep into her skin that blood was steadily trickling down her arms. She tried to console him and keep him quiet, but that was impossible since he was barely a year old and not capable of understanding what was occurring. None of us could.

The bombing went on for what seemed like forever, but we appeared to survive in our cold, dark cellar. Nothing had happened to us, although the whole house shook, and everything upstairs rattled. We knew we had survived when finally we heard the long wailing that Mama said indicated everything was all clear. She told us it meant people could come out of their bunkers or basements and see what devastation had occurred. Although we were still frightened, curiosity piqued our interest, so we slowly climbed the stairs into our apartment. None of the bombs had actually fallen in our area. They hit the city of Rüsselsheim, but none of them touched the village where we lived. We were grateful that the angels had watched over us during our first night of sheer terror.

Even though the bombs didn't hit near our home, the intense air pressure did a great deal of damage. All of our pictures had fallen from the walls, and items that were on shelves and counters were thrown to the floor and smashed. Dishes were broken and our windows were not only shattered, but the wood had also splintered around them. Chairs had been thrown and turned upside down, and it seemed as though everything was destroyed. But other than the bloody punctures on Mama's arms and the trauma—especially to Siegfried—none of us suffered any physical harm.

The following day while walking to school, we saw true devastation. Many homes and buildings had been torn apart or completely leveled. Litter was piled high in the streets, concrete building blocks were thrown, and windows were broken in all directions. Everyone was outside taking in the aftermath. Some of the businesses had been completely blown into oblivion, and in their place, nothing but smoldering, gaping holes. Telephone poles were knocked down with wires wildly strewn throughout the streets. It was dangerous simply walking about.

Many people were stunned, walking in a daze, or perhaps a state of shock. Everyone handled the new day differently, some were silent and numb, while others screamed, collapsing to the ground. No one really knew how grave the losses were, but from what we saw, they were significant. On our long walk into the city, we pondered the fate of our school. When we finally made it through the obstacle course, the formerly clean and well-paved streets of Rüsselsheim, and arrived at school, we found that other than broken windows, nothing had happened to our building. I really enjoyed learning, but a couple of days without the beatings going to and from school would have been welcomed. Sadly, we heard numerous people had been killed, and the bombings would most likely continue. They warned us to be particularly careful, as the air raid sirens were no longer practice drills, but sounds to fear, carrying destruction and mayhem in the dead of night.

After the first bombing, the taunting by the children continued, even heightening when it was reported on the news that it had been the English who had bombed Germany. They were blaming *us* for the bombings, believing that England and America were the same. After all, we both spoke English, and the children didn't comprehend the difference.

The bullies continued their torment, calling us "dirty Ammies," and frightening us to a higher level. With the bombing, the stakes had raised. Some children were presumed dead, and the survivors thought to avenge them by torturing us.

For the most part, we were safe in the school. Attempting to avoid harm's way, we'd get there early, so we wouldn't encounter the kids making our lives miserable. Likewise, we tried to rush out of school the minute the bell rang and run home as quick as we could, so we wouldn't encounter their wickedness in that direction either. If something prohibited us from fleeing immediately, we'd wait until long after the others had gone, poking our heads out the door, looking left, looking right, and if the coast was clear, we'd head home. But even the slightest noise from behind prompted us to look back out of fear.

By that point, we were incurring daily assaults. Sneaking up from behind, children would knock us to the ground, spit on us, throw dirt and rocks, and scream obscenities at us. Some of this treatment came from kids we had previously considered friends. "Dirty Ammies, dirty Ammies, dirty Ammies!" We couldn't comprehend the meaning of these words, let alone understand how we had become that meaning.

Although each night we lay in bed waiting for the unthinkable to happen, we didn't experience another bombing until after Christmas. Still, the holidays were a sad and meager time for us. Again, there was no tree to decorate, and no treats. In fact, there was very little of anything. Mama made a new dress for my doll, and once again, Peter's wagon received a fresh coat of paint, but she and Papa had no gifts for themselves.

Nonetheless, we were content and thankful to have survived the holiday without incident. We learned not to ask for anything, knowing our parents couldn't provide any more than what they had. The love in our home made up for everything, and as long as we were together, we seemed to be fine.

After Christmas, when the next array of bombs was showered upon us, we were more aware of what was in store. Fear shot through my system at the first alarm, surpassing mortal terror. It turned my insides out, triggering nausea and vomiting followed by diarrhea. When there was nothing left but dry heaves, I rushed to the basement and huddled praying and hoping that we would make it through.

Mama grabbed a suitcase in each hand and headed for the stairs. Just as she reached them, the air pressure concussed our home and threw her to the basement floor, right over the stairs. Exactly as she held the suitcases at the top, she held them at the bottom, only now, she was on her butt. She was more frightened than anything—and so were we, fearing what could have happened to her. The bombs hit closer to home that night, and the horror intensified tenfold.

Every night, we wondered if we'd see another morning, whether or not a bomb would collapse our home, and if we were going to die. After all, the last bombing had led many people to meet their maker; why should we be different? Perhaps, the next time was our turn. But thankfully, we knew if our number was called, we'd all be called together. If we were going to be blown straight to heaven, at least we'd do it, with the five of us holding hands for the journey.

The government had ordered us to wear gas masks to aid in our survival, but the masks were frightening in and of themselves. They were big and black and reminded me of gruesome monsters that I was sure would jump out of my closet in the middle of the night and savagely devour our entire family before the light of day. I despised the very sight of them, whether or not they could benefit us in some way. They were uncomfortable, cumbersome, and they stunk.

Siegfried was especially terrorized this time, shrieking in desperation for Mama to make it stop. Knowing there was nothing she could do but wait it out, she covered his ears as tightly as she could, but the forceful tremors sent violently through his tiny body with each hit were unforgiving. She held him tight to her chest, rocking back and forth, while praying out loud, hoping that the sound of her voice would give him some comfort.

It was well below freezing in our cellar, and there was no heat to warm it, so we wrapped blankets around us and huddled together to create body heat. It seemed like time stood still and the bombs would never cease. But finally, the all-clear siren let us know we had managed to make it through another attack. We picked our way to the top of the stairs, only to find there was much destruction to our home, undoubtedly more than the first time.

The windows were all blown out, and the walls and our freestanding closets in the bedrooms had pieces of glass embedded in them. We couldn't touch anything with our bare hands, since glass shards were abundant and could cut our flesh to shreds. Judging how hard and far the air pressure threw glass, there was no way a human being could stand in a room and withstand the force. The bombs themselves killed people in the immediate area, but the concussions from the air pressure killed and wounded more than one could imagine.

Sizing up the damage, folks walked around wrapped in bandages where glass had splintered and harmed them. We saw bodies lined up in the streets. Perhaps they were surprised by the sirens and tried to seek shelter in a doorway or a bunker but didn't make it in time.

There were so many dead bodies needing burial, the few available gravediggers were not only running out of time, but also space for disposing of them. Hospitals were filled with the injured, including children. They were overcrowded, and people feared what would happen next time. And when would next time be? Now, a horrible fear of the bombings was added to our fear of the Nazis, fear of starving to death, and fear of being harmed by other children on our way to and from school. Having no alternative, we learned to live with fear, our constant companion.

Hitler was on the road to world domination. He believed that if he could conquer Europe, he would own the world and be able to grant Germans the "living room" they desired. The Allies however, were determined to destroy Germany's will and capacity to fight, hence the repeated influx of bombing raids, civilian casualties or not. While we were standing knee-deep in the midst of it all, it was difficult for us children to understand what was taking place. We had no idea why anyone could be so angry that they'd start killing and destroying homes and property and the lives of so many innocent. But we learned that was what war entailed, and people did everything and anything to stay alive during the hellish times surrounding these indiscriminate bombings.

People began building huge concrete, holding tanks. The tanks held gallons upon gallons of water and were placed into basements to provide a water supply in the event of fire. The people worried about coals from the stoves causing an entire home to be engulfed with flames during the explosions and completely destroyed.

There were three types of bombs being used. There was what we called the *Spreng bomb. It* could drive itself into the ground and lift everything from underneath when it exploded. If the *Spreng* bomb entered a structure, there'd be nothing left at all. They were dropped to try and get into the bunkers and underground factories, creating monstrous craters in the ground where the structures formerly stood.

The second type of bomb was the *Luftminen,* otherwise known as air mines. Immediately upon impact, they destroyed everything in their vicinity. Sometimes as many as thirty to forty homes were completely blown away and wiped out without a trace.

Third, the White Phosphorous or WP bombs came in a canister resembling a huge umbrella. They were narrow, and upon contact, a propeller like device shot out, throwing white phosphorous. Wherever WP hit, fire ignited. If it happened to fall on a human being, the only way to put it out was to smother it with sand or dirt. If water was thrown on top, the phosphor spread, as a grease fire would, running down the skin with the water pushing it along and perpetuating the burning.

We had to make sure we brought our rabbits inside during the night, fearing that air pressure or phosphor would kill them. Phosphor was poisonous and if it landed on the vegetables growing in our garden, we could no longer consume them. Unfortunately, we couldn't see if they had been contaminated, so we had to use our rabbits—that we'd planned on eating as a last resort—as guinea pigs to test our food.

We would pick a few leaves from different vegetable plants and feed them to one of the rabbits. If she survived, it meant the phosphor had not gotten on our vegetables and we could continue eating them. However, if she died, it meant that the vegetables growing above ground had been contaminated. Only potatoes, beets, carrots, and things that grew underground would be of value. We hated to use our rabbits that way, but it was a true case of do or die.

We were frightened of all the bombs, but especially of WP bombs—people hit with that phosphor rarely survived. Sometimes we sat in the cold cellar with wet blankets around our heads and shoulders, in the event that phosphor was released, we could throw the blanket and flee, trying to protect ourselves from the horrific, skin-melting chemical. It was difficult to comprehend that men could fly over a village full of innocent women and children and drop a weapon that would burn them alive, leaving their bodies to mesh with the tar on the roads that had likewise melted. After a phosphor attack, fires blazed in all directions, leaving the distance lit with amber-glowing flames of death.

How terribly frightening each day had become. We understood that there may not be a tomorrow, so when we sat at the supper table at night and said our prayers, we thanked God for another day, and we begged him to let us live yet one more. Perhaps that evening while we slept, he'd spare us from another bombing and give us the grace to stay alive. The only thing we had to hold onto was our faith, our prayers. Nothing else could come and save us.

After the second bombing and the destruction of numerous businesses, rations became more scarce and filling them increased in difficulty. Mama needed rations for thread, needles, buttons, and everything else. In order to obtain bread, we had to stand in line, receiving one loaf on Monday, one on Wednesday, and one on Friday. On Monday mornings, we'd get up early and take turns waiting in line. Often we'd arrive at six o'clock in the morning, as the lines increased in size and people arrived earlier to beat each other. Peter went first while I prepared for school, and when I finished, I walked down to relieve him, giving him an opportunity to get cleaned up. When it was time for me to leave for school, Mama walked down with Siegfried to take my place in line.

The bakeries didn't open until nine o'clock in the morning, and they were only allowed to make so much bread per week, and so much per day. If we were too far back in line, we'd miss our opportunity for that day and our ration card would no longer be valid. Standing outside became a problem during frigid winter months, and often it was all for naught.

We didn't have the opportunity or the ration cards to buy boots, which we needed for the heavy snow, so we wore our high-leather shoes, and stood dancing in line, trying to keep warm. Just when it seemed as though our toes would break off, they simply went numb. There was no relief in sight. It seemed as though all we could do was struggle through each and every day, praying constantly that our troubles would cease and that better days would soon fall upon us.

A month or better had passed before the next bombing. Trapped in an endless night, I yearned for the light that signified a new beginning was near. Tiny flecks of light did shine through one afternoon when we learned via letters that the rural areas had not been bombed so far, and remained safe from the atrocities. At least my grandparents had been spared, which was a relief. I longed to be back on the farm with them, free from all my fears. To be in a warm home that was safe, free from splintering glass and deafening noise.

Papa tried to minimize the damage done to our apartment. The government gave us rations to have our windows replaced, so he went to retrieve the glass to do so. Knowing that luxury wouldn't last long, he realized that if he opened the windows before we went into the cellar during a bombing, and kept the shutters closed, that the air pressure most likely wouldn't break the glass. However, during winter months, it made for a very cold house, especially for the baby.

It seemed like we were never going to thaw out. It was bitter cold, yet Mama was afraid to leave the stove going during the night because of the ever-present fear that a bomb could trigger the hot coals to ignite. When climbing into our bed at night, it seemed as though we'd freeze to death before the sun could rise. As usual, Mama used her ingenuity and she starting putting bricks in the oven before we turned in. They heated to extreme temperatures; then she wrapped them with towels and placed them under the feather blanket at the foot of our bed. During the night, we placed our feet on the bricks, and miraculously, we could sleep. If a bomb happened to fall during the night, we took the bricks down in the cellar with us to provide a tiny bit of heat as we huddled together under cold, wet blankets. Thank God we had the bricks; there were times when we'd return upstairs and ice had actually formed on the walls.

As cold as we were, there were others who were worse off. People emerged from their cellars with no homes at all. With tears in their eyes they would try to stack crumbled bricks back into some kind of shelter for the next day. Fear and sorrow were visible in their eyes; happiness and joy had become extinct. It became difficult for people to survive, both mentally and physically. There was no one to make us feel at ease about what was happening. People had to struggle on their own. There were no counselors, and no Red Cross to help us. We made the best of what we had, becoming a bit more hardened each day. Fortunately, in Germany it was mandatory for homes to be built out of concrete blocks or brick. Not wanting to risk the forests being destroyed, people weren't allowed to erect wooden houses. Wood was used for finishing the home inside and making furniture, but as long as alternatives were available, it was not to be used for the main structure. As it happened, it was a good thing, since homes built out of concrete blocks and bricks were much more resilient to bombings. The few wooden structures that had been erected were simply blown away, as if they had never existed at all.

When we weren't being bombed, it wasn't because the bombing campaign had stopped. It had just moved on to other cities. Mainz, Frankfurt, Dusseldorf, Mannheim, Bremen, Cologne, Trier, Essen, Berlin, and all of the big cities shared a similar fate. As surely as daylight was to happen upon us, so was another bomb. Each time Rüsselsheim was besieged, it became more severe and increasingly difficult for Peter and me to make our way to school.

All of the children in the Hitler Youth were blaming us more than ever for the attacks on their city. It became harder for us to attend school and get home safely. The throwing of stones, fist fights, tripping, pushing, and running us over with bicycles was worse than ever. Often we fell and scraped ourselves. We'd have bloody knees and bloody elbows, which frightened me. I was afraid of catching *Wundrose* again and facing the threat of losing an arm or a leg or perhaps not surviving at all.

Even though we tried to fight back, we had become so beaten down that we went home and begged our parents, "Why can't we just join the Nazi party? Why is it that we're the only ones not allowed to be part of their organization?" Our father arduously replied, "No! First of all, they don't want you, and second, it is better that you never have any contact with that organization. There's no way you'll ever join, so just take your bumps and bruises the best you can and make the most of it."

There was just no help for us in any way or from anyone. We had to learn to live with the constant taunting and the abuse that we endured. We didn't understand why our parents were being so cruel to us. Why couldn't we join? We just wanted to fit in and be like all of the other kids. We were tired of being ridiculed and beaten, but our parents were too afraid to tell us why, too afraid to utter anything negative against Hitler.

Meanwhile, the adult Nazis similarly continued badgering our parents. Mama was still being asked to make the long trek into the city several times a week where they'd ask the same questions over and over again. They kept her for hours, let her go home, and sometimes came back and required her return to headquarters the same day. They might leave her alone for a few days, and then start the cycle over. But she continued doing whatever they asked of her.

The trips back and forth were time consuming and difficult for her, so she'd leave Peter and me at home with different jobs to help out. I made the beds and swept the kitchen, and Peter went outside to weed the garden. Anything to keep us occupied. She was concerned about the long walk into the city and worried about trying to find shelter for all of us in the event of a bombing. We had been fortunate that the bombings had not yet begun during the daytime—it was always during the middle of the night. But we never knew when that might change, and she wasn't willing to risk our safety.

With no manpower left to man the watchtowers, young people were being deployed to protect our city. Fourteen, fifteen, and sixteen-year-old Hitler Youth were used as sentries, not eligible to be drafted until they reached seventeen. They sat high up in the towers with a responsibility that no child should be saddled with. As the hands of the clock moved round and round, so did the young men whose job it was to man the search lights, identify approaching enemy planes, lock their sights in, and annihilate them before they had the chance to do unto us. Enemy planes lost over our city and shot down were done so by children, as there were no official soldiers left at home.

From an early age, first grade and on, these kids were taught about warfare, making them feel superior. They were obnoxiously arrogant; even the humblest of children began to believe that the blood running through their veins gave them freedom to wreak havoc in Hitler's quest for purification of the so-called "Aryan" race. Many of the mothers had become concerned about the difference in their children's personalities and how they were acting toward their mothers, grandmothers, females in general, and especially non-Nazis. The Nazis' mission to take over the school system and force-feed a new set of values and beliefs left the Hitler Youth with hostility and intolerance toward anyone outside of their circle.

If the truth be told, as much as I hated the young Nazis who made it part of their daily routine to torment us, I was also glad that they were protecting our city. I could have cared less who they were, as long as they could do something to make the bombings cease, or at the very least, warn us of the inevitable. The way I saw it at age six: More power to them if they can spare our village from a forthcoming attack. And if the Allies wanted to kill me in cold blood, then I said, *Let the Hitler Youth kill them first.* Self-preservation is no crime, after all.

A new order was announced that the Hitler Youth group would start meeting on Sunday mornings. However, with only two Catholic priests to preside over the entire city, Sunday morning was the only time Catholics could attend a church mass in Rüsselsheim. Mass was subsequently eliminated for all of the children of the youth group, because missing meetings was not an option.

After that order, our priest had no altar boys available for mass. He asked Mama if she'd help instruct Peter in Latin, so he could fill the position. She was honored, and Peter became an altar boy at the young age of seven. He was proud to serve the church during mass, and the priest was thrilled not only because he was the only person available, but because he was a fine, upstanding young man. When Peter officially began his duties, we had to arrive a bit earlier, which also enabled us to avoid some of the taunting by the Hitler youth, because even when our parents were with us, it didn't diminish much. They still continued with their malicious behavior, even calling our parents names.

Papa used to walk with a German goose step. He was very tall and very fast, but I was always running right along the side of him. I didn't want him to spend one minute alone, so I hustled to keep up. Peter came along later with Mama and Siegfried. However, with the onset of the taunting, Papa had to slow down, making sure he stayed alongside all of us to protect us, which gave my little legs a break. He wanted to ensure they wouldn't throw stones at my baby brother or Mama. Seemingly, that worked out well for all of us.

One early Sunday morning, while waiting for mass to begin, Mama noticed that our young priest wasn't present. She was concerned that he might have fallen ill, so she asked the elder priest of his whereabouts. Nervously he told her that he had no idea, and that he had simply vanished. The preceding Saturday morning, a German girl came to church to marry a Nazi officer. The officer was not Catholic and therefore wasn't permitted to stand at the altar. They had to stand on the other side of the altar rail. The young priest, without realizing the severity of what he was saying, asked her why she couldn't have waited for the soldiers to come home to marry a nice Catholic boy. Not having swayed her decision, he proceeded to marry them, but the Nazi had overheard his question, and within hours, the Gestapo entered the church and told him that there was something they needed to discuss at headquarters. He never returned.

The elder priest traveled to Nazi headquarters and delicately inquired about his young associate, but they denied any knowledge regarding his whereabouts. During his conversation with Mama, the elder priest was visibly shaken. He reiterated that it was very important not to say anything derogatory against the Nazi party at any time. "No matter how aggravated you become, or how many times you wonder why things are happening, be very careful with whom you discuss it. Somehow," he continued, "I have a feeling that we're being punished for not going along with everything Hitler wishes. If we try to go against him or anything he stands for, I have a feeling that we will disappear—and where they're taking people, I don't know."

Our fears were intensified, but we didn't dare inquire about anything or anyone. We certainly couldn't ask things like, "If we're winning the war, why are we being bombed so often? Why is there so little food and fuel, and why can't the soldiers come home on furlough?" Mama said her brothers had been gone for two years and hadn't once been back. But we couldn't ask, "Why weren't they allowed to return to their cities on vacations? Why were the members of the Nazi Party receiving food, yet the people that didn't belong weren't? Why are they watching us so closely, when we're not doing anything wrong?"

We might have pondered those questions, but we certainly never spoke them aloud. We minded our own business and kept our mouths shut; people around us were starting to disappear. But on one occasion, we learned a serious lesson ourselves—the hard way. It was Mother's Day, and I had been allowed to go into town and purchase a card for Mama. I knew that Papa couldn't do anything special for her, so when I located a card with a man sitting with a small girl on his lap, I thought it would be perfect to purchase it for her from both myself and Papa. I got the card on Friday, and of course I couldn't wait until Sunday to give it to her. I was so filled with happiness to do something nice for Mama that I was bursting at the seams, only to feel totally dejected after she opened it, as she asked me to exchange the card for one with a flower on it. In a depressed manner, I made my way back to the store and politely told the man, "Could I please get a card with a flower on it? My mother doesn't like the man on this one."

Without explaining why, the man closed down his shop and walked me home. He had a serious limp, but a determination to make the trek, nonetheless. Mama was quite surprised that I hadn't brought home a new card, but instead brought home the storeowner himself. "Mrs. Adams," he said, "could I please have a word with you?"

"Of course. Has Marlies done something?"

"No, but you have. I don't know if you are aware, but the man on the front of this card is Goebbels, Hitler's propaganda minister, and your daughter came into my store, telling me that you didn't like him. Are you aware of what could happen to yourself or your family if the wrong ears had heard those words?"

"Oh dear, yes, yes I am very aware, and I am so sorry," she answered.

He told her, "I have seen your family in church. I know you are good Catholics, and I only came to warn you to be much more discrete."

"Thank you, thank you, we will."

The people who belonged to the church still seemed to be good Catholics, and the storeowner was certainly one of them. There were many German people who never joined the Nazi Party that remained good people. Those who did join were asked to inform on the others in order to receive food and continue getting Nazi privileges. They did so, often not realizing that what they were doing was causing harm to the German people themselves. The young children never realized what they said in Hitler Youth group meetings could actually harm their parents and their families, but did it ever.

7
Life Goes On in War Time

The Underground Economy

There were farm villages on the outskirts of Rüsselsheim. Reaching them meant a long walk, but sometimes early in the morning, Mama prepared items that she had sewn and repaired, which she tried to exchange for food. She packed us up for the journey, putting Siegfried in the wagon, and off we went in search of a day's meal.

We'd head out early in the morning and walk for miles in search of someone to barter with. Apples, potatoes, or any type of food were welcome exchange for the items she made. Some of the farmers got to know her, and the kind ladies on the farms occasionally offered a basket of fruits or vegetables. With the baby in the wagon, we could put one basket with him, and she'd carry the other. Or she could carry Siegfried and put both baskets in the wagon. Either way, he was too small to walk the long distance. She carried the heavy items for miles. The many long trips took their toll, as she thinned out by the day. She didn't have enough food for us, let alone herself; Mama put everyone else's needs first, always.

I often went into the garden and ate fresh vegetables right from the ground—after making sure they weren't contaminated. I ate the carrots, peas, broccoli, cauliflower, beans, and anything I could find. When there wasn't anything edible growing in the garden, I ate weeds. There are plenty of weeds that taste quite good, but when you're famished, almost anything tastes good. Somehow we managed to survive the winter, and when spring arrived, it meant going back to Kell and my grandparents' farm. That was synonymous with Heaven as far as I was concerned.

There were no bombings in Kell, and the children were still kind to us. There was no stone throwing or attacks of any kind, and it was peaceful. There was so much love and warm-heartedness in that small village that the weight of the world was lifted off my shoulders, if only briefly.

I felt sad leaving Mama and Papa in the city. And even though we were in a place where we were free of our own worries, we still worried about them. While we were gone, the bombings continued there several times, and we were worried about their well-being. But with her usual reliability, after each bombing, Mama immediately wrote a letter to let us know they were all right. My grandparents had heard about the severity of the bombings, but they hadn't actually experienced or witnessed one first hand. They asked us a lot of questions about the war, and Oma became frightened. She couldn't believe we were in so much danger. "Maybe it would be better if your mother and you children came to live here on the farm."

Mama, however, wouldn't hear of leaving Papa. "He's my husband," she said, "and I'm not going to leave him in the city to struggle alone. We're a family and we'll stay together. I can't walk away from the responsibilities of being a wife, and if God wills it, we'll survive. If he doesn't, hopefully, he'll take us together." That's the way she was, and no one was going to change her mind. She took her commitments seriously. But for us kids, the time spent with my grandparents in the summers was enchanting, when we could again be carefree children loving every minute of life. Unfortunately, it always ended too soon. In the blink of an eye, summer was over and back to the city we'd go.

Me and the Gestapo

When we returned from our grandparents' to spend the winter in the Rüsselsheim, we immediately started school. Peter was eight, and I was seven. Siegfried was still too young. There was, unfortunately, a twelve-year-old boy named Dracker between us and school. The son of the Gestapo officer in charge of our town, he was a heavy-built delinquent who didn't show any sufferings of hunger throughout that period. He was entirely nasty and he often enticed the other children to pick on Peter and me.

One afternoon, Mama had been called into the city to see the Nazis. Peter and I were left home alone, and I was in the house making the beds, dusting, and sweeping the kitchen floor. All of the sudden, I heard Peter hollering, "Stop, stop!" from the garden. I went to the window and saw Dracker holding Peter down on the ground. He was sitting on top of his chest with his knees pinning his arms to the ground, while pounding his face with his fists.

Peter started bleeding the minute something touched his nose and all I could see was a small human laying there covered with blood. I couldn't even recognize his face as he kept screaming, "Stop, please, stop!" Dracker was pummeling his face with both fists, and I was seeing red—not only from the blood—as I picked up our broom and ran out of the house. I hurried into the garden and proceeded to slam the broomstick against Dracker's head and back. I repeatedly hit and beat him. I wanted to kill him. And all I had in my mind was that I was going to keep beating him until he died at my fingertips. I hit him across his face, his hands, and his back. I hit him hard. He continued trying to ward off the broom, but I couldn't be stopped. I had so much anger for what he had done to my brother that I continued beating him until he mustered the strength to crawl on his hands and knees out of our garden, running home.

I decided to let him run, only because my brother needed me. I picked Peter up and helped him to the house, wondering how I'd stop all the bleeding. His nose was gushing like a waterfall, and his eye, deeply cut just beneath, was also bleeding. I managed to help him into the bedroom and put cold washcloths on his wounds. I was only seven; I didn't know what to do. But I got him into bed, agonizing for my mother to return. What was I going to do with my brother? I began to cry, not knowing how to help him, and feeling deeply saddened for him. I knew Mama could remedy anything, if she could just make it home. Every time she left the house, I worried about her not returning, but this day had an even greater sense of urgency. I cried, "Please Mama, please hurry."

After running back and forth between Peter and the window, for what seemed like forever, I finally spotted her coming down the street. "Peter, don't worry, Mama's coming."

I met her at the door and started to cry. "Peter's been hurt badly! You have to come and check on him."

She hurried into the bedroom with shock written on her face. Grabbing for a towel to stop the bleeding, she cried, "What happened here!"

"Mama, Dracker came over and beat Peter."

She began tending to him, but by the time she had come home, his eyes were completely swollen shut, his face was twice its normal size, and his nose was visibly broken. He was still covered with blood. I had done the best I could to clean him up, but to no avail. Thankfully, Mama was more skilled than I, and she stopped the bleeding.

When she finally quieted Peter, she asked me for details. "How did this all begin?"

I told her, "I heard Peter hollering and looked out the window and that's when I saw what was going on."

"What did you do, Marlies?"

"I took the broom and went out and gave him a beating. And I hoped that I had killed him, but he ran away."

Mama pleaded, "Please don't ever talk that way. God forbid, what's going to happen to us? You know Dracker's the Gestapo's son!"

"Yes, I know that, but he was killing Peter!"

She became frightened, "Oh dear God, what is going to happen to us because of this?"

When Papa came home, she told him what occurred, and that was the first time I ever saw him shake and turn pale, looking physically frightened. He looked at Peter and me and just as Mama had, he uttered, "God forbid, what is going to happen to us?"

Just as we expected, it wasn't long before there was a knock on the door. When Papa answered it, there stood Dracker's father, completely suited in his Gestapo uniform. He didn't ask to be invited in, before pushing his way into the kitchen. He had Dracker with him, and I could see a huge welt that went across his entire face. His eyes and nose were swollen, and we could see where I had hit the broom handle across his face. One eye was swollen shut, and while I admired my handy work, the Nazi turned around and barked, "I would like to know who did this to my son!"

I stood there, looked him square in the eye, and proudly answered, "I did."

"You hit my son?"

I answered, matter of fact, "Yes."

"Why?"

"Because he beat my brother."

"Couldn't your brother defend himself?"

"No, he couldn't. Dracker had him pinned down in the garden."

"Where is your brother?"

"He's in bed, in the other room."

"Tell him to come out here."

Mama interrupted, "He's very ill, he can't see because his eyes are swollen shut."

Dracker's father pushed open the bedroom door and stepped inside. He looked at Peter lying there on the bed. His face, so destroyed from the beating that he didn't look human.

The Gestapo officer stood there and looked down at Peter and asked, "Exactly what happened to him?"

"Your son hit me."

He turned around and looked at his son and said, "Did you hit him like this?"

"Yes."

"Why?"

"Because they're Ammies!"

"What did he say, or what did he do to entice you to hit him like this?"

"He said nothing. He's just a dirty Ammie, and we don't want them here."

His father turned around, "They're here because we want them here, and they are not going anywhere. If he didn't say anything against the party, Hitler, or any of the Nazi organization, then you had no reason to beat him."

Dracker insisted, "He's just an Ammie, and we want them away from us. They're the ones causing the bombings."

"He's only a little boy, and he's not even half your size, and you beat him just because he's an American?"

"Yes sir, I did."

"I don't ever want to see this again. Unless he says something against the Nazi Party, you're not to touch him." Then he turned to me, "You have to promise me that you will never hit my son again."

"As long as he promises to leave my brother alone, then I won't have to touch him."

Out of nowhere, Papa proceeded to slap the attitude right off my face. He was frightened, but with no one else standing up for Peter, I didn't care. The Nazi officer made his son shake hands with Peter and me, but as we shook, I warned him under my breath, "Don't ever touch my brother again." He looked at me with new respect, and they walked out of the house. Fortunately, we never heard another word about it.

After the fight, walking to school seemed a little easier, because Dracker told the other kids to leave us alone. "Forget the stone throwing, just leave them alone." He became—more or less—someone who looked out for us, someone who occasionally helped us out. Whenever Dracker wasn't with the other children, the taunting commenced; the pushing, shoving, stone throwing, and name calling continued. But whenever he was present, it didn't happen, so we tried to calculate exactly what time he went to school, and we tried to leave then too. He had become a sort of watchdog for us and never again touched Peter or taunted me. In fact, some of the children began harassing me when Dracker warned, "Leave her alone; she's really mean."

In early 1942, just after Christmas, an announcement came over the radio that all children over the age of five had to leave the city to live in the country, because the bombings had become so severe. We were getting bombed constantly, and the fear was unbearable. Parents were afraid for the lives of their children. The only safe places had become the underground bunkers, but with the Spreng bombs that went underground and tore the bunkers to shreds, nothing was totally safe. There really was not any peace of mind. Hitler was concerned about the children living in the city, because so many were getting killed or severely maimed. He was losing his young people—his future soldiers—and he could not let it continue.

Since the rural areas weren't yet under attack by the enemies, he decided to move the children to the countryside. He made the rule stating that rural people had to take in so many children, and he was enacting this for one year. The farmers took the children and their ration cards to provide for them in their new homes.

By the beginning of March, all children had to be moved out. Some had actually started moving to the country as early as January. My grandparents sent us a letter as soon as they heard the news report. Oma said they could take us for a summer, but not for an entire year. It would be impossible for her to provide for both Peter and me year round.

The government had given them a French prisoner to help work on the farm, knowing that Opa was no longer able. Additionally, Opa needed someone to stay at home and take care of him, because he was bedridden most of the time. That meant two people on the farm were no longer available to work, yet, more food was being consumed. They couldn't possibly provide for everyone. As much as it broke her heart, Oma decided that she could only take one of us.

We also received a letter from Papa's sister who lived along the Rhine district as well, but in the opposite direction. I had never met the woman—none of us children had—but she contacted Papa by mail saying she wanted me to go and live with her, because she needed three people in her home to butcher a pig for the year's food supply. Since there were only two—she and her husband, who was wounded in the first world war and not capable of fighting again—they needed a third individual to live with them.

She supposedly owned a small farm, but needed someone to care for the animals and help with working the land. The woman, whom I had never laid eyes upon, was all of a sudden very interested in me. Mama decided that since Peter was older, he would be a bigger help to Oma, so he'd live there, and I'd live with my aunt. Another reason she agreed was she was afraid the Nazis would find a home for me where the family might entice me to talk about Hitler. She worried that they'd make Nazism sound appealing, and that they'd convert me to their way of thinking. It was a big concern, and she couldn't voice her opinions to anyone other than Papa, so happily she agreed. "Thank God I'll be able to send my children with family members. Now I won't have to worry about them."

Arrangements were made that in early March we'd be removed from our home. Peter would live in Kell, and I'd live with Aunt Lena in a small town called Holtztum. I was anxious, but not actually concerned, since Mama's family had been so loving, kind, and gentle. Going to live with another relative didn't scare me, but I knew I'd be lonely without Peter. That was my greatest fear. *What will I do for an entire year without my brother?* Not to mention, I'd miss Mama and Papa and Siegfried too. It seemed like such a long time to be away from home and the people I loved.

I had a cousin that was working in the hospital in Rüsselsheim. She was Papa's brother's daughter, and she had made contact with us. Occasionally when she had a few hours on a Sunday, she'd come to our house to visit. Her name was Ann; she was seventeen years old, and she was absolutely lovely. While working in the hospital, she contacted us in regard to me living with Aunt Lena. She had received a furlough for two weeks to return home and spend time with her parents, so she offered to take me along and drop me off at Aunt Lena's. That way, Mama could take Peter to Kell.

I remember that morning as we walked together to the train station to meet my cousin. She promised to make sure that I got to Aunt Lena's, telling Mama, "Don't worry about Marlies, and have a safe trip to Kell."

As we prepared to go our separate ways, I said my good-byes to Mama, Peter, and Siegfried at the train station, which wasn't easy. I couldn't imagine being away from them for that long. I pleaded with my brother, "Peter, please don't forget me."

He answered, "Oh my gosh, no, I would never do that."

Mama hugged me tight. My train was scheduled to leave first, so I finished up my good-byes and stepped onto the platform with my cousin Ann. Mama told me my train would stop about seven miles from my final destination, the village of Holtztum, and that I would have to walk the rest of the way. Ann wanted to make me feel better, "It shouldn't be too bad; it's only seven miles to Holtztum, and Aunt Lena will be waiting to walk you home."

Seven miles didn't bother me; I could walk that standing on my head. All I was concerned about was which one of my aunts would she be most like? Would her personality and mannerisms be similar to Aunt Ann, Aunt Clara, Aunt Ida, Aunt Mary, or even Aunt Rose? I couldn't find fault with any of them, so I was sure Aunt Lena would be equally wonderful.

As our train slowly pulled into the station, I looked out the window and into the crowd, taking notice of one particular woman staring back at me. She was very tall and thin, and she looked frightening. She had huge, dark eyes that were sunken into her forehead, and she appeared repulsive. Her long, black dress covered her lanky body and arms that extended to her long bony fingers. Her hair was tightly pulled back, revealing her pasty, wrinkled, ashy skin. I turned to Ann and whispered, "Oh my goodness, did you see that ugly lady? She looks just like a witch." My cousin didn't say anything.

When the train stopped, we headed down the platform with my suitcase and an extra bag that I carried with me. As we approached the end, I noticed the ugly lady pushing her way through the crowd. The closer she got, the more nervous I became. She finally stopped directly in front of me, and Ann proceeded to horrify me with the words, "Marlies, this is your Aunt Lena."

My heart sank to my feet, while my breakfast was about to come out of my belly. I had no real justification; it was simply an inner fear of the frightful woman. I felt extremely uncomfortable, not liking her from my first impression. And it seemed as though she had the same feelings toward me.

She looked at me with no affection, but as she parted her pursed lips, exposing her stained yellow teeth, she said, "So, you're John's girl. Put your suitcase in the wagon."

Ann grabbed for it and proceeded to do so. Then Aunt Lena inquired, "Can you pull the wagon?"

"Yes, without any problem."

"Fine then, we'd better be on our way." I continued staring at her, interrupted briefly by the conductors' "All abroad."

I looked away and turned toward my cousin. She knelt down and stared into my eyes, smiled and gave me a big hug and kiss. I hugged her so tight. I wanted to tell her I was scared and that I wanted to go home, but I couldn't say the words.

"Be happy, Marlies."

I tried to smile, while holding back the tears, and with my lips quivering said, "Okay."

8
The Hell that Was Holtztum

My cousin re-boarded the train and was gone. Alone and scared, I turned to look at my aunt. Her face was lifeless. I smiled, hoping she would in return, but her expression never changed. She just looked down at me and said, "Let's go."

As we walked, not a word was spoken. It was the first time we met and yet, she didn't ask about my family. She didn't ask me anything. As the long walk wore on, the wagon became heavier and heavier. Just like Papa, she walked so fast, it became almost impossible to keep up. I had to walk through part of a village and a forest that led into the small town of Holtztum, all the while dragging my load through the often-difficult terrain. The wagon bounced up and down, sometimes lifting off of two wheels and almost tipping, until I would twist the handle to force it back down. Each time one of those close calls occurred, she made tracks farther and farther ahead of me.

As she exited the forest, I pulled with all my might, trying not to lose her. I turned onto the main road and was thankful to see she was still there. I couldn't understand why she never looked back and why she wouldn't walk—or talk—with me. Had I done something wrong or was she mad at someone else? I was relieved when she turned, finally, off the road and onto her property, yet I was filled with questions, uncertainty, and fear.

Her farmhouse sat on a large plot of land. It was a run-down two-story home, made up of dark bricks and dirty windows. To the right of the house stood a large wooden barn, also in need of repair. The barn was connected to the main house by a large set of wooden stairs that led to the living quarters. On the other side of the barn was a smaller area that looked like a barnyard. As I looked around, she pointed, "That is where the pigs are housed."

"All right." I could see that on the other side she kept her wagons and two cows.

"Let's go upstairs and I'll show you where you'll be staying, and by the way, put the wagon in the barn."

I walked to the barn and opened the door. I could smell the filth from the animals and wondered how Oma would feel if she could see how poorly kept the grounds were. I put my wagon away and pulled the suitcase containing a year's worth of clothing onto the ground. I dragged it out of the barn and looked up the long steep stairway leading to the main house. Frightened of losing my balance and falling far below, one step at a time, I finally managed to make it to the top.

As I made it to the landing, she was standing in a long hallway. On the right side were two doors. She pointed and said, "The first door is our bedroom, and the door next to that is yours."

I left my suitcase next to my door, and she showed me around. On the other side of the hall, across from the bedrooms, were two other doors. The first door led into a large living room. Two big couches, a couple of big chairs, a cabinet dressed with dusty trinkets, and a large table-and-chairs set, sat atop the old and deteriorating carpeting that covered the floor. The dingy curtains hanging on the windows prevented the sun from coming in, and as a result, the room was dark and unpleasant.

Off the living room was a door that led into another area. She told me that was her husband's workshop. He was a carpenter and, at the time, was making small furniture and dollhouses for children. I smiled and hoped that maybe he'd like me and make a dollhouse for me to play with. He stepped out of his workshop, looked at me, and mumbled, "I'm Uncle Henry, and you must be John's daughter, right?"

"Yes, I'm Marlies." I said with a big smile.

He looked at me and grinned and then, straight-faced, looked at her. "Lena, are you going to make something to eat?" Nothing else was said as we walked out of the room.

The door next to the living room led to her office. As we walked out of the living room back into the hallway, she approached the office door and told me in a stern voice. "Nothing in there is of any use to you, and I don't want to find you in there at any time." I nodded my head in agreement, and we moved on.

Next, she proceeded to take me into the kitchen. It was a long space, seemingly comprised of the whole back of the house. Similar to the rest of the house, it was not very inviting. There was a long counter that faced me as I walked in, and at the end of the counter on the right was a huge cabinet where she kept her dishes, pots and pans, and supplies. There was a sink with a pump, and a machine that was used to homogenize milk. Next to that were a big, black coal-and-wood stove and a counter that continued to the end of the wall. To the left in one corner was a small stool that sat next to a huge, black cast-iron kettle. The kettle sat, keeping warm, on top of a low potbelly stove with a small fire burning inside.

Upon entering the kitchen, on the right-hand side of the floor, there was a trap door. She opened it, pointing out, "This is where you will go to feed the animals." I looked down the rickety steps, and she continued, "It goes directly into the barn; this way you don't have to walk outside." She closed the door and walked into another room.

Hungry and wondering what was cooking, I stepped onto the small stool and peeked into the kettle. There were quite a number of items in there: scraps of meat and vegetables floating in some sort of liquid. As I stood wondering what it was, my aunt walked back into the room. Startled, I asked if the kettle contained our dinner. "No. It's slop, and you'll use it to feed the pigs." I stepped off the stool and continued to look around.

Next, we walked outside and Aunt Lena showed me the grounds, before taking me back into the barn. They had two cows—one white and a little cranky, and one brown and friendly—quite a few tools, and a couple of big wagons in an area where she kept the straw and hay mounds. There were sweet beets mixed into the hay to feed the cows. I was thrilled to be around animals again.

Next, she took me around back and showed me the pig stalls. Upon entering, I was surprised to find such a dark, dingy atmosphere, and I was overcome by a stench that permeated the air. There were four, individual stalls with doors, and she opened them to show me the pigs lying in the back of each one. They were difficult to see—the only light that entered the stall was from a small, muddy window that hung overhead. She pulled on the dirty light fixtures that hung from the ceiling and illuminated filthy stalls. Being built partially underground added to the darkness of the damp, unkempt area where manure was piled high. I could see there was no fresh straw for them to lie in, so silently, I thought, *The first thing I'm going to do is clean out those stalls and make them look like Oma's.*

The cows weren't in much better shape. They looked a little healthier than the pigs, but not by far. We proceeded back up the stairs into the kitchen, before she took me into the small bedroom designated for me. There was a small bed, a dresser, and a freestanding clothing closet. She grumbled, "There are hangers, so go ahead and hang up your clothes while I make something to eat."

I looked down at the suitcase and thought about Mama. She had made so sure everything I needed for the year was with me. I missed her already, and my suitcase was still packed. I told myself to be strong and not cry and began to unpack my belongings. I removed the ribbons and the brush for my hair. I placed them in the small dresser near the bed. Next, I removed the beautiful dresses and aprons Mama made for me, placing them all on the bed. I began to pick the one I'd wear to dinner, after all, it was my first evening in Holtztum, and I thought it was proper for me to look sharp.

In Germany, aprons were a tradition, worn when you dressed to go to someone's house, church, or any kind of special occasion. I picked out a nice dress with a small, white apron made with lace and ruffles around the bottom. Not being able to reach the bar in the closet to hang the rest of my clothes, I looked around the room and was happy to find a small chair. I pulled it close, removed a hanger, and one by one began to put away my clothing. While I completed the task, I began to cry. I didn't know why, but all of the sudden I felt very lonely and overcome with an eerie feeling. I didn't want to be there; I missed my family and wished that someone would come and rescue me.

Aunt Lena stepped into the bedroom, looked at me, and instantly knew that I had been crying. It didn't matter though; she had no idea how to comfort me and made no attempt to do so. "We're having fried potatoes and sour milk. Do you like them?"

"Yes, that's fine." Sour milk was better than no milk, and I hadn't had any since the previous summer. The only time I had been able to enjoy a fresh glass of milk was at Oma's, so I looked forward to having it again.

Fried potatoes were also a rarity, since we had nothing to fry potatoes with. We had little pats of margarine that couldn't be wasted, so frying potatoes was not an option at home. So they did sound inviting. I hadn't had anything except for a small slice of bread before I left home early that morning, so I looked forward to eating. My stomach was rumbling and I was all too hungry.

After hanging my clothes, she called, and I ran into the kitchen and sat down. She had sour milk in one bowl and fried potatoes in another, and she proceeded to put some on my plate. Uncle Henry came in and sat down, and I was surprised that he didn't bother washing his hands before eating, but he didn't. Since I was used to silence at the dinner table, I wasn't too surprised when they didn't speak either.

However, I was shocked that no prayers were said. At every meal I had ever eaten, prayers were said before and after. We always thanked God for the food he had given us. Since there were no prayers said out loud, I silently said my own and ate my food. Not one word was spoken throughout the entire meal.

When we finished, I helped her clear the table by putting the dishes in the sink. She had a kettle of water going, so we washed them together. She washed, I dried, and she told me where to put them. Not until after the dishes were done, did she say, "I think you've had a long day, and it's time for you to go to bed." My uncle walked out of the kitchen and back into his workshop. That seemed to be a routine for him. He spoke very little to her and even less to me.

My first encounter with Uncle Henry and Aunt Lena was cold and not very encouraging. I went into my room and started writing a letter to Mama. It began, "Mama, I can't stay here; please come and get me. I don't like it here. It's very dingy and not very inviting. Aunt Lena and Uncle Henry barely speak and they're not friendly at all. Aunt Lena frightens me, and she looks like a witch."

Big tears were falling down onto the paper as I folded it and wrote our address on the outside. I walked out of my room and handed it to Aunt Lena and asked, "Do you have any postage?"

She grabbed my letter, "I'll take care of that for you."

"Thank you, good night, Aunt Lena."

"Goodnight."

I went to bed for the first time in my life without hugs or warm, goodnight kisses. No one said a prayer with me, and no one tucked me in. I had all of those things at home; yet here, all I had was a lonely feeling creeping over me, and I was frightened. I couldn't wait for Mama to receive my letter, knowing that she would retrieve me immediately.

Upon waking up, I realized that it was Saturday morning, so I asked if I should go down and feed the cows.

"I don't expect you to live here without doing any work, so that would be a great idea," she replied sarcastically.

She didn't give me any breakfast, so right away I went down into the barn and began cleaning out stalls. I filled their pails with water and began the arduous task of taking the manure out before replacing it with fresh straw. I also knew how to feed them, so I went ahead and did so. I began talking to the cows as I worked, when I suddenly realized there was someone else in the barn.

He was the old gentleman who lived next door. When I first encountered him, he didn't speak at all. He was crotchety, and continually made grumbling noises. I didn't even know if he was able to speak, but he must have been, since he kept going upstairs into her office. They discussed what had to be done throughout the day, and she'd give him instructions. After quite some time, she told me that his name was Joseph and to make sure that I stayed out of his way.

"He doesn't like to be bothered, and I don't want you wasting any of his time. Don't start any conversations with him. He doesn't like children."

"All right, Aunt Lena."

Every morning he came over to milk the cows. I didn't know why he hadn't been drafted into the service, why he was there, or who he was to my aunt and uncle, but when something on the farm needed repair, he stopped by and took care of it. With Uncle Henry not being much help, I'm sure she had to pay him for his efforts. I don't know what was wrong with Uncle Henry, but he had difficulties breathing. It seemed as though he was always short of breath and struggling for air. He was sickly and more or less happy to be confined to working in his shop.

The gentleman next door also took care of planting the crops. When it was time for harvesting, he made sure that the proper amount of grain was given to the government and a certain amount was delivered to the mill and transformed into flour. With my arrival, I alleviated a lot of Joseph's workload. I fed the cows and pigs, took care of the barn, and if necessary helped him in the fields. Aunt Lena would take me out and show me where he was and what I needed to do to help him, continually reiterating, "Don't bother that man; leave him alone; and stay out of his way."

Teaching the Pigs to Walk

It was depressing not having anyone to talk to, so I cherished taking care of the animals. I spent time with the cows, trying to get to know them and letting them get to know me. When I entered the pig's stalls, I knew it was going to be a big job to clean them out. Determined, however, I found a pitchfork and started throwing the manure into the wheelbarrow. There was a garden hose, and I proceeded to clean as much as I could into the cobblestone courtyard. I was soaking wet, and my shoes were saturated with dirt and water, but I was on a mission. I did my best to clean the area, and I put food in a trough for the pigs, but they lay in the stalls near the back wall and didn't advance toward the food. I thought it was odd that they weren't coming out to eat. They were grunting and doing a lot of wiggling, but they wouldn't stand up.

The more I started cleaning the stalls, the more I noticed that all four pigs were just lying there. It dawned on me that they were crawling on their bellies trying to get to the trough where the food was. All of the sudden I realized that those pigs couldn't walk. None of them walked. I ran to the house and yelled, "Aunt Lena, don't your pigs walk?"

"No, they don't walk."

"Well, how come?"

"I don't know, but they are getting fat, and they'll be getting butchered, so there is no problem with whether or not they can walk. All I care about is that they get fat."

"Maybe the reason that they can't walk is because it's too dark in that room."

"That has nothing to do with it."

"My grandmother said animals need light, fresh air, sunshine, and exercise. Maybe that's why they can't walk."

"That's not your concern; just go and feed them."

Disheartened, I returned to the barn, but feeding them was difficult for me. I had to take small buckets of food down the stairs, through the barn, and around the front of the house into the stalls. Wanting to make sure the animals were fed properly, I had to make several trips. If I was stronger or taller, maybe I could have done it all in one trip. But I had to take small buckets one at a time—it took at least four or five trips per pig.

Later that evening, I sat down at the supper table, and my aunt gave me a slice of bread and a glass of sour milk. I had taken my shoes off each time I went up the stairs, not wanting to get manure in her kitchen, and when I was finished, I asked her where I could wash them. She told me to go down the barn and wash them, meaning I had to go back down and put the shoes on over my wet socks and go into the cold barn to wash up. When I completed that task, I asked her, "Where can I put my dirty socks?"

"If they're dirty, go wash them."

I found a bucket and put some cold water in it; then went downstairs and stood in the barn barefoot to wash my socks. Some of the spots didn't come out, but I finished the job and hung them with a piece of rope that I managed to find. When I finished, since the floor was chilly, I went back upstairs and found another pair of socks to put on. It was only March, and everything was still quite cold.

I had worn my coat to clean out the barn, and I was so afraid that dirt would get on it that I tried to be extra careful, but I always managed to get something on it anyway, and that meant I had one more thing to wash. I quickly found out that coats are difficult to dry.

When I finally sat down to eat supper, she and Uncle Henry had already finished, so I ate by myself. While she was puttering around the kitchen, I told her that I would like to ask Uncle Henry a question.

"Like what?"

"Well I wanted to know if he could build something for the pigs."

"Build what?"

"I would like him to build a fence around the pig barn. Perhaps I could get them outside and once I do, then maybe I can get them to walk."

"How will you get them to walk?"

"Well if he'll build it for me, I'll get the pigs out. Somehow I'll manage to get them out."

With a nasty smirk on her face, she said, "Let me talk to him; I'll be back."

She placed sour milk and fried potatoes on the table for me, and I sat down and began eating. Uncle Henry came into the kitchen.

"You wanted something?"

"Yes. Uncle Henry, could you build me a fence around the pig's stalls so I can coax them outside? I want them to have fresh air and sunshine, and maybe then they'll learn to walk."

"I'll see what I can do."

For the first time in Holtztum, I had something to look forward to. I said goodnight, washed myself with cold water from the sink, and went to my room.

As I sat on my bed, I realized how disheveled I was becoming. Mama always braided my hair. She did a beautiful job, but without her, I had difficulties keeping my braids together. There were no mirrors in the house, yet I could tell they were slowly becoming unraveled. I twisted them into long rolls and put rubber bands around the ends. As hard as I tried, they didn't look very nice, and I couldn't quite remember how Mama styled my hair so effortlessly.

After struggling with my braids, I sat down at my desk and started writing another letter. This time I cried harder than I did the night prior. The paper became covered with tears as I told her again that I didn't like where I was. I had no one to talk to, and I was so lonely. I begged Mama to come get me as soon as possible. I dried the tears on the page and put my letter in an envelope. Again, Aunt Lena told me to put it on the kitchen table and she'd make sure that it went out with the morning mail.

The following day was Sunday, so I asked, "What time is church?"

"The bells ring at eight and twelve o'clock."

"Won't it be too late to go if I wait to hear the bells?"

She took me to the window and pointed at the steeple, which was about a quarter of a mile down the street. "If you want to go, there it is."

As I walked back to my room, I was filled with a sense of relief, knowing that Mama would soon read my letters and come to my rescue.

When I woke the next day, I was looking forward to going to mass. I tried to make myself presentable by putting on my new dress, made especially for the trip, along with my coat and shoes. The shoes were still damp from the night before, but I had to wear them. They were the only pair I had. Thinking I had cleaned up pretty well, I walked into the kitchen feeling proud, wearing my new dress. "I'm all ready to go to church." To my utter disbelief, no one else was ready to go. In fact, I had the distinct impression that they never went to visit God, and if I was going, I had to make my way alone. So I did.

As I approached the front of the church, I could hear the bells ringing, and I was pleased I made it on time. As I entered, I saw many children, and surprisingly, the priest made them sit down in front. There were rows of kneelers that the children sat and kneeled upon throughout the mass, and since I too was a young child, I had to go down in front like the others. It would have been much easier if I could have snuck in unnoticed and blended in at the back of the congregation. That, however, was not an option, as I was escorted up front.

I smiled at many of the children, said hello, and told them my name. They seemed friendly as they reciprocated my kindness.

"Are you going to be going to school here?"

"Yes. Yes I am."

One of the girls told me where the school was, and they asked me where I was living. I told them that I was living with my Aunt Lena, Lena Wolf. All of a sudden, the children walked away. They didn't want to hang out with me, and I felt kind of strange. I didn't understand what was happening. One minute they showed me kindness, and the next, I was shunned.

After mass, I walked home, and again she gave me a slice of bread and a glass of sour milk. Afterwards, I went down and fed the cows and pigs and cleaned out their stalls. By the time I finished and came back upstairs, they had already eaten lunch, and she didn't offer me anything. I wasn't going to get fed until suppertime.

In the meantime, I decided to spend time with my favorite cow. She was gentle and seemed to enjoy having me there. I talked with her and sang some songs and enjoyed spending my time with her too. I decided that since we would be spending a lot of time together until Mama came to get me, that I would call her Kushen.

That evening, I again wrote a letter to Mama, and this time, one to Oma. I included a letter for Peter, telling him how lucky he was to be with Oma and Opa and how I wished I could be with them, rather than the horrible place I ended up. I imagined all of the wonderful things Peter was doing, all of the wonderful conversations they were having, and most important, all of the love that was being showered upon him. I desperately longed to be there. I missed being on the farm with the people I loved, the people who loved me.

After I finished my letters, I folded them nicely before deciding to turn in, since I had to get up early for my first day of school. It was difficult to sleep, wondering what tomorrow had in store, eventually though, my brain was tired of the whirling thoughts, and I nodded off.

With the light of day and the rising sun, I got up and washed my face and hands and tried to clean up the best I could. I dressed myself and Aunt Lena gave me a slice of bread to eat as she walked with me to school. Since we couldn't see it from the window, and she had nothing to point to, I suppose she felt obligated to show me the way.

As we walked, she proceeded to tell me I shouldn't come home at lunchtime even though all of the other children went home. She'd be very busy and wouldn't be able to take time to prepare anything for me. I was to stay in school until the day was over, without so much as something to snack on.

"I want you to do this every day. There's no reason for you to come home."

"Then who'll take care of the pigs?"

"You can do that when you return after school. As long as they eat once a day, that's all that's necessary. Just give them extra food and don't worry about the pigs."

"Well, what about the cows?"

"From now on, I want you to get yourself up early enough to get ready for school and to feed the cows before you leave. I told you Joseph didn't want to do that anymore, he has enough trouble milking the cows and taking care of what has to be done in the fields."

As we entered the school, she introduced me to the teacher, who seemed pleasant enough. She invited me into the class and introduced me to the other children, as I sat down at my new desk. When lunchtime came, the teacher was leaving to go home and told me that I wasn't permitted to stay in the classroom without supervision. I left the room and sat down on the steps in the hall. Alone and hungry, I just knew this would become my daily routine, if Mama didn't arrive soon. I thought about many things that first day of school but my hope for the picket fence I requested kept me going and filled with anticipation.

That did in fact become my daily routine, but on that first day when I returned home from school, I was elated to find that Uncle Henry had built my fence. It was a perfect picket fence, covering a large area, and he even incorporated a gate on one side. I was so pleased that he had taken time out of his day for me, and I immediately mapped out my plan of attack.

I pulled the troughs partially out of the stall area and put food in them. The four pigs each crawled over to the feeding area and lay there. I cleaned out all of their stalls and added fresh straw. Every day when I arrived home from school, I moved the troughs out a bit farther, until I finally had all four pigs out in the hallway leading to the front door. Before the end of the week, I had coaxed each one outside. I made sure to keep the cobblestone area clean and covered with fresh straw for them. They even relieved themselves right where they were lying. They couldn't even get up to do their dirty work. Their muscles had nearly completely given out. They were lucky they could still crawl, and luckier that I had arrived to try and save them from their dismal existence.

People had told me pigs were dirty and sloppy, but I knew it wasn't true. The only reason pigs wallow in dirt and mud is to stay cool. Otherwise, pigs go into one area and do their duty and keep the areas where they eat and sleep clean. These pigs, however, couldn't walk and had no choice, so I moved the trough for them and tried to clean up where they had been lying.

I asked my uncle if he could make one big trough, so I wouldn't have to fill four of them. I could keep it in one area and it would be a lot easier to clean. He agreed and built it. I was so thankful that he was helping me. Otherwise, I don't know what I would have done with myself. I took the four, small troughs back into the stalls to store them, since they were empty and the pigs were all outside.

I closed the doors so they couldn't get back in, and I left them outdoors. It was cool out, but I figured that it was better than being in the dark, dingy barn. They must have agreed, because they made no attempt to go back in.

I proudly finished for the night and went inside and tried to wash my underclothes and socks. Aunt Lena had a big sink and let me wash whatever I had, but not once did she make an attempt to wash my clothing for me. My meals continued to consist solely of sour milk, bread, and fried potatoes, yet as I looked into the pig's kettle, I saw pieces of sausage, pork chops, vegetables, potatoes, and potato pancakes. The food in the slop bucket was much better than what I was offered.

Even though the pigs kept me busy, it hadn't gone unnoticed that an entire week had gone by, and yet I had received no response to the letters I had written to Mama and Oma. I didn't understand why. It couldn't possibly take that long for a letter to get to Holtztum. It never seemed to take that long for letters to come from Kell, every other day we received a letter when we lived in Rüsselsheim. Now that I was in Holtztum, when I really needed one, it seemed as though the letters might never arrive.

I asked my aunt how long it should take for delivery, and she said, "Well, you know we are in the middle of a war, and sometimes it's difficult for letters to be delivered promptly. I wouldn't be expecting one for quite sometime if I were you." Regardless, I continued writing every night, and I continued crying over them.

The children at school were not any friendlier. They spoke to me when they had to, but it was usually forced, and I had the clear impression that no one wanted to associate with me. When they played games, our teacher told them they had to ask me, but other than that, they never voluntarily invited me to join them. I didn't understand why, except that maybe I had become the smelly child that no one wanted to befriend.

Deciding which Is Worse: Shame, Filth, or Loneliness

After being in Holtztum an entire week, I asked Aunt Lena why I hadn't taken a bath. "Don't you take baths?"

She replied, "You want to take a bath? Well, after you come home from school tomorrow and take care of the cattle, then you can take a bath."

That's exactly what I did. I came home and took care of the pigs and spent time with the cows. Kushen, the brown one really seemed to be a friend. She spent time looking for me, and as I entered the barn, she always made a funny little noise. I'd hug her, and she'd nuzzle me with her wet, slimy nose as she licked my face. It seemed as though she craved my attention, and without her affection, I wouldn't have had any.

When I finished and went upstairs, Aunt Lena told me to take my clothes off. There was a big tub sitting on the kitchen floor.

"While you take your clothes off, I'll put hot water in the tub."

She had given me a towel, and as I came out of my room, I dropped the towel and climbed into the tub. It was nice and warm, and so soothing.

"Aunt Lena, could you wash my hair?"

"You're in the tub; wash it yourself."

I was surprised by her answer, but she had given me soap, so I tried to wash my own hair. The difficulty was removing the suds without fresh water to rinse with. She picked up my towel and placed it at the far end of the counter. The kitchen was cold, but instead of placing the tub near the stove, she placed it across the room. It didn't take long before I got quite cold sitting in the tub, and having a wet head made it worse.

As I was about to climb out, the doorbell rang. She answered the door and three young Nazi officers came into the house. I had seen those same men go into her office on prior occasions, but this time was different. She brought them into the kitchen, and they sat down at the table. She was joking and talking ever so nicely to them. I hadn't realized that she had the ability to treat anyone with decency, but the Nazis must have cast a kindness spell on her. She gave them coffee, something we didn't have at home, so I was amazed to see that she had it. *Where on earth did she get coffee and why did hers smell very different from the grain coffee that Mama made?*

They drank and conversed about all kinds of things. Being naked, I was too embarrassed to listen to the things they were saying. More important, I was focused on how I was going to get out of the tub. The water started getting very cold, and I started to shiver. After what seemed like forever, I finally interrupted, "Excuse me, Aunt Lena, may I have a towel?"

"The towel is at the end of the counter; go get it."

I was too ashamed to stand up in front of three, strange men and climb out of the tub. That would never have been allowed at home. Nakedness was covered, and we never walked around without clothing in front of anyone. I had never seen my parents or my brother naked, and I was not about to change my way because my aunt was a lazy good-for-nothing woman who was trying to humiliate me.

I sat in the cold water shivering so badly that I could hear my teeth chattering. Finally, one of the Nazi officers remarked, "That girl looks like she's freezing to death." He walked over, picked up the towel, and assured me, "You can get out, I won't look. I'm just going to wrap you in this towel." I stood up, and he did as promised, wrapping the towel around me while he looked the other way. I ran straight to my room, climbed into bed, naked with tear-filled eyes as I lay there hoping to stop shivering.

When I finally withdrew from the safety of my bed and got dressed, the Nazi officers had gone. She said, nonchalantly, like nothing had happened, "You'd better eat. It's getting late and nearly time for you to go to bed. Tomorrow's Saturday; there'll be a lot of things for you to do, and Joseph is expecting you to help in the fields." She didn't say goodnight to me; she just walked into her office, after having given me the usual sour milk and fried potatoes.

Having had just about enough of her sour milk and fried potatoes, I walked over to the pig's kettle and proceeded to take out pieces of food and put them on my plate. It was something different, and as I chewed on the pigs' slop, I realized that it tasted a lot better than what I had been getting. I'd had an entire week of sour milk, fried potatoes, and sliced bread. I hadn't had any meat or vegetables, which I loved, so I looked forward to having something different.

Aunt Lena received vegetables from the market, eliminating any need for her to grow a garden. But she never offered them to me, and since she was so unfriendly, I was too shy to ask. I longed for the days when I could walk into the back yard and pick fresh veggies. She always put the same food in front of me and never asked what I wanted, even though I knew there was a plethora of alternatives available.

In addition to my troubles, I was having a hard time keeping my shoes clean. I tried to keep the manure off of them and keep my clothes clean as well, but I really didn't know how to do it properly, giving me another reason to cry at night.

I sobbed, "Mama, please write me a letter and tell me how to wash my clothes. I don't know how to do it. Aunt Lena has soap, but I don't know how much to use. I rinse them and put them in water, but I don't know how to keep them clean. Please write and tell me what I have to do, and how often do I have to wash my clothing?"

My dresses were dirty and my coat spotted, but finding time to clean them was impossible. The temperature outside was very cold and washing them meant wearing wet clothes and gloves the next day. I tried keeping them somewhat clean by using a damp rag to brush the spots, but somehow I knew I was fighting a losing battle. I made a decision that staying warm and dry with dirty clothes was better than being wet and cold with clean clothes. Topping everything off, my head began to itch as my hair and body became as dirty as my clothing.

One evening, I noticed, while lying in bed, that small bugs were crawling on my pillow. Horrified, I jumped up and pulled the blanket from the bed curling up in the corner only long enough to creep back over to see what had gotten into my bed. As I looked at the small brown bugs, I realized I had lice. *What was happening to me? How did I become this dirty bug-infested girl?* I convinced myself that I must have gotten the lice from school, and I hoped that someone would help me. I curled up on the floor and again cried myself to sleep

The following week after I had suffered the entire weekend, the teacher checked me and told me I definitely did have lice. She gave me a small bottle of medication and told me to take it home and have Aunt Lena put it on my head, so the lice would perish. When I went home, I immediately told her I had lice, and she needed to put the medication on my head.

"If you have lice you brought it from home."

"No, Aunt Lena, I didn't have lice at home; Mama always made sure. She checked my hair and took good care of it, I didn't have lice then, but I have them now, and this is what my teacher told me to do. She said it had to be placed on my hair carefully and then wrapped in a towel and left for a period of time before washing it out." It was the only way to kill the lice, and I told her that the teacher also said, "You have to keep them confined under a towel."

After I told her all of that, she scoffed, taking the bottle and dumping it on my head. "There's no need for that, just put the stuff on and wait until it dries. By that time, your bugs will be dead."

All I wanted to do was get rid of the lice. I needed to get rid of them, and I was so upset, I wanted to scream, but I couldn't. She frightened me more than the bugs.

Medicine or not, she didn't help me wash my hair this time either, so I went into the kitchen and tried to use the pump to rinse it out, but the water was ice cold and I couldn't endure it for long. I didn't wash it very well, but I was afraid to ask for a bath.

In all the time I spent with my aunt, I never asked for another bath, and she never offered one. I became a filthy, foul mess. The lice continued to flourish on my hair; I was constantly itching. And worst of all, the other children noticed. Other than at Kell, no matter where I went, I just couldn't catch a break and connect with other children. I tried to be good. I said my prayers and always thanked God for providing for me. I was kind to others and especially kind to animals, so why in heaven's name did everyone despise me so?

I had been there three weeks, and I hadn't received a response from Mama. I couldn't believe it, my 8th birthday was approaching, and not one letter or card came. I became very concerned and I asked my aunt why I wasn't getting any mail. "Why isn't Mama writing?" She shrugged her shoulders and walked away, but she must have been thinking about a better answer, because shortly before it was time for me to go to bed, she dragged me outside by the arm as we heard airplanes flying over. She yanked me aside with her teeth clenched, and with a low, throaty voice attempted to enlighten me, "Do you see those planes going over? They're headed for Frankfurt and Russelsheim, and if you haven't heard from your parents, they're probably already dead. They've been killed by the bombs."

I started screaming, "No. That's not true! That can't be true. Somebody would let me know! Mama and Papa and Siegfried are not dead!"

"Of course they are. Have you heard from them?"

I cried, "No, not even a note."

"That's why! They're dead. And you better get used to the idea. And if you have any plans on running away, I suggest you think twice, since you have no place to go to."

"I'm going to go to Oma's!"

"Your grandmother has her own problems, and before you make any decisions about going anywhere, you better write and ask them if they even want you."

That's exactly what I did. I could barely see through my tears, but I ran into my room and slammed the door behind me. I was sure my heart would break as her words played over and over in my mind.

Could Mama and Papa possibly be dead? I started to realize that what she said must be true, because if they were alive, I knew Mama would have written to me. Mama would never have forgotten my birthday, and even if she did, she would have let me know something. Yet I had not heard one word.

I started believing that the bombs had surely killed them.

My heart was broken, and I thought I would die. Like all children, my family was the most important thing in my life. Knowing that I would see them again was what kept me alive, and struggling to survive. With one devastating blow, Aunt Lena destroyed my very reason for facing another sunrise.

As I wallowed in my sorrow, I lay down on my bed to cry. As I lay there, lice began crawling on my pillow, and that frightened me.

At that moment, feeling totally alone, everything frightened me, but still I sat down to write a letter to Oma. As I wrote, the lice fell from my hair onto the paper, and I killed them by smashing them with the back of my thumb, but they were falling onto the paper faster than I could snuff them out.

That was when I realized exactly how bad the infestation was. As I climbed back into bed and saw the movement on my pillow, I couldn't tolerate one more minute.

I picked up my blankets and went down to the barn where I lay on the straw next to my cow, and as I cried, she turned and licked my face.

She seemed to sense my loneliness, and she nuzzled me and moved her legs so I could cuddle against her warmth. Wrapped in my blankets, for the first time in weeks, I was comfortable.

Kushen didn't hesitate to give me a place to sleep. From that moment on, I no longer slept in my lice-infested bed. I stayed in the barn each night with my only friend, my cow. In the morning, she'd wake up early and nudge me, becoming my trusty alarm clock. I didn't know how to face another day without my family, but all I could do was keep myself busy with the one thing I cared about, the animals.

The first thing I did when I woke was prepare her food and clean her stall. Afterwards, I went upstairs and tried to wash myself the best I could. I put my hair into rolls since I still hadn't mastered braiding; then washed my face and hands. I put on one of my dresses, even though they were all badly stained, and tried to clean my shoes the best I could, and headed off to school.

It was hard to focus that day, but I still had to face my usual problems. I had become so filthy that my teacher wouldn't let me sit with the other students any longer. She said my lice were too pronounced, and she was concerned about the other children catching them from me.

My teacher tried to help, "Marlies, please take these bottles of the medicine home. Why can't you seem to take care of your problem?"

I told her what Aunt Lena had done, and yet she didn't say another word. She simply continued giving me bottles of medicine to take home, all the while making me sit alone in a corner in the back of the room.

The other children started making fun of me. They called me "dirty pig." Outside when they played games, the teacher no longer asked them to have me join, and when they jumped up and down with their jump ropes, or held hands and sang songs together, I was left to sit alone. Even worse than not being included, when they played ball, they usually took it and threw it at me. I had become a moving target as well as their source of amusement. They'd trip me and laugh and poke fun for their enjoyment, and no one befriended me. In fact, I had no friends at all, not a single person had one ounce of kindness to spare.

Believing my parents were dead, it didn't matter if I had friends or not. It didn't make any difference if children were friendly, if they spoke with me, or if they spent any time with me. I couldn't have cared less. But I did care about one thing: I was praying for a letter from Oma to let me know that Peter was all right. I never stopped hoping that they'd come and rescue me.

I hated my aunt. She never looked for me, never took care of me, and couldn't care less if I was cold or hungry as long as I had the same old sour milk and fried potatoes every night. My uncle was no better; he never sat and ate in my company, nor held a conversation with me. There were no stories, no prayers, and no attending church. There was nothing. My uncle rarely came out of his shop, and I knew he made a lot of toys for other children in the village, but he never made a toy for me. He wouldn't even allow me in his shop. In all of the time I was there, I never once saw what the inside of his workspace looked like.

9
Nazis in the Family

I noticed the Nazis visiting the house quite frequently and that the people in the village avoided Aunt Lena at all costs. Whenever she went to purchase something and needed help carrying it home, she'd drag me along—that's when I realized that no one spoke to her.

She had no friends in town and no regular folks ever came to visit. However, the Nazis came, and they always brought boxes of items. Afterwards, she'd have a bottle of oil, butter, pork chops, sausage, and all kinds of meat in the icebox. She had soap for washing clothes and for washing her hair, paper products, and paper to write on.

These items and others were virtually impossible to find in Germany, but she had all of them. She even had toilet paper, all the necessities. Yet I never saw her go to the market and take out a ration card. She simply went to the butcher and the grocery store and asked for things. They'd give it to her immediately; she'd pay and walk home with everything her black heart desired.

As young as I was, I began to understand what was going on. She had become the very thing Opa had warned us all against, a Nazi, and she was informing on the townspeople. She used to stand by her window with binoculars and watch people. She also gathered information in town by asking questions. Many people shunned her, fearing what she could do to them. But it didn't seem to bother her, and she chose to live her life accordingly.

As I walked home from school, the children stayed way behind me, or they'd run in front of me trying to avoid contact. They didn't want to reap the rewards of her wrath, and if it kept them from beating me up, then so be it. I noticed that when I returned to the house and into the barn, she'd come down the steps. I could hear voices and see her talking with the children, asking them questions. She'd say things like, "I hear your sow had baby pigs." If they answered yes, she'd continue her inquisition, "How many little pigs did it have?" She'd continue, "Have your chickens hatched any baby chicks lately?"

The children usually answered honestly, "Yeah, we have a lot of baby chicks, two of our hens have hatched their eggs, and we have twenty-three baby chicks." She'd pump them for incriminating information to find out if the farmers were hiding things from the Nazis or lying outright to them. She informed them who had baby chickens, pigs, etc. If the people were somehow able to hide a pig somewhere—like my grandmother was doing—she'd rat them out to the government.

She also asked the children if their family members ever talked about Hitler. Saying things like, "I bet they're getting dissatisfied with all of the things they have to give away."

The children replied with statements like, "My mother's mad because she says Hitler is killing us; in fact, he is destroying us."

Coincidentally, after she pumped the children for information, suddenly, some of the farm people disappeared. Sometimes just the farmer, but sometimes the farmer, his wife, and their children vanished from town. The teachers made general announcements in school that the children had moved away and were no longer attending our school.

The strange thing was they didn't move. Their farmhouse with the furniture and the animals and everything was still there. The Nazis would suddenly bring a new family in from the city. The new residents took over the farm as if they had been there forever, and no one ever knew the truth of what happened.

The people who moved into the homes and took care of the farms were always Nazis. They were strangers, and the townspeople isolated themselves from them. It became harder and harder to live with them, and it didn't take me long to understand what my aunt was doing and why I was being shunned. I had become guilty by association. The townspeople had informed their children not to say anything to or bother with me, because they knew that she was an informer. I finally understood why she was given food and supplies from the Nazis. All the pieces were fitting together.

German people were starting to disappear just like the Jews did, and people were frightened by what was happening. This, combined with the fact that I had become a very dirty, unkempt little person, made people disgusted in my presence.

No one was taking care of me, and after sleeping in the barn without having a bath in months, I had gone beyond filthy. I tried to keep myself clean by washing my feet, hands, and body; but it seemed like there was always something scaly starting to grow somewhere. Even with the cold water and soap, I wasn't able to do a good job of washing myself. As the warm weather of summer approached, the more I smelled. My head was completely covered with lice, and still no letters arrived for me from anyone.

I had succumbed to what she had said—my family was dead, and they were never coming for me. I never heard from Oma either, but I hadn't realized until later that I didn't know her name. I only knew her as Oma. In Germany, a grandmother is Oma and a grandfather is Opa. I had never really paid attention to what her real name was since my mother called her Mama, and my cousins and I called her Oma.

I used to hear people come to her house and say, "Hello Ann," or "Good morning, Ann," but I didn't pay attention; to me she was just Oma. When I sent letters to my grandmother, I wrote to Oma in Kell. When I lived with Mama, we all wrote letters, but they were placed into one envelope, and she sent them out together. We didn't have to know the address. Mama always took care of it, so we could save on envelopes and postage. I assumed that was why I wasn't hearing from her.

The summer was difficult, but as time went on, I noticed the small things meant more to me than ever before. I came home from school one afternoon and went to the barn. As I walked in, the pigs saw me and dragged themselves across the floor of the pen using their front feet. I was thrilled, and I bent down and hugged them. "You're doing excellent, and it won't be long till you will all be able to walk!"

With each passing day, the pigs' condition seemed to be improving. Some were starting to stand on their own, and others were still trying. But all of them were always happy to see me. Less than six weeks later, all my pigs were walking. They were in the front yard running around and happy to be alive. When it rained, I tried to get them into the barn where it was warm and dry, but they wouldn't hear of it. And who could blame them? All summer they enjoyed being outside where it was warm during the day and cool in the evening. They all became frisky, happy, and healthy; and I was proud of myself. I knew they loved me for helping them, and I loved them more; they had given me something to feel good about.

I loved all the animals in the barn, but the cow had become my best friend. She was there for me constantly and always happy to be in my company. I told her everything there was to know about me. While she listened, she'd make funny, grunting noises, gentle bellowing sounds, as if she were saying hello. Sometimes, I swear she was trying to talk to me. I'd hug her and give her big kisses, and she always slobbered all over me with her runny nose. We played together often, and I know she enjoyed, as much as I did, the small games I'd make up for us. I'd sneak underneath her and stick my head out between her front legs and play hide and seek. She'd put her head down, nudge, and lick me, never knowing how crucial her friendship had become for my survival. Without the animals, I truly had no reason to live and no one else cared if I did or not.

One night I saw potato pancakes in the food bucket for the pigs, and I finally got up the courage to ask Aunt Lena if I could have potato pancakes too. "If you want potato pancakes, you can have potato pancakes." I was surprised by her response. As I walked away, I thought to myself, maybe all I have to do is start asking for things. But since I had never asked, maybe it was my problem. I kept that thought in the back of my mind for future reference and could hardly wait for dinner.

Later that day when I came home from school, she was in the process of making the fresh potato pancakes. She was frying them on the stove, and from the supper table I could see that she had them buried in over an inch of oil. I didn't remember Mama or Oma ever making potato pancakes like that. Even when we lived in America, Mama used very little oil for frying. Likewise, when we were on Oma's farm, she also used very little. Aunt Lena's were different though. When she put them on my plate, they were saturated and dripping from simmering in oil for so long. However, I was hungry, and since she had made them for me and they smelled good, I proceeded to eat them with enthusiasm. Unfortunately, they didn't last in my stomach very long—I became downright sick. I couldn't stop vomiting, and of course the pancakes came right back up.

My stomach felt like it was on fire, and every time I felt like vomiting, I'd get a harsh burning in my throat. It took an entire month for the raw sensation to completely diminish. For a long time, I couldn't eat anything other than bread and water. I'm not sure what was in or on top of those pancakes, but I never asked her to make me anything again, and she never offered.

Winter was just around the corner, and I was becoming excessively thin. My old, dirty clothes were hanging loose, the children still made fun of me, and still no one wanted to be near me. When I went to church on Sunday mornings, I was no longer allowed to sit with the other children. I was asked to stand in the back of the church near the door. The lady in charge of the children didn't stand anywhere near me either. She stood off to the side, and when everyone else had gone for communion, she'd look at me and say, "Go ahead now." Thankfully, I was still permitted to walk down the aisle and up to the altar to receive the host. Perhaps the priest had some sympathy for the pathetic child who week after week entered God's house alone, but he was the only one.

As the body of Christ dissolved on my tongue, I made the sign of the cross before turning to retreat down the aisle; only to hear the children snickering and making "PU" noises while holding their noses and moving clear of the aisle. Trying to remain solemn, I kept my head bowed, but occasionally as I raised my eyes just a tad, I also saw adults moving off to the side whenever I neared.

There were no mirrors in our house that I ever saw.. If they had one, it was hidden in their bedroom, so there was no way for me to see what I actually looked like. Sometimes, when I looked into a glass window, I saw a reflection of myself, but it didn't show much—just a girl with a tremendous amount of hair hanging loose. I couldn't see exactly how dirty my hair and face were, but apparently everyone else could.

Saved! But not Rescued

I had arrived in March. Spring and summer were both behind me, and we were in the midst of late fall. As usual, I was in the barn. I came home from school and started taking care of the cows. Apparently, Joseph had come home from the fields early, and I didn't have to help him put hay on or unload the wagons.

Grain had been gathered from the fields and a big thrashing machine had been sent to the farms, one by one. The thrasher separated the kernels of grain from the stalk, and the stalks were used for straw. It had already been to our farm, and the miller was scheduled to come and gather the sacks to be stored for the government.

There was a monstrous, round building outside of town built of cement and brick that acted as a holding area where the grain was stored. Even the grain on my aunt's farm was turned over to the Nazis, so she didn't look suspicious. That was one of the reasons she had me come and live with her, so she would be able to butcher and keep a pig. Actually, she didn't need to butcher a pig, as her food supplies were plentiful, but she had to make a showing for people to keep them from suspecting her of being an informer. The others from the village had to give away so much of their products that she, in turn, had to do the same. I was aware of the particular day that the miller was coming only because she had informed Joseph and me that we were to be there to help place the sacks of grain on his wagon.

That day, I arrived home from school and went into the barn to visit my cow, when I was startled by a strange noise. I didn't realize what it was, but it sounded like something had fallen in the shed next to the cow stalls. I turned around and opened the door to see what the noise was and where it came from, only to find Joseph standing there urinating, right in the shed. I surprised him as much as he did me, and he became very angry. In fact, I'd never seen anyone as angry as he was at that moment. He kicked the wooden wall and started cursing. He was using terribly foul language, words I had never even heard of, but I knew they were bad. Very bad. As he was hollering, his face became distorted with anger. I turned away quickly, trying to leave, apologizing the whole while, "I'm sorry, Joseph; I didn't mean to walk in on you."

My instincts told me to run, to run fast and hard, but an overwhelming urge made me turn back for one last glimpse of the angered farmhand. In the split second that it took to rotate my head and catch him in my peripheral vision, I saw him pick up a big piece of wood and start to chase after me. I stood there, unable to move, like a deer caught in headlights, just as he hit me on the side of the head with the wood. The blow knocked me unconscious, and all I remember was everything turned black.

As color returned to my world, I was in my bed upstairs and instantly knew something was very wrong. I hadn't slept in that bed in months; someone else had put me there. But why? As I tried to open my eyes, everything was hazy, but I was able to make out the images of the miller, a doctor, Aunt Lena, and another woman whom I had never seen before. They were all standing around talking as if I weren't there. I was dizzy and in so much pain that I closed my eyes again. I had no idea how much time had passed, but judging by their conversation, it had been a great deal. As I gained consciousness for the second time, again not knowing how long I was out, I saw that the doctor and the strange lady were still there. She gently told me that I had a nasty head injury, and that I should lie quietly.

As I turned my head, I began to vomit. I couldn't control myself, and it went all over the bed. "Aunt Lena, I'm sorry. I'm so sorry. I'll clean it up."

Quickly, the strange lady comforted me, "Now you don't worry, I'll take care of everything."

I felt relief hearing those words, but again, I couldn't help myself and dozed off. It seemed each time I opened my eyes I'd start vomiting. The next time was no exception. It was dark in the room as I became sick again, but this time there was no one there to help me. I tried to get up to clean the area, but I couldn't raise my head, so I lay there in the warm, murky liquid as it turned cold. Smelling the putrid odor made me more nauseated than I had been originally.

The next time I woke, it was morning, and again, that strange lady was there. She looked blurry to me, and I still didn't know who she was. As she talked gently, she lifted me from the bed and into a chair. That's when I noticed that there was a large, blood-soaked area on the lower part of the bed. I had been bleeding profusely, but I didn't understand why. She tried to give me fluids, but I couldn't keep anything down. With the saddest expression, she kept repeating, "You poor thing, you poor, poor thing." Later she asked, "Marlies, do you know where your mother is? Maybe I can get in touch with your parents. Your Aunt Lena won't give us much information, and I was wondering if you could tell me how I could contact them?"

"My parents are dead. I have no parents."

"Oh my goodness! Who told you that?"

"Aunt Lena told me they were killed in a bombing."

"Is there anyone else?"

"I have my Oma who lives in Kell."

"What's her name?"

"Just Oma."

"Where's Kell?"

I uttered, "I don't know, it's just a nice little town," before I again sank into a deep slumber. Seemingly all I could do was sleep, especially after such an exerting conversation.

While I slept, the doctor returned. He waited for me to wake up, and after his final examination explained, "Your sickness is going to end soon, and you'll recover, but you have to continue to lie very still."

It's normally difficult for any eight-year-old, but especially me, to lie still, but with the pain I was experiencing, it was easy for me to abide by his wishes. Days passed without so much as a sighting of my aunt, but the lady kept coming, and eventually I was starting to feel better. I don't know how long I lay in that bed; I don't know how long I had been sick, but I knew it was a long time. Days passed slowly as I tried to muster the strength to move. Frustrated, I couldn't even lift my head from the pillow.

Happily, at last the vomiting ceased, and the headaches began to recede. It seemed like I was starting to get better, but my whole body continued to ache, especially my lower half. My legs were in excruciating pain, but I still couldn't understand why. I knew why my head was aching—I had been beaten with a piece of wood—but why did the rest of me hurt? My aunt never said anything, nor did the lady or the doctor give me any reasons for the pain or the excessive blood.

For the first time, I recalled the lady telling me her name was Anna Adams. "You know I go to school with an Anna Adams."

"Yes, I know. That's my daughter. Did you know that we're related to you?"

"Nope, I didn't know I had any relations here other than Aunt Lena."

"Well, we're not a very close relation, and we don't get together." She said she was a cousin, and that her family had also come from Oberemel, where my father was born.

I was so happy to have another relative, "Maybe when I get better, I could come and see you sometime." Her reply saddened me.

"No, I don't think that would be a good idea. You just stay here and do what your aunt tells you to do."

Just when I had a glimmer of hope, she sucked the wind from my sail. Nonetheless, I was grateful that she was helping me through my difficulties. She tried to keep me clean, and I hadn't felt that way in months, so I knew she must have given me a bath. I couldn't remember taking one, but suddenly I was no longer disgusting, even to myself. I was wearing a new nightgown that she had brought to me from her daughter. My sheets were changed, and I was feeling like a normal little girl again, except for my hair. I could see her staring at my head as she asked about my lice.

"You have an awful lot of lice, and you had better start using the medication the school sends with you."

"Aunt Lena uses it, but I don't think she's doing it right."

She shook her head and walked out telling me, "Marlies, I will be back tomorrow, but it will be for the last time."

As she promised, she returned the next day for my final checkup. "The doctor says it isn't necessary to have me come anymore. I wish you health. Marlies. Try to be happy."

I felt like I was losing the only compassionate human being that I had known in such a long time. She was the only person that showed any concern for me, while everyone else went out of their way to avoid me. She never came again, just like she said.

I slowly started getting up from bed, and little by little, I was able to walk around my room. I started feeling better, but when I got ready to turn in for the night, I realized how many lice were still crawling on my pillow. Unable to bear the movement, I went down to the barn and lay with my cow, all day and night. She hadn't forgotten me. She was still my best friend, and just like before, she kept me warm. I lay there and cried, wondering if I was going to die too, but it didn't happen. I became better, and in the morning went back upstairs.

Aunt Lena told me, "The doctor wants you to stay home from school at least until the end of the week."

"What day is this?"

"Wednesday!" She was very abrupt with me and very angry.

"Aunt Lena, I am sorry that I haven't been able to take care of the cows or the pigs. Has Joseph been able to take care of them since I've been sick?"

"No, Joseph hasn't been able to take care of them, thanks to you!"

"Why, I don't understand."

"Joseph's no longer here."

"Where did he go?"

"He went with the police. They took him away."

"Why? When is he coming back?"

"He's never coming back!"

"What did I do?"

"I don't know what you did, but whatever happened to make Joseph so angry had to be your fault. I've never seen him angry or unkind to anyone. That's why we don't have him any more, and now I have to find someone else to do his work. I never should have brought you here. You're nothing but trouble."

She blamed me for what happened, but I had no idea what I had done, leaving me to sink even deeper into the depths of my sadness. She became even colder, not spending one minute with me, she didn't even speak unless it was absolutely necessary. However, at slamming pots, pans, and doors, she was quite proficient and more than happy to oblige.

Angels in Our Ears

Just when I thought I would have to take on all of Joseph's responsibilities with Aunt Lena, an elderly man arrived one morning. He was there to help out on the farm, which was wonderful news, since his mere presence would keep her out of the barn. As long as someone else would do her work, I could have some peace in the only safe haven I knew. She might have owned the barn financially, but I owned it in the ways that truly meant something and preferred that she didn't invade my space.

The new farmhand appeared a bit more amiable, but he didn't go out of his way strike up a conversation either. Perhaps after the ordeal with Joseph, I should have feared the old man, but I didn't. I feared the silence I was living in abundantly more. He'd say hello and ask me how I was, but the conversation was short and not of any great importance. He kept to himself, but every now and then, I'd have to help him in the fields. On one occasion, while spreading manure together, he asked me, "Sweetie, what happened to your parents?"

"I don't know. They lived in Russelsheim, and my aunt said they don't write to me because they were killed in the bombings."

"How long will you be staying here?"

"Probably forever. I don't know where I'm supposed to go, because no one writes to me, which makes me think my grandparents are dead too." I started to cry.

"Don't cry. Don't you cry; things will get better."

I didn't see how they could. What was getting better? My aunt wasn't talking to me at all. She no longer put anything on my hair, she wasn't washing my clothes, the food put in front of me was always the same, and I was eating out of the pigs' slop. I couldn't believe it, pigs' slop was more or less what kept me alive. At breakfast, she wouldn't even come in the kitchen to give me a piece of bread. I'd try to cut myself a slice, but a few times, I cut my finger instead, using old rags to stop the bleeding, not knowing what else to do.

Nightfall upon nightfall, my life was becoming increasingly difficult to endure and the loneliness was numbing. With each new day, I prayed for just one person who'd show some compassion, but each day ended the same, with no one wanting to be in close proximity. I was just a dirty louse-infected little girl who had no one to speak to except for a cow. I loved her immensely, as she was all I had, but I desperately sought a human being to talk with and discuss things, anything.

The taunting from the children at school continued, and I was still separated from the others by the teacher, but while not being allowed to play any games, I did the best I could with my studies. If there could possibly have been an upside to any of the nightmare, it was that I was doing very well in school and on my homework assignments. After all, I had no activities to distract me. I was merely an onlooker where the games of childhood were concerned. My life had never been so depressing, so I continued writing letters to Oma, hoping that someone would eventually receive one.

I also continued hearing airplanes going over and knowing that cities were being bombed. I thought the world was on a steady path to its end. The Nazis continued visiting the house, always being welcomed with endless amounts of time spent socializing, but Aunt

Lena never had one second of kindness for me. She was as ugly inside as she was outside, and I loathed the very sight of her. But as miserable as things were, I had one bright spot: my pigs were doing well. They were happy and playful and glad to see me. At least the animals adored me!

As it usually happened, my nights were not filled with pleasant dreams. On the contrary, one night I had a horrible nightmare. I don't know why, but when I saw Aunt Lena in the hallway, I told her that, in my dream, the grain tower caught fire and all of the grain burned.

"God forbid," she said, "don't even mention something like that. It would mean the farmers would have to make up the difference, and there isn't anything to make up the difference with. I think you're a little bit touched in the head. You don't know what you're talking about. Dreams are dreams."

Far surpassing any coincidence, when I arrived at school, we heard fire engines, and I found out that the grain tower was *indeed* on fire. When I arrived home, Aunt Lena was infuriated. She pushed me into a corner screaming, "What did you do, try to make your dream come true? You set that building on fire!"

"Aunt Lena, I never did that! I've never been near that building. I see it when I walk to school from a distance through the fields, but I have never been near it."

"Well, that building started on fire, and they are coming here to ask you about it, because I told them what you said. I believe you're responsible for setting that fire. And if they prove you are, you're going where Joseph is, and no one will ever see you again."

I was trembling from fear, knowing I hadn't done anything. But would anyone believe me? I couldn't fathom that she thought I was guilty, yet sure enough the Gestapo trudged up our walkway, entered the house, and headed straight for the kitchen. They sat down at the table, and interrogated me as if I were a hardened criminal. "So, your aunt tells us that you torched the grain tower."

Sitting across from them, with her hovering to the side, my pulse skyrocketed with the accelerated beating of my heart. I was clenching my fists under the table, feeling the sweat pool in my palms. But I didn't cave; I stood tall and told the truth. I told them I knew nothing about it, that I had dreamed the building was on fire, but I didn't go there and set things in motion. After taking notes and staring pensively, the two poker-faced agents decided they had gotten all the information from me that they could, warning that they'd return to speak to me again. Three or four days later, the men returned, telling me that they'd found the person responsible for the fire with all the evidence pointing away from me.

"We can't blame you. From what we understand, you were in school when the fire started at approximately ten o'clock in the morning. We know there's no way for you to have pulled it off; so you're off the hook."

With a glare that could melt ice, she looked at me saying, "You got away with this one, but don't ever attempt to do anything wrong. You're in deep enough trouble as it is, and I'm watching you."

I realized how truly evil she was. From that moment on, I'd never speak to her again. She was all too eager to turn me over to the police for something I hadn't done. Creating conflict while ruining relationships had become the highlight of her dank, dreary existence, and I prayed I'd never end up as she had.

If I wasn't in school or church, without hesitation, I headed for the barn where the animals never judged me; They simply reciprocated my affection, never making issue of the fact that my lice problem had become so severe that the vermin had eaten my entire eyebrow, leaving a disgusting sore that was constantly draining pus. My hair looked like that of an unkempt, straggly old woman. It was long and had turned entirely white from the eggs that clung to every inch of each strand, and everyone could see it as plain as day. I couldn't get a comb through it, as it was strewn with straw and other foreign objects. Comparing it to a rat's nest would be an insult to the rat, as I officially lost the battle of trying to keep myself clean.

Each night, after doing my homework, I continued sitting in my room writing letters. The pages had a bumpy texture, from where my tears dried, combined with the remains of the lice that I crushed the life out of. When I finished my letters, I followed the same routine that I had followed for months: I put them on the table for my aunt to take care of, as she always said she did.

I never missed Sunday mass, and if standing in the back of the church through the entire service while the children snickered, was what I had to do to get God to listen, then I was willing to pay the price. I continued going and kept praying that God wouldn't forget me. Maybe somewhere there would be someone who cared, someone who would give me a clean place to live, and maybe, if I was lucky, I could take my cow with me. Dreaming of better days was nice; although I doubted very much they'd ever come. Still, I never gave up on the hope that God would send a guardian angel to take me away from Aunt Lena, while I cursed the day that Adolf Hitler sent me to Holtztum to live in squalor.

10
Rescue

When the couple and their young child arrived on her doorstep, Aunt Lena was absolutely shocked to see them standing there. Nervous, she welcomed them into her office. She sat down with them, striking up idle chitchat, before excusing herself to make coffee. I saw her open the trap door, checking the basement barn area to make sure I was down there. Of course I was with my cow. She closed the trap door again and proceeded to make the coffee, racking her brains to conjure a story they might believe.

Not happy with her evasive behavior, the woman beckoned from the office, "Lena, where is Marlies?"

"I am sorry, but she has gone to a nearby village to spend a few days with friends. It's quite a long walk, and I won't be picking her up until Sunday night. But you mentioned that you have to get back to Rüsselsheim tonight, isn't that right?"

"Yes, that's right."

"Well I 'm sorry to see you miss her, but you won't have the opportunity to see her—she's not here. If we had known you were coming, we could have made other arrangements."

The woman became agitated. "Lena, how could you allow her to go to a village when you know that they are starting to bomb them too! God forbid she should be in one of the villages and something happens. What if someone was killed there or something happened here? Where would she go? Where would she live? What if she were injured? How could you allow her to leave and go away overnight? The bombings are so severe now; how could you allow it?"

"Oh, she's done it many times. The friends she stays with are very nice people; they take good care of her. In the event that something should happen, I've given them your address and they know how to contact you. So there's no problem." She continued telling them lies, trying to divert their attention.

The woman's focus changed briefly as her curiosity piqued, "Where on earth do you get coffee?"

"From doing a favor for someone. I have been saving it for a special occasion. Since this is the first time my brother and his wife have come to visit me since he went to America, I consider this a special occasion to serve coffee."

Unbeknownst to me, my parents had *not* been killed in a bombing. And God must have been listening to my pleas, as he sent one of his angels to whisper in Mama's ear one night as she slept. I later learned that she had a dream so vivid—as real as the one I had about the grain tower being engulfed in flames—of me sitting at a desk and writing a letter with tears streaming onto the paper. But tears were not the only thing on the pages; there were also bugs. She saw an open sore over the top of my eye, and I appeared dirty, sad, and lonely.

Abruptly waking from her dream, she shook Papa, "John, I can no longer tolerate why our girl doesn't write to us." Mama had been writing to me on almost a daily basis. Evidently, Aunt Lena had been taking the letters out of the mailbox and destroying them. She never let me know that even one letter arrived. As for all the letters I had written, she amused herself reading them, but never sent them on to their intended destinations.

Making matters worse, on occasion she'd write to Mama telling her how happy I was and how well I was adjusting. She went on to say that I had lots of friends, so I didn't have time to write, but to give my regards and everything was fine. She told her I was happy and looked forward to being reunited with my family in maybe another year or so, when the children were permitted to return to their homes. She wrote all the letters under the guise that life in Holtztum was grand.

Mama didn't want to believe that nonsense any longer. She had constantly spoken to Papa about it. However, he had always tried to ease her mind by saying, "Well it could be true … you know how children are. She's getting a little older; maybe she's enjoying herself and can't take time to write."

Mama wouldn't relent this time, "John, I'm extremely concerned about her; my dream was too real. It was like an omen that I can't let go. I have to go and see my girl. No one has heard one word from her, not even a note. Peter and my mother have sent many letters, and she doesn't even bother to take the time to say thank you?"

At approximately the same time, announcements had come over the radio stating that children could be returned to their families. Many of the villages were also being bombed now. There really wasn't any safe places left, so the children might as well go home and stay with their parents. The bombings had increased everywhere and were dropping, on average, every other day, even though there wasn't much left to be destroyed.

"John, it's been nearly a year; some of the sanctions have been lifted regarding the children. Let's see about going to get Marlies. First thing tomorrow, please ask for permission to leave the city; I can't wait any longer." If she's happy, maybe we'll leave her for a while; but if she's not, we'll bring her home."

Papa could never say no to Mama, so he made arrangements with the Opel factory and went to see the Gestapo. They gave him permission to leave for one day. He could go to Holtztum that morning, but he'd have to be back the same evening. Additionally, when arriving at the train station, he had to go to Nazi headquarters and let them know that he had arrived and what time he would be leaving. They made plans to leave by train early Saturday morning. There was no time to notify Aunt Lena.

Mama didn't sleep at all Friday night, nervously anticipating their trip. Bright and early, she was packed and ready to go, hastily doing exactly as they had planned, careful not to waste one moment's time. They boarded the train whose final destination was Holtztum, riding in a fair amount of silence, not knowing what to expect upon their arrival. Papa already knew the way to his sister's home so, as the train pulled into the station, they prepared Siegfried for the seven-mile walk that would pave their way to horror and disillusionment.

None of us could have imagined what would happen in the following moments. As she sipped from her cup, Mama commented, "This coffee is excellent. I haven't had any since the beginning of the war. I'm shocked to find that you would have something so precious in your home." She served the coffee with cream and sugar, and Mama was amazed to see those items as well. "Lena, we haven't had sugar throughout the entire war."

They continued talking, but Siegfried was exploring. Being three years old and very inquisitive, he walked throughout the entire house. I was still in the barn, but it was time the pigs were fed. So I went up to the kitchen through the trap door, closed it, and proceeded to start gathering a bucket of food from the kettle of slop on the old stove. I was helping myself to some of the scraps, when I heard someone behind me. I turned around and saw a little boy standing in the kitchen. I was caught off–guard, since no one but Nazis ever entered her home.

I wondered what on earth would a little boy being doing here? Not one child other than myself had ever crossed the threshold into her house, so I tried to befriend him and figure it out.

"Hello, who are you?"

I had interrupted his progress through the house, while he stared at me as if he was frightened and uttered, "Oh, you are so dirty! Who are you?"

I didn't know who he was, or what to say in response, I just lowered my head with embarrassment, knowing he was right, and just as quickly, he turned around and ran into the office. The office? No one was ever permitted to walk into the office; yet, this strange little boy was walking in as if he had a right to be there.

I set the kettle down and crept across the kitchen floor listening to the voices coming from behind her door. "Oh, that's just a girl that comes here and helps out once in a while; she's probably feeding the pigs. Don't pay any attention to her." I had no idea who the voices belonged to, but I was curiously trying to find out.

"Well, I'd like to go and see the little girl and ask her about Marlies."

"No, that won't be necessary, just sit down!"

"Lena, I want to talk to that young girl."

A man's voice snapped, "Is there any reason why Elisabeth shouldn't talk to her?"

"Mommy, you don't want to talk to her; she's filthy—so dirty I don't think you are going to like that girl."

As the office door opened, I didn't want to get caught eavesdropping, so I ran back across the kitchen to the trap door. And as I took my first step, to retreat down the hole, I realized that someone was standing behind me. I slowly turned my head and saw what I was sure to be the ghost of my mother standing before me and I started to scream, "No, no, I don't want the ghosts to take me! I don't want to go! I don't want to be dead!" I started crying, just then my legs collapsed from underneath, and while on my knees, I began to pray. "God, please don't take me away and let me die. I know I have complained a lot lately, but please don't let me die." In the midst of my hysteria, I realized that the ghost was screaming too.

As she hysterically stood there, yet trying to calm herself, the man burst into the kitchen, took one glimpse of what she saw, grabbed his head, and started to shake. "Oh my God, how in heaven can this be possible?"

With the speed and force of an animal on the attack, he spun around, grabbing Aunt Lena by the throat. "For this, I'm going to kill you!" He shoved her into a chair in the kitchen and furiously continued choking the life out of her. She was turning shades of reddish blue, and as she struggled to pull his hands from her throat, I realized God hadn't come to take me to meet my parents in heaven. They weren't dead at all! They were very much alive! And Papa was about to kill his sister! Knowing he could be harmed, I screamed, "No! No, please let go of her, Papa, please! She's with the Nazis! They're going to hurt you. Let go of her!"

He stopped, as if I left him breathless with one good sucker punch and looked at me through loathing squinted eyes. "What did you say?"

"I said she's with the Nazis. She's friends with the Nazis. Please let her go, don't hurt her, or they'll make you disappear!"

His hands dropped to his sides, Aunt Lena gasped for air, "Is that the truth, what she said? You're a Nazi?"

She sat up very straight in the chair, looked him square in the eye, "If you ever lay another hand on me, you won't live to see another day. I'll make sure of that."

"Do you mean to tell me you've become an informer?"

"What I do to stay alive is my business. That's no concern of yours."

Papa stood shocked, repulsed, and in disbelief, but she had anger of her own to spew, "What right do you have to judge me? You're nothing but a filthy deserter. When you left Germany for America, you gave up your rights. And making matters worse, you took a good German girl with you. You and your whole brood should be eliminated as far as I'm concerned."

Mama was initially speechless, until a barrage of self-directed insults flowed freely from her quivering lips. A steady stream of tears were running down her face as she cried, "What have I done to my children? What have I done to cause all of this harm? All I wanted to do was see Papa before he died. What kind of a state have I put my children in? What kind of a horrible self-serving mother am I?" She was so desperately sad over what she saw, I thought she was going to break down right then and there.

"Mama, please don't cry; it's not your fault. You didn't know, and I still love you."

The little boy was standing there looking at me with disgust. As he stared at me, a smile came across my face as I began to realize that he was my baby brother Siegfried. I wanted to hug him, but I knew he was afraid, so I simply looked at him, smiled, and said, "Hello Siegfried, it's me, Marlies; you look nice."

The long curly hair he used to have was cut short, and he looked so clean and healthy. I couldn't believe how much he had grown.

They had all changed so much. How thin Mama had become, and how much older she appeared, with long, white locks covering her head where a shiny, black mane used to flow.

Siegfried looked at me, and without saying a word, moved closer to Mama and grabbed onto her dress. She looked at Papa with a sense of urgency, "We have to get out of this house. We have to get out of here right now. I can't tolerate being in this dungeon for one more minute." She turned her attention to me, "Marlies, let's get your things together. We are leaving."

We hurried into the bedroom, "Where are your clothes?"

"They are hanging in the closet."

When Mama went over and opened the clothes closet, she began to cry again.

"These are not clothes. These are filthy rags. Is this what you have been wearing all of this time?"

"Yes, Mama, I tried to wash them; I tried to do the best I could."

"Oh my Lord, leave everything right where it is. These pungent rags should be burned, don't even touch them."

She walked over to the bed, picked up the blanket that was lying there and wrapped it around me. "We're leaving, and we're leaving right now."

"Mama, I have to say good-bye to my cow. She's been my only friend. Please, I have to say good-bye."

"Don't worry about the cow; the cow will be fine. You come with me; we're leaving immediately."

I so badly wanted to say good-bye, "Please, what will happen to her?"

Mama assured me that she'd understand why I left so suddenly, but it was Mama who didn't understand the depth of my relationship and the struggles I shared with that old cow. Walking out on her was the hardest thing I ever had to do. I wanted to look into her big, brown eyes and thank her for all the months of welcoming me into her heart and safely warming my body while I slept next to her in the stall. If I could have wrapped my arms around her just one more time, I could have told her how sorry I was for leaving her alone to fend for herself in what was surely to be a foul feces-infested sty. I knew Aunt Lena wouldn't take care of her any more than she had me, but Mama didn't get it.

Everything was happening with whirlwind speed, and I couldn't take it all in fast enough. As we walked back into the kitchen, Papa spun around, looked at his sister with hatred in his eyes. I didn't know he knew how to hate, but he knew how to hate her. And just as he was going to say something, Uncle Henry walked out of his shop and into the commotion-filled kitchen. Papa turned and looked at him with the same eyes, "Henry, I always knew you were a mouse. You are nothing but a worthless human being to let something like this happen to a little girl, while you sat back and did nothing."

"John, you know I have no say in this house. I have no right to open my mouth about anything."

"I don't care what type of a man—even a crippled man has a right to say something to his wife. You let her do what she has done to my little girl, and never intervened, which makes you a pathetic excuse for a man." He turned back to Lena, "I have nothing to thank you for … except nearly destroying my only daughter; so don't you dare contact me in any way, ever. I no longer have a sister. From this day on, you are dead in my eyes.

He turned, giving Mama the signal that he was through, as he continued to stare into Lena's eyes. Mama took hold of my hand, Papa grabbed Siegfried, and we stormed out of the house, nearly shattering the filth-covered windows as I felt the door slam for the last time. As soon as we reached the street, Mama put her arms around me and hugged me so tight I thought my ribs would crack. She cried so hard, and Papa did too. He hugged me and asked, "Marlies, are you all right? Will you be able to walk to the train station?"

"I can walk to the end of the world, now that you've saved me! You're here! And you're not dead! You know that she told me you were dead."

Mama let go of me and asked, "What do you mean we're dead? Where did she get such an idea?"

"Mama, I have known you were dead for so long. She pointed to the planes overhead and told me they killed you. I never heard from you, and no one ever wrote to me or even answered my letters, so I believed her."

On the way to the train, she told me she had written daily. If there was ever a day when she didn't write, it was because she was prevented from being home by the Nazis. "I was sick to think that you never even sent me a note. Why didn't you write and tell me that this was going on?"

"I did, I have been writing to you since the day that I left. She looked like a witch and I was afraid of her, so I begged you that first day to come and get me. I wrote that I couldn't stay here. I sat down at my desk every night to write while I crushed the lice that fell onto my paper. The pages were always wet from the tears I cried, and I wondered how you'd read my words."

"That's exactly how I saw you in my dream. I saw you sitting exactly at that desk. I saw the sore over your eye; I saw the lice; I saw the tears; and I saw you writing a letter. That's why we came. The dream was so vivid, I had to come and see for myself that you were being taken care of."

"Mama, I knew the guardian angel would send someone. I prayed to the angel every night, and I prayed to God that he wouldn't forget me, and that's why he sent you. I knew somehow that God was listening."

Mama cried several times, and so did I on that long walk to the train station, but I was happy. And for the first time in nearly a year, I knew my family was alive and that someone other than the animals loved me.

Due to my condition, Mama wouldn't permit me to go back to the city, so she told Papa, "You go on ahead and catch the next train to Rüsselsheim, and I'll go to Kell to see my mother and Clara. We'll see what we can do to clean this child up and get her back to health. John, you do understand—I have to go home to the farm."

Papa understood what had to be done and gave me a big hug as he headed for Rüsselsheim, while Mama, Siegfried, and I headed to Kell. No one knew we were coming, so it was going to be quite a surprise, in more ways than one.

Recovering in Kell

While on the train, we kept a blanket wrapped around me. Someone asked why I was wrapped so tightly, and Mama politely replied, "My daughter's ill, and I need to keep her warm." Of course, the train was filled to the brim with people, many of whom stared at me wondering what my fate had been, but everyone had their own problems and issues, so with the help of the blanket, I wasn't such a big deal for long. There were many sickly people, along with a few refugees who were lost and trying to find a place to belong. There was no room on the train for us to sit, so most of the time Mama held Siegfried who was drowsy from his two long walks. He acted as if he didn't want to be anywhere near me, as frightening as I was. He just stared at me.

When we finally arrived in Trier, we were able to catch another train to Kell. Surprisingly, some of Mama's friends were traveling on it too. They were filled with questions, but she said she'd explain another time. She was very deep in sorrow, and they instantly realized it, so no one pushed the issue. Placing their hands on her shoulder, some said simple things like, "This war is terrible; it's terrible for everyone," and they'd turn and walk away.

We arrived at my grandparents' and knocked on the door. Oma came out with a look of disbelief on her face. "Oh my God, Elisabeth, what's happened?" Aunt Mary and her children were also there helping out with Opa's care and the farm work. She often spent the night to relieve Aunt Clara who spent countless hours at his bedside.

The first thing I did when we arrived was go into the courtyard to find Peter. After believing I'd never see him again, my eyes filled with tears of happiness the moment I saw him. Sadly, the feeling wasn't mutual; he didn't recognize me. He looked at me with disdain, appearing as though he might get sick, and wouldn't come anywhere near me. "Are you really my sister?" he demanded.

"Peter, yes. It's me!" I took the blanket off, and they saw how white my hair had become. I'm sure they all realized what louse eggs looked like, but they had never seen anyone so gruesomely infested.

My hair had transformed from a lovely chestnut to pure white, and the horrible sore over my eye made me appear distorted. When Oma and Aunt Mary looked at me, they simultaneously gasped with utter disbelief and shock. They couldn't believe a little girl could be so pitiful. Even with all of the lice I had, Oma didn't hesitate to rush to my side and hug me, while questioning, "Elisabeth, what happened to this child?" Mama filled them in on the few details that she had concluded, and Oma grabbed me by the shoulders and assured me, "We'll take care of this and clean you up, and you'll be the same little girl we had before. All of the bad things are going to be left behind and forgotten."

They removed all my clothes and my shoes and took them outside to burn them; then immediately fixed a tub of warm water, scrubbing me so clean, I thought that they'd scrub the skin right off my body. There wasn't a spot on me that hadn't been scoured with a brush, and I was beet red when I climbed out of the tub. For the first time in months, I didn't itch from head to toe due to the filth.

Aunt Mary sent my cousin Marlies, "Go on home and find some clean dresses, and bring them right back." Marlies and I were about the same size, so I knew her clothes would fit. I was amazed with my cousin; she was one of the few who didn't shy away from me. She came over with tears in her eyes and took my hand, "I'm so sorry; you must have had it badly, but I'll be right back." She took off through the fields faster than I had ever seen her move. When she came back, she brought me her nicest garments and was kind enough to bring me a new coat. Aunt Mary had just made it for her, and she hadn't even worn it to church yet. I felt bad that I had previously accused her of being selfish. I realized it was just her way to be a little cranky, but all was forgotten upon my return from Holtztum. She showed me the kindest gesture I had received in over a year, and I loved her for it.

My cousin Carly whispered, "Do you really have lice?"

"Yes, I do, so don't come anywhere near me, because I don't want any of you to catch it."

Aunt Clara told Mama that in order to get rid of all of the lice, they were going to have to shave my head. I started to shake as I thought, *Oh dear God, what's going to happen to me when I have to go to school? If I don't have any hair, the people in Kell won't want me either! It'll be just like it was in Holtztum. It'll start all over again, and no one will want me.* I started to cry, imagining myself without hair. I imagined Aunt Rose without hair, but she was a nun, and she wore a habit to cover her head. I wouldn't able to do that; what would I use to cover my head?

I couldn't stop crying until Aunt Clara uttered what I needed to hear, "All right, Elisabeth, we can't cut off her hair; we have to find another way. I'm afraid shaving her head might cause a severe breakdown after all she's been through." Wiping the tears away with my sleeve, I started to smile. I loved her too, and was so pleased that she'd find another way.

"Let's go upstairs and talk to Opa. He doesn't sleep much at night since he's been ill, so we won't be waking him. If there's a solution or any kind of answer, he'll be the one to think of it." Step by step, as I made my way to the top, my emotions were torn. I was delighted to see Opa again, but a tad frightened of how the cancer might have deteriorated his body—and very frightened that my appearance would scare him even more than his would me. But the moment our eyes connected, I saw, he too had tears rolling down his cheeks. And all my fears vanished when he spoke. "I have always known there was suffering in the world, but for a young child, you sure have had your share—and that's certainly not fair. I'm on my deathbed, and I should give mercy to all. However, forgiving your aunt for what she's done to you will be difficult at best. Now come over here and give me a hug."

"Opa, you'll catch my lice."

"I've had lice before—in the first world war. I'm not afraid of it, and at my age, they don't want to come near me anyhow. Now just get over here and give me a big hug!"

"Alright Opa." As our cheeks meshed together, I felt safe and comfortable.

He looked deep into my eyes and spoke to my heart, "You're special to me, little one, and I know sometimes you wonder if God has forgotten you. But don't you ever believe that he will. He has done so many kind things for you. He let you keep your arm. And he'll let you make it through this war too. You've had a sad experience, but these are the crosses that God sends us. Don't lose faith in him—he has brought you home to people who care about you, and he has kept your family alive. There are always going to be evil people in the world, but we have to remember to forgive them. Forget what happened and move on. It'll make you a stronger person."

"Opa, I could never forgive her for what she did. I can never ever forgive her."

I could tell that he knew how I felt, but he said, "A time will come that you will be able to. We have to make peace with whatever goes wrong in this world, before we can go into the kingdom of heaven. It's hard for me here on my deathbed to forgive all of those who have sinned against me, too, but I have to find a way. God punishes those who harm others; it's not up to us. Leaving the punishment in our heart ... that only makes us bitter. Forgive and forget and look forward to and remember the *good* things. You are a strong little girl, and I love you with all of my heart. And I will pray for you."

"Opa, I'll pray for you too. I don't ever want God to take you away from us! We need you!" He gave me a smile that melted my heart, and I asked, "Is there something they can do so they don't have to cut my hair off?"

"Of course there is. They're not going to cut your hair off—not while I'm still alive.

"Now Clara, go down into the barn and get the Cuprex. It's what we've been using to keep lice off the cattle and the pigs. Put it on her hair with a toothbrush, cover her head with a towel, and leave it on until it begins burning her scalp. When she complains of the burning, wash her hair, and by that time, it should have done its job without harming her. Afterwards, take a louse comb and remove all of the eggs from her hair. It'll be a big job, but take the time to do it right, and don't worry about me up here."

I ran over and hugged him so tight, I never wanted to let him go. When everything seemed desolate, he had a solution to offer. I thought he was the greatest human being on earth.

Mama, Aunt Mary, Aunt Clara, and Aunt Ida all began working on my hair with toothbrushes. They worked the Cuprex onto every strand of hair and wrapped me in the towel just like Opa said. While we were sitting there waiting, I told them about the past year's events at Aunt Lena's. I felt bad telling the stories to those sad faces—it looked like someone had put a knife through their hearts. They were so sad and so sorry, especially Mama. She sat sobbing, "I simply can't believe that this has gone on for so long."

I was telling them that I was thankful that God was gracious enough to return me home, when all of the sudden my head began to burn. They took me outside to the barn and dunked my head into a gigantic, wine barrel cut in half, a makeshift trough for the cows' water. It was cold, but it didn't matter one bit, as Aunt Clara had washed my hair with lye. When she finished and I stood up, there were undoubtedly a million lice floating on top of the water. It was remarkable how many came from my little head.

With the clothes and shoes from my cousin Marlies, I was starting to feel like a human being again. We all went up to my room, and they sat up all night with louse combs trying to remove the eggs from my hair. For the first time, in a long while, I didn't see any crawling on my pillow or sheets, and I felt as though I was on top of the world.

Before I went to sleep, I knelt down and prayed to God, thanking him for giving me another chance at a decent life. I also prayed for my cow. "She was just a simple-minded animal who didn't know any better, but she was my best friend, my only friend. God, please make sure that if she dies, you'll watch over her in heaven, because she has a right to be there. She gave so much of herself to me. She was kinder than any human being had been; so please take good care of her, and please don't let her suffer before she gets old and dies." I also prayed for Opa, asking that he'd get better. I finally fell asleep, believing that my grandparents' home was heaven and all of the people within were angels. Surely, I had arrived that night on a one-way train, straight from hell.

The next day, as I was looking more human, Peter no longer backed away from me. He finally came over and hugged me. "I'm sorry I couldn't do it before, but I couldn't stand to see what had happened to you. If I was bigger, I'd go and beat Aunt Lena for what she did to you."

"Oh, Peter, you could never hurt anyone, but I appreciate your concern." My little brother, Siegfried, also came and sat by me. "Marlies, do you still have lice?"

"Nope, not anymore, Siegfried."

Everyone was gentle and kind and understanding, but what made me feel really good was to see my Mama's smiling face. That's what was worth so much, to see her smiling at me as I started to look human again. I had a bandage over my eye, a nice clean dress, clean socks, and clean shoes. I became so happy that I was smiling too. I ran around feeling like I had just been born, and after an entire week of grooming my hair, they removed each and every one of the eggs. My hair looked vibrant, clean, and shiny again—just as it had the day I'd arrived in Holtztum.

Oma told me that she had also written me many times, and that she had put her address on the envelope so that there wouldn't be any confusion, and I'd know exactly where to send my letters. It dawned on me that Aunt Lena was taking my letters and destroying them because she knew how I felt about her. She knew I didn't like her, and that's why she treated me the way she did. I was like the plague to her; only there for one reason: so she could butcher and keep one of her pigs. Uncle Henry, realizing she didn't care about him either, spent so much time alone in his shop and eventually lost interest in life completely.

11
Changes at Kell

After a week passed, Mama said she had to return to Papa. "I can't leave John alone any longer. I have to get back, but Marlies, you stay here until the start of the new, school year. Since it's only March, you'll finish out the year with Peter. In the fall when school starts again, you'll come back to Rüsselsheim."

That was fine with me—to be able to stay on the farm—but I would miss Mama very much, so I begged her. "Mama, please don't let anything happen to you and Papa and Siegfried. Don't let the bombs get you."

Little did Mama know, as she boarded the train, that in less than one month's time, she would be back in Kell for her father's funeral. On April 2, 1943, in the middle of the night, Oma was awakened by a rustling in the barn. She woke Aunt Clara, and together they went outside to determine what caused the cows to be so restless. Their bellowing was cause for alarm, but after thoroughly checking the area, they found no reason for the disturbance. "Mama, I don't see anything, and I think they're calming down, so let's go back to bed."

Upon returning into the house, she went upstairs to make sure the clamor hadn't disturbed Opa, only to find that my beautiful, warm, loving, and gentle, grandfather had died. No one knew the exact moment that he'd passed on, but somehow, the animals knew, and they'd found a way to let the rest of us know too. Without their bellowing, Opa would have lain there alone until the crack of dawn when Oma went to check on him before beginning her chores. They decided to wake all of us and break the news. I felt as though I had lost one of the truest friends I ever knew. I loved him infinitely, and he suffered for so long before dying. Mama and my uncles were all notified by telegram, but none of his boys were permitted to come home while they fought Hitler's ridiculous war around the world. Not even one of them was allowed to return to Kell.

Likewise, Aunt Rose was notified at the convent, but Mother Superior told Aunt Clara over the telephone that there was no way Aunt Rose could come home. She had already had her vacation, and they would not grant her the time to come home again. If she tried to return, it meant breaking their rules. Aunt Clara inquired with furor, "Are you people so heartless that you wouldn't let a daughter come home for the funeral of her father, a father who loved his daughter immensely. How could you be so cruel?"

"These are our rules, and the rules that all the nuns must live by."

Aunt Rose cried on the telephone as she confirmed what Mother Superior had said to her sister, "I cannot go against her orders. I have given my word for complete obedience. This is the life I have chosen, and this is what I have to do. I will pray for Father, but I will not be able to come home for the funeral."

Opa was placed in a casket and laid out in the living room for viewing, as was the custom. A steady stream of people came to pay their respects. People came not only from Kell, but from all of the surrounding areas. They wanted to say one final good-bye to a great man, to an unsung hero, a man who cared for others so generously. There was no one who didn't love Opa, and he was greatly missed.

They were such a close and loving couple that it seemed as though part of Oma had died with her husband. It didn't show in her work, or the things she did, but the grief in her was deep, and things were never the same.

Part of me went with him too. I couldn't sleep the next night, so I went downstairs and knelt by his casket. With two candles burning and many flowers surrounding, I began to speak with him. I wasn't afraid because he was dead, or because his body was in our living room, I just needed to talk to him. "Opa, I love you so very much, and words can't describe how much I am going to miss you."

With the creaking of the stairs, suddenly, I turned and saw Oma standing behind me.

"You shouldn't be down here all alone, you are just a little girl and you should be in bed."

"Oma, I had to spend some time alone with Opa. I love him so much."

"I know you do, and you can always love him. But he's moved on to live with God, and I am sure there's a wonderful place for him there." She helped me up the stairs and back into bed, and I prayed for him again, making it seem as though I was more at peace.

Opa was laid out for three nights. On the second night, I woke as I heard a noise. I was in the front bedroom near the hallway, and people had to walk through my room to get to the other bedrooms down the hall. As I heard the noise, I reached up and turned on my light and saw Uncle Johann. He had gotten up to go to the bathroom, and on his way, stepped into an applesauce kuchen.

During our mourning, many folks brought food, for the family and guests to eat. At the time, the kuchen were lined up along the wall in my bedroom and covered with a clean, white sheet. Seeing Uncle Johann standing with applesauce squishing out between his toes was the funniest sight I had seen in a long while. He accidentally kicked the sheet back, tripped, and landed right in the middle of the kuchen. He continued repeating, "What did I do, what did I do, what did I do?"

His voice became increasingly louder, until eventually waking everyone in the house. One by one, they came in and had a big laugh. Aunt Clara helped him clean his foot, and they threw the kuchen into the pigs' slop. It was good to see everyone laugh, even for a brief moment, during our time of mourning.

Vazil, the Russian Uncle

When all was said and done, and Opa was laid to rest, we needed to forge forward on the farm. The work wouldn't wait for any occasion, death or otherwise. In order to complete the workload, French prisoners of war had been sent to the farm to help out, but the majority of them proved to be useless. They refused to work, and even though they were being fed, they were worthless to Oma. One by one, she took each of them back and asked to be given someone that would actually earn his keep. They finally brought forth a young Russian prisoner. He couldn't have been more than eighteen years old, but he had features of an old man. His hair was long, and much of his face was covered with a long beard. He wore a heavy, fur coat made of bearskin that was secured around his waist with a rope. His shoes consisted of rags wrapped around his feet and covered with bearskin hide.

They asked Oma if she'd like to give him a chance. She looked deep into his eyes and liked him from the first moment she saw him. "He has kind eyes, and I like the way he looks. I'll take him home with me." When he first approached the farm, he was less than desirable to me, resembling a wild, mountain man. He was tall, yet possessed gentle, intelligent eyes, so Oma tried communicating with him the best she could. Although he clearly did not speak German. She showed him to Uncle Matthew's bedroom, "This will be your room; the place where you'll sleep." He stood motionless, never making a sound.

She took him into the kitchen, showed him the sink, and gave him a bar of soap to wash with and a razor so he could shave. Although he didn't speak our language, he was familiar with the items. She demonstrated with hand gestures, using Uncle Johann as an example of what she wanted him to do. But again, he watched in silence.

He was in desperate need of decent clothing, so she brought him a clean shirt, pants, socks, boots, and a jacket from Uncle Matthew's room and placed them on a chair in the big living room. When it was time to sit down for dinner, Aunt Clara indicated where he should sit and to take his heavy coat off. With his head hung low, he slowly drew his eyes up to meet hers as he held the coat close to himself never setting it down. As we began our meal I wondered what the young Russian would be like? Would he fit in with our family? Would he work hard? Did he have a family of his own? What was his name? All questions that were answered in time.

It was about three days later when he finally walked over to the chair and picked up the boots, the shirt, and the pants and entered the chimney room. He came out with a pail and headed to the sink. It looked as if he was going to pump water to take a bath. Oma gave him a big kettle of hot water to pour into the pail, and as he took it, a gracious smile emerged on his face. They brought bucket after bucket to help him make bath water. He went into the room and shut the door, and when he came out, he was refreshingly clean and dressed in Uncle Matthew's ensemble.

He took the fur wrappings from his feet, placed them in the coat, and rolled it into a bundle, which he placed in the shed. He returned to the house where we sat waiting for his return before beginning our meal. As Oma began to pray, he sat and listened, still not uttering a word. With my head bowed, I glanced up to sneak a peak at our new quest, and noticed his left hand appeared crippled. His knuckles and fingernails were injured quite badly, but while I was gawking, he caught me. As a matter of fact, there was little he didn't pay attention to. He was observant, spending a great deal of time watching everything around him. His name was Vazil, and for some reason, I took a liking to him.

When he finished his meal, he stood up, nodded to Oma, walked into the hallway, and looked at Aunt Clara. She communicated to him which chores he should do next, and he seemed quite efficient. He did what he was told, and he did it quickly, perfectly, and neatly. Aunt Clara was pleased with him, and almost instantly, Vazil became family. We all took a liking to him even though he was subdued and kept to himself. Aunt Clara reminded us, "I bet he understands a lot more than we think. Being in a German prison camp, he's picked up a lot more German than we think. He's probably just feeling us out, the same way we are him." She was right. It wasn't long before he began answering us in German and became a big help on the farm. After a short while, it seemed as though he had always been there.

Vazil showed an enormous amount of respect, gentleness, and love for Oma. He made believe she was his mother, and with all of her sons strewn throughout the world, she was happy to take on that role. He constantly tried to please her. One morning she placed a piece of liver on a plate to cool, and a neighbor's cat bolted across the street, crept into our kitchen, and stole it. Oma chased the cat into the courtyard, extremely upset, but he managed to stay just far enough ahead of her. Vazil saw how agitated she was and tried to comfort her, "Don't worry Mother, Vazil take care."

"Oh Vazil, take care of what? The piece of liver is gone, and we have so little food to begin with."

He tapped her on her shoulder and smiled, "Vazil take care."

The following Sunday, we were getting ready to go to church, and Vazil was standing in the courtyard making noises to attract the cat. I told him, "Vazil, you'll never trick that cat; she's wild and nasty." He continued making the noises, and before long, I saw the cat come out and slowly move toward him. He reached out to touch the cat and with lightening quickness, grabbed it by the tail, wrapped it around a pole, and killed it. He threw the cat on top of the manure pile and looked at Oma with a smile on his face, "You see, Vazil take care."

Oma stood in shock, "Vazil, how could you do that? How could you kill that cat?"

"That cat no longer steal from Mother."

Oma was worried as she looked away and quietly mumbled, "Oh dear Lord, he killed that cat. Is that his way of dealing with things that causes harm?" She turned back to Vazil, "Thank you, you are right, that cat will no longer steal from anyone."

She went to church and prayed for him, "Lord, please don't let him have a cruel heart. He's always been kind to the animals, but his way of rectifying a wrong scares me. That is what he truly believed he should do."

I was shocked too, and didn't know what to say. I never liked the cat—it was nasty—however, I wouldn't have wished it dead. But Vazil didn't give us an option. What he did wasn't right, but that's the way he was, loyal, dependable, and trustworthy. Some would argue to a fault.

The following Sunday, we sat in the living room crocheting and knitting. We were all busy and focused on the task at hand, when Vazil came in from the barn with a pair of scissors and a comb. "Clara, cut Vazil hair, and take hair off face." Aunt Clara was surprised, but was happy to oblige.

When she was finished, he was absolutely debonair. I was proud of him, "You look great Vazil, just like my uncles! I'm happy to see all that hair gone. You look young, like you should."

He rubbed my head and gave me a hug and said proudly, "Vazil look like German."

Aunt Clara said, "Yes, Vazil, now you look like a Hans, a real member of this family."

He stood tall, "Vazil member of family." He pointed to Oma and continued, "That my mother."

Oma got up and hugged him, "I couldn't love my own sons more than I do you, and it has been an honor to have you on this farm. You're a hard worker and a trusting person, and I wish you could stay here with us forever."

His smile faded, "Vazil never go back to Russia. Vazil stay in Germany."

Out of nowhere, Aunt Clara asked him the question we had all been wondering, "Vazil, why don't you pray with us?"

"Vazil, nix pray."

"Why?"

"When I became soldier, I made promise to Stalin that he is my only God. Vazil never break promise."

"But Vazil, if you don't pray, you will never get into heaven."

"Vazil nix go to heaven, Vazil stay in Germany." We all laughed, but still, he never prayed and that worried us.

Aunt Mary often received letters from Uncle Karl, and occasionally he sent cigarettes along. Since no one smoked, she gave them to Vazil. Usually at the supper table as we prayed, he sat quietly with his head down and a cigarette in his hand. When we finished, he put the cigarette out, and we ate our meal. He never left the table when we said our thank you afterwards; he simply sat quietly until Oma finished the prayer, and then he'd walk out. While cleaning up one night, Oma mentioned that he may not be praying, but he certainly is listening.

Having Vazil on the farm was like having *two* men. Uncle Johann respected him and they liked working together. He was a true member of our family and never considered a prisoner in our home. Although having him on the farm was a major relief, missing Opa never became easier.

Testing Oma and Learning a Lesson

Even with Vazil on the farm, there were jobs he wasn't expected to do, like knitting. That was left for us women to manage, and knitting became the source of the one and only occasion in my life when I became angry with Oma. It was summer, prior to school starting, and I knew that I had become quite proficient at knitting, so I asked Oma if I could begin a pair of socks.

She started the stitches for me, and I was knitting with four needles—which had become second nature. When I had a quarter of the length finished, I dropped a stitch, and rather than going back, I simply added another. Every so often Oma picked up my work and checked it to make sure I was doing things right, but she never critiqued out loud. She simply asked, "How do you feel about your work?"

"Oma, I'm very proud, I'm doing a good job, but when it comes time to make the heel, you are going to have to help me."

"I will."

Finally, after a long struggle, I finished my sock. I was so proud. I wanted to holler to the whole town that I had actually created my very own sock!

Oma took it for observation, "Yes, you've finished; now let me check it." She pointed out the dropped stitch near the beginning.

"Oh yes, but I added another one and that will never show so that doesn't matter. After all, it's my first sock, and everyone is expected to make mistakes."

Sternly, she disagreed, "Not in my house."

She proceeded to open the sock and unravel it all the way down to the beginning, as I stood in front of her completely appalled. "Why did you do that, Oma? Why did you unravel my whole sock?"

"You made a mistake, and if you had taken care of that mistake in the beginning, you wouldn't have wasted all this time. I don't want my children making mistakes and continuing from there. You have to rectify your mistakes immediately. Now you'll start all over, remembering this moment all of your life: do it right the first time, and you will waste little time doing things repeatedly."

Even Vazil looked at her. I could tell he felt sorry for me, so when she finished her sermon, I used his pity to look her in the eyes and say, "You know, Oma, I used to love you, but I don't even like you anymore. Because of what you did, I'm never going to make another sock again."

She responded, "That's entirely up to you. However, as you go through school, you'll be expected to make them and, Marlies, you won't make anything else as long as you live here with me, unless it's another sock. Until you're ready to do that, there will be no knitting. You can put the knitting needles and the yarn aside, and you'll have nothing to do in the evenings."

I was so angry with her that I went to my room and cried. I felt sorry for myself, and that continued for a good two weeks. Thankfully, my anger started to subside, and I thought to myself, *I'm going to make a pair of socks. I'm not going to make one mistake, and I am going to show her.*

In the evening, lights had to be out, and there were no longer any radios, since they'd been confiscated. The only news received was through town meetings, or if someone else heard something and relayed the message back. Most of the news had stopped altogether, because Hitler didn't want people knowing how seriously the towns were being destroyed, how many people were being killed, how many were disappearing, and how hard it was for the soldiers to keep fighting without food, ammunition, or warm clothing. He didn't want people knowing exactly what was occurring. So, through prohibiting radios, he was able to keep us in the dark. Without having alternatives, knitting and crocheting became the only things to do.

I didn't have anything else to make, so I got on my knees and asked Oma if she would start another sock for me. She rubbed my head saying, "I knew it wouldn't take long for you to come around. All of the things I do aren't to be nasty or mean; they're all done to teach you something. So yes, you and I are going to start again. And this time, you'll make a perfect pair of socks, something we'll all be proud of—especially you. I promise you'll be prouder of something done right, than of something done haphazardly."

I proceeded to make my socks with Oma's help, and when I finally finished, she was right. I was as proud as a peacock, knowing there wasn't one single mistake. All of a sudden, all of the love I had for Oma was right back, blossoming like it had before. I couldn't even remember what it felt like to be mad at her, but I knew that it had filled me with sadness.

Killing the Fatted Pig

A wonderful surprise occurred the summer of 1943. Uncle Matthew was unexpectedly permitted to come home for vacation. He had recently earned his second Iron Cross for bravery, and it was his first time coming home since the war began. It was a big surprise to Oma, but as happy as she was to have her son return, she worried that there may not be enough food. Not only did she have Peter and me to feed, but now Uncle Matthew as well. She talked it over with Aunt Clara.

"We need food for Matthew. He's going to be home for two weeks, and I don't want anyone going hungry." They knew what needed to be done. It was time to butcher the pig hidden in the attic

Uncle Matthew's return rejuvenated our family, but Vazil looked frightened as he walked into the house wearing a German uniform. Since Vazil was a Russian prisoner, they were supposed to be enemies, but it didn't take them long to become good friends. Vazil and my uncle were a lot alike and thankfully, Uncle Matthew only considered you an enemy if you were shooting at him.

The day after his arrival, he and Vazil went into the attic to butcher the pig. While they were upstairs, one of my uncle's old classmates, a high-ranking SS Officer came by to say hello. They had been friends for many years and he wanted to congratulate him for being awarded the Iron Cross. As he came up to the house, he didn't see anyone in the courtyard, so he asked Uncle Johann where everyone was. Without realizing what he was saying, Uncle Johann answered, "Oh, they're all up in the attic butchering the pig." That was the worst thing he could have said, because Oma had already butchered her pig, and the others had been sent to the government. New litters were being born, so how could they possibly be butchering?

The officer commented, "Well that seems very interesting. Now let me have a look."

He came to the top of the stairs in the attic and I turned around and noticed him. "Uncle Matthew, look!" He turned and saw him standing there looking very pompous with his hands on his hips, "Well isn't this a beautiful sight. What a surprise. Today must be my day, as I came to congratulate you on your medal of honor, and instead I find that I'm going to have to begin writing up arrest warrants."

I thought Oma was going to collapse as she stood gasping for air, and my aunts were each turning pale as fear overtook them. Uncle Matthew, with a huge butcher knife in his hand walked up to the officer and asked, "How are you today?"

He replied, "Like I said, this is a big day for me." Uncle Matthew walked closer, put the knife to the Nazi's throat and warned, "I'm going to tell you one time and one time only: if word of this gets out of these four walls, I promise you that I will walk all the way back from Russia, and I'll cut you from here down. This is a promise."

It wasn't mere talk, and knowing Uncle Matthew from the time they were children, he knew my uncle was a man of his word who always followed through. The yellow-bellied officer wouldn't have known the first thing about bravery, and I could see he was visibly frightened. He knew Uncle Matthew meant every word he said, as he reiterated. "If my mother finds trouble or has any problems because of what you've seen here today, I promise you this. Somehow, I'll return to hunt you down. You know me well enough to know I never go back on a promise."

The Nazi gazed around the room at each of us with fear in his eyes and answered, "Matthew, I came to congratulate you on your medal and on what a fine job you are doing. So congratulations. I wish your family health, and I'll be seeing you." He turned around and retreated down the stairs, and not one member of my family ever heard another word about butchering the pig—which surely could have meant imprisonment or worse.

When Uncle Matthew stood up to him the way he did, he was an authentic hero in my eyes. With a commanding air about him, he feared nothing and no one, and certainly never sought anyone's favor. He was an honest man and a German soldier, but he was not a Nazi. He never joined their party, nor did any of my uncles. They were merely soldiers, drafted and fighting, whether or not they agreed with why we were at war. To label all German soldiers as Nazis was wrong, because many of them were only doing what they were ordered to do: fighting for their country and their families. I had always placed him on a pedestal, but now he was even more important in my eyes. He didn't show fear, and because of that, we were able to pull it off, which meant another year without having to worry about starving.

At night as we knitted, Uncle Matthew delighted us with his stories, especially the one of how he earned his medal. We sat fascinated, hanging on every word, as he told how he and twenty-six men had been surrounded by the Russian army. They were in a ravine, and the Russians swarmed above with their vehicles. All combined, the German soldiers only had a few bullets left, while the Russians, celebrating with vodka, were waiting to go in for the kill.

Uncle Matthew was in command and decided they'd wait until the Russians were drunk. "They're going to have to sleep it off, and we'll rush them during the night. If daylight comes, they'll butcher us, as they've done with all the German soldiers they've captured. So we have to move swiftly."

They heard stories of how German soldiers were tied to two separated trees. The tops of the trees were bent to the ground with ropes forming a taut arch. One leg was tied to one tree and the other leg to the other tree. As they released the trees to spring back to their upright position, the soldiers were literally ripped in half, with body parts hanging from the ropes attached to each tree. Others were skinned alive, many were left with their toe and fingernails pulled off, their tongues cut out, nails pounded into their faces, and swastikas burned into their foreheads and chests. "My men had no part of that. After taking prisoners into custody, we took them away to prison camps, but never tortured the enemy."

They'd seen atrocities many times, and that's what they were facing if daylight broke. They didn't want to die, especially not that way. When nighttime fell, they climbed up out of the ravine to where the enemy soldiers had passed out. They rushed them with their bayonets, killing many of them while seizing their weapons, before holding the others at bay. They disabled all of the vehicles, except for the one they needed for escape, and out of the twenty-six men in the ravine, nineteen made it out alive and back to safety.

Because of his bravery and saving those nineteen lives, he was awarded the Iron Cross and allowed to come home. I had heard of German soldiers being considered "Nazi animals," but they weren't the Nazi army, they were merely the German Army. Nazis were a different breed who indeed destroyed human beings.

The two weeks of his furlough passed quickly, and as Uncle Matthew prepared to return to Russia, he shook Vazil's hand and addressed him as brother. "I hope to see you again someday when I return." It seemed as though part of the family disintegrated, and our security diminished. We all felt the loss, but Oma feared she'd never see her son again, or any of her sons, as she wondered what their fate would be.

What held Oma together were the letters that were delivered that gave her a general idea. One stated that Uncle Peter had been wounded and almost lost his life. He tried to help a fellow soldier, and a grenade exploded, causing shrapnel to penetrate his face. He was blinded and his hearing was lost, but while recuperating in an

English hospital, a young nurse had written Oma explaining that hopefully his eyesight and hearing would return.

Uncle Joseph had been lucky. He was also deployed in Russia, but all reports had indicated that everything was going well with him, with the exception of the cold and hunger he endured. My uncles tried to write letters that didn't frighten Oma, which meant they didn't always tell the truth. They didn't want their mother to suffer any more than she already was, and apparently others didn't want her to know the whole truth of what was going on either because we could tell their letters were censored by scribbled-out sentences they had originally written.

Thankfully, the war didn't touch Kell as much as it did the cities, and in my mind, it remained a magnificent and safe haven. Even though the time I spent there was always too short, it was also beauteous, inspiring, and living there always contributed to making us better people.

One thing I couldn't help but notice was the high number of refugees and beggars that were coming through our village. Oma always tried to oblige them whenever possible, and many times people asked for shelter in our barns, and she'd never turn them away. Providing shelter was an easy request, opposed to those who begged for food, but she always gave her most to those who had the least.

One afternoon, Peter and I were in the barn pitching hay when we noticed something way up in the rafters that looked like a wild animal. After close examination, we realized it was not an animal; it was Vazil's coat. He had rolled it up and stuffed it way up in the rafters.

I always wondered why he seemed to be so mysterious. The curiosity was eating at me. When we were out in the field, I finally got up the courage to ask him what happened to his hand. I'd asked him many times before, but he always avoided the question saying, "One day, I tell you."

I figured it was as good a time as any, and for some reason he must have agreed. On that particular day, he'd praised me for all of my hard work, and as we sat under a tree eating our sandwiches, he began to explain. He was eleven years old when he and his two brothers tried to find food. His father was fighting in World War I, his mother was alone, food in Russia was very scarce, and they were near the point of starving.

Vazil and his brothers went to a farm and were in the process of stealing anything they could find, before someone saw them and called for the police. Unfortunately for the brothers, someone did see them and two officers chased them on foot. Vazil's brothers were younger, only five and seven years old, so Vazil told them to run in the other direction, so they'd be hidden. Vazil stayed in the open to divert the officers' attention, and when he finally made a run for it, it was too late. They easily grabbed him.

He was taken into police headquarters and interrogated to find out who was with him. He refused to give up his brothers, so the police took his hand and placed it in the doorway. They repeatedly slammed the door trying to get him to break down. The result was a severely crippled hand, but he proudly said, "Vazil nix talk. I nix talk; I tell them I go alone. They slam door on hand so hard, I believe it going to break off." The pain was great, but they couldn't make Vazil talk.

After a good beating, they wanted to throw him in prison, but only being eleven years old, they brought Vazil home and told his mother what occurred, leaving her to tend to his mangled hand. I sensed he was still bothered by the incident, as he had difficulties talking about it, but it showed me what a kind and good man he was not to implicate his brothers in what they had done to survive. I loved Vazil and related to how he felt, knowing there wasn't anything I wouldn't have done to protect my brothers either.

Our time spent on the farm was filled with life's lessons. The people kindly taught us to do what was right as we worked hard in the fields and at home. We helped Oma to keep everything clean and beautiful. We were taught to be kind to others, no matter who they are—for instance, Vazil. He was an enemy, and my uncles were fighting the Russians, however, he was only a young man drafted into the service to protect his country, the same way my uncles were, and my father was in WWI.

He'd never break a promise to anyone, he was trustworthy, and he taught me not to judge people based on where they came from or what they had. Rather I learned to judge based on their character, their work ethic, and the goodness that was within.

Mixed Blessings, Going Home

Although the lessons we learned were invaluable, it was time to head back to Rüsselsheim. Peter and I needed to be instructed on our first Holy Communion, return to our parents, and begin school. I was sad to leave Oma and the farm, but I didn't want my parents to be alone any longer either.

The war and the bombings continued to intensify. The English were bombing during the night, sometimes two and three times a week, and the Americans were bombing during the day, also two or three times a week. Returning to Rüsselsheim also meant returning to the taunting, standing in lines for hours to receive food, and again worrying about saying or doing something wrong in front of the Nazis. It seemed as though there was a constant cloud of gloom hanging over our heads, and to top it off, we always went to bed hungry.

Receiving instructions for Holy Communion meant that we would have to go into the city on Saturdays, as well as weekdays for school and Sundays for mass. Seven days a week, we walked into the city. There would be no reprieve, and Mama was looking frail, thinner by the day, and she very seldom looked happy anymore.

12
With Friends Like These,
Who Needs Enemies?

Nazis vs Women and Children

While I had been away in Holtztum, my family made friends with a lovely, Catholic woman, with whom they walked to church on Sundays. Her son had been forced into the Hitler Youth Group, and during a meeting before Christmas, all of the children were given a Christmas present. The present was a picture of Adolf Hitler.

They were told to go home and hang the picture in a special place. When he had returned home from youth group, his mother was visiting her parents, so he decided to hang the picture himself. The best place he saw was above the fireplace where a crucifix hung, so down it came, and in its place hung the fuehrer. When she returned home, he was excited, "Look Mother, look what I did!"

She was infuriated. She took the picture down, threw it on the floor, and put her crucifix back up saying, "That man will never replace God in our home."

The following Monday, he returned to youth group and the Nazis asked the children how their mothers responded to the pictures. The little boy, without knowing any better, told them how his mother reacted. He was told that she acted that way because she didn't understand how important Hitler was to the German people, and they would in turn instruct her on the importance, but they needed to know how to locate her. He told them she'd be at her parents' house, and he gave them the address. The Gestapo went to pick her up, claiming they had questions to ask, and she was to accompany them without hesitation. She asked her father to go to her house in case she didn't return in time to pick her son up. She left with the Gestapo, but mysteriously never returned.

Her father went to headquarters and inquired of his daughter's whereabouts, only to hear that they had sent her home and had no idea where she would have gone. Not believing their story, he—and everyone else, including my parents—was extremely concerned. Rumors spreading wildly as to her demise, but no one ever determined where she went. Within two short months, her own ailing mother died of fear and a broken heart, leaving her father to raise his grandson, alone.

Children were inadvertently turning their parents into the Gestapo without realizing the consequences of their words, and people were disappearing as a result. Mama was overcome with fear, "Never say anything derogatory against Hitler or the Nazis, ever." There were two clearly different factions: the good German people and the Nazis.

In the fall, food had become so scarce, that we'd wait in line at the bakery for hours starting at six o'clock in the morning. Often, they'd close while we were still in line. Not only were we left with no bread, but we would lose our rations for the day as well. Sometimes, we'd go two or three weeks living on one loaf of bread, which clearly, was not enough to sustain five hungry people. Food in the grocery store was measured down to the gram, and you wouldn't receive one gram more than you had rations for. I can't remember how many times I walked by the bakery with my mouth watering, wondering what rolls tasted like, but never having the opportunity to find out.

If we had the good fortune to go to the orchards early in the morning, we might be able to find some fruit lying on the ground, but instead, we usually had to stand in line at the bakery or be on our way to school. We couldn't find time to get to the orchards until after school, and by that time, they had been completely picked over.

One night, Peter and I made an agreement that we'd go out after a windstorm. It was past nine o'clock and more than a mile to get to the orchard. There was a path that led into the woods, but as a result of the bombings, there were obstructions and bomb holes we had to watch out for while trudging through the difficult terrain. Luckily, the trees were lit with moonlight, so we headed down the path. When we arrived, we found very little fruit on the ground. We agreed that picking the fruit from the branches was stealing, however, if Peter climbed a tree and the fruit should happen to fall, that would be a different situation, and we didn't consider that stealing.

As Peter climbed higher and higher, the branches started shaking and the apples began falling to the ground. I gathered them as quickly as I could, and our sack in the wagon was looking quite healthy, when Peter spotted a tall man dressed in black coming down the path. He whispered, "Marlies, there's someone coming, quick, we have to get out of here before we're caught."

He jumped out of the tree, and I was worried that he was hurt, but he landed right. "Come on run, hurry, let's run!" He grabbed the front of the wagon, and I grabbed the back, and we ran with all of our might in the opposite direction through the fields without getting back on the road. We thought maybe the lady upstairs saw us leave and called the Gestapo to look for us. As a hundred thoughts raced through our minds, our bodies began to shake. Going out at night in search of food was not permitted. If we'd gotten caught, our parents would have gone to prison … or worse.

Suddenly Peter hollered, "Marlies, look out!" My foot slipped into a bomb hole, and I was hanging on for dear life to the back of the wagon. Luckily, he was still hanging onto the front and pulling. The holes were big enough for a house to fall into, and once created, they filled up with water and mixed with dirt, forming a quicksand type of substance.

I believed myself, the wagon, and all the apples were going into that hole and never coming out as my feet slipped off the muddy walls, preventing me from gaining a foothold. There was no one to help us, but Peter held onto that wagon and with all his might, he pulled me up and away from the hole. We didn't stop for one second, but from that moment on, I ran with my head up looking to see where we were headed. Every now and then, we had to pick the wagon up and pull it over rocks and fallen trees, but we finally made it home. How we managed to get there and who the mysterious man was, I have no idea, but fear and adrenaline kept us going. We became stronger than we ever imagined we could be, knowing I could have drowned in the thick murky water if Peter hadn't been there to pull me to safety.

Once we were safely home, we leaned against the rabbit pen, and all of a sudden, I couldn't breathe. Peter had the same reaction, telling me, "Put your hands over your mouth, and breathe slowly." I began vomiting from fear before finally catching my breath. We sat there and shook violently, tears running down our faces, unable to control our emotions. It was the most frightening thing we had been through, knowing our parents could have suffered as a result of our actions. If it was our fate that a bomb should kill us all, at least it would be of no consequences of our own. However, this was different; we'd put the events into motion, and the results would be directly tied, and we knew it.

It seemed like it took forever to be able to breathe right and stop shaking, but we didn't want to go into the house and frighten Mama and Papa. We could never let them know the details—especially that Peter had been up in the tree. We wanted to forget what had happened, but as we strolled in acting nonchalant, we could see their concern. It was after eleven. They looked frightened, but we tried to cover by telling Papa that he should come outside and see all of the fruit we'd gathered. He was amazed, "Elisabeth, they have almost an entire burlap bag full of apples. This should last quite a while. You can make applesauce, and the children will have something to eat. It's amazing."

Mama began taking apples out of the sack. "This looks like awfully good fruit, are you sure that you didn't pick it from the tree?" We shook our heads back and forth and told her that not one apple had been picked, and that was the honest truth. She didn't buy in that easily, "Why would these apples fall from the tree? They don't look very ripe." That time, I bent the truth a bit, "Well, remember, Mama, we had a big windstorm … and the trees got shook up pretty bad. The fruit wouldn't have fallen if it wasn't ripe enough."

"Well, what on earth took you so long then?"

Peter piped up, "There were so many trees! And going from one to the next took quite a while, and then we tried not to rush coming home."

We got away with our story that time, and Papa was so pleased. He went into the bedroom and came out with a piece of licorice for each of us. Where he had gotten it, I had no idea, unless it was sent from one of our uncles. He'd been saving it for a special occasion. I'm sure Siegfried would have liked one too, but Papa had saved it especially for us, and we weren't complaining about the sweet chewy surprise. While we sat eating our licorice, he told us that we had done a fine job, and he was proud of us.

We thought we had gotten away with our little white lie, but not long afterwards, he took me aside, "You want to tell me the truth about the fruit? Did you pick any of those apples from the tree?"

"No Papa, we didn't pick a single apple, and I promise that's the truth."

"Well you got the apples somehow, and I don't know how, but I doubt that the wind blew that many unripe apples to the ground. But I'll believe you since you've never lied to me before. As long as you say you didn't pick them, then I'll go along with that. But tell me, what took you so long?"

"Oh, no, it's just like Peter said. It took awhile to pick up all those apples." I don't think he ever believed those words, but the apples were such a blessing to our family that he desperately wanted to believe. We had fruit and applesauce, and Papa took an apple to work each morning. For the time being, we had food in our stomachs, which made it all worthwhile.

Even though we had a little nourishment, it wasn't always easy to keep it in our stomachs, as the bombs continued to drop. One night as the alarm began to wail, fear shot through me, and I ran to the bathroom. If I was quick enough to be the first one to reach the toilet, I'd be spared from vomiting or defecating in the pot that was hidden beneath our beds. We each had one, and with only one bathroom, they were a necessity—keeping an otherwise messy cleanup to a minimum.

Knowing I had little time, I was leaving the bathroom, trying to pull my pants up and head for the basement, when a horrible rumbling came about. It seemed as if an airplane was tumbling toward the ground. The sound grew stronger, seemingly piercing the air directly over our house. It was so powerful, I was thrown against the bathroom door with my pants pulled just above my knees, yet the full alarm had never gone off. As the sound traveled further away, an explosion like no other pierced my eardrums. We never found out what type of bomb it was, but thankfully it was the only one that night. When it made contact, it blew away more than a hundred homes, as if they had never existed.

Many lives were lost. The full alarm sounded too late. The following day, as we went into the city, wagons were being filled with the dead. With no time to conduct proper burial ceremonies, they were taken away and dumped into mass graves. Even if time allowed, there were no sites available to put them in. There were as many as twenty-five people piled high per grave—and not many left to mourn them.

When the bomb exploded, nearly everyone within its vicinity died. Those fortunate enough to survive walked around wrapped in red-stained bandages, with blood gushing from their extremities. There were people leaning against buildings for support who had lost limbs. Nearly everyone I looked at was bleeding from one orifice or another, their suffering immeasurable. Some of the dead were covered with sheets, but others hadn't been, leaving horrible images that would always haunt me. I wondered if I'd ever again experience precious moments of carefree living, as I once had on West Avenue in Naples, New York. Those moments had become nothing more than distant memories, as our mind-bending journey through hell continued. Papa dismantled a cupboard in the basement in an effort to block cold air from entering our apartment. There was no use even trying to replace the glass that had many times before been blown out.

The Allies vs Children

Just as we were recuperating the best we knew how, the Allies struck again, this time perpetrating yet another horrific element. Fountain pens and dolls were found lying on the ground, and true to form, deprived children ran for them as they would in an Easter egg hunt, seeking a prize. Excited, children picked up the dolls, and as they said "Mama," they'd explode. Many children were maimed or killed as a result of this despicable act of war.

Afterwards, there were town meetings that warned parents and children not to touch any items strewn about the lay of the land, as they were most likely explosives. Somebody was supposed to go through the region in search of them, but just in case something was overlooked, parents were warned to check all areas where their children played. One of the little girls living three blocks away was not so fortunate; her eyes wide with excitement as she happened across a petite, baby doll lying on the ground. Her joy would last but for a brief moment, as the doll exploded in her arms, blowing off one hand and severely mutilating her young face as blistering burns melted her tender flesh. Her pain and suffering ended three weeks later, as her life was snuffed out during a subsequent bombing.

Living in Germany during the war meant a complete mistrust of everyone and everything. People were turning each other in for anything they did, and our freedoms were so restricted, I was surprised they didn't develop a method for reading our minds and arresting us for our thoughts. Fortunately for me, it hadn't come to that, otherwise I would have suffered the consequences long ago. I loathed every minute of what was happening to us, primarily what was happening to my little brother.

Siegfried was especially terrified by the bombs, so Mama never left him alone. She knew she was his only hope for comfort and wouldn't dream of denying him that. He usually wrapped his arms so tight around her neck that bruises were visible on her skin, yet, year upon year, I never once heard her complain. She was sincerely thankful to survive each attack, no matter how much pain she had to endure.

Mama had made another acquaintance down the street who had a six-year-old daughter. She was concerned about whether she'd be able to find shelter for the both of them when they journeyed out from the safety of their house.

"Elisabeth, would you mind keeping Christa when I go into town? This way, I can be sure she'll be safe in your cellar."

"Of course, we'll take good care of your little girl."

Many times Christa came over and spent time with us in our cellar, but one afternoon, again, the Gestapo came to the door, ordering Mama into the city for questioning. She didn't want to take all of us children with her, so she asked Peter and me to watch Christa and make sure we made it into the cellar if an alarm sounded. Sure enough, shortly after she left, the alarm did sound. We grabbed Christa and dragged her downstairs, and without her mother, or ours, we could see she was visibly frightened. We all were; our hearts pounding with more force than usual. We were alone with no parents to shelter us, but I was older than Christa so, as Mama usually protected me, I would in turn protect Christa. Her eyes rapidly panned the room, before locking into mine. I asked her, "Christa, have you been baptized?"

"No, we don't even go to church."

"You know you should because if something ever happens and you die during a bombing, you might not go to heaven. You might go someplace where you'll never see God. Wouldn't you like to see God and spend time with him?"

"I don't know much about him."

"You should learn about him and how special he is, and you really ought to be baptized."

I began reflecting on a conversation I'd had with Mama, when she told me that if we knew of people who hadn't been baptized, in the case of an emergency, anyone could perform a baptism.

"Mama, how would I baptize someone?"

"You simply take holy water, make the sign of the cross, and say, "In the name of the Father, and the Son, and the Holy Spirit, I baptize you (and say their name)."

"Will that really work?"

"Oh yes. This is a legal baptism in the case of an emergency, and if that person should die, they will surely go to heaven."

Being alone in the cellar when the alarm signaled that the bombs had been released, I was convinced that this constituted an emergency, and I needed to baptize Christa. Mama always kept holy water in a small bottle, so I hurried over to retrieve it. Not thinking it was enough I poured it into a pail of water and dumped the whole bucket over her head. I proceeded with, "In the name of the Father, and the Son, and the Holy Spirit, I baptize you, Christa."

Soaking wet, and squinting, as she rubbed the water and hair out of her eyes, she asked, "Marlies, does this mean that I will go to heaven if we die?"

"Yes, this means that you are now a soldier of God, and you'll go to heaven. And he'll have a beautiful place for you if we don't make it. This is what God promised us. We'll all be up there, and maybe we'll see each other again."

A sense of relief came over her as we huddled together, alone and frightened. Peter and I began reciting all of the prayers that we had learned, including one about the angels. Even though it wasn't time for bed, I wanted to teach her the prayer. So we began:

Now I lay me down to sleep,
Fourteen angels watch will keep,
Two at my head, two at my feet,
Two at my left side, two at my right side,
Two to cover me, two to wake me,
And two to take me to heaven some day.

I told her, "If you learn the prayer and say it at night, the angels will come and watch over you. In case they can't protect you from the bombs, they'll make sure that you're taken to heaven, so we can play together again."

We stayed in the cellar and prayed and hoped that our mothers were alright, and that they'd found shelter somewhere. We were also hoping that Papa was safe in the Opel factory. The bombing ceased, and the first thing we did was run to the corner to sit and wait for our mothers to come home. It seemed like we waited forever when we caught a glimpse of Mama hurrying down the road with Siegfried, and not long afterwards, Christa's mother also scurried along.

Christa's mother had never paid much attention to prayer, but she was beginning to believe that there was a God somewhere. She truly desired a sense of faith and belief in God and wanted to instruct her daughter on religion, but she didn't know the first thing about it. Mama offered her a book that would teach her fundamental religious instructions, telling her, "Whatever religion you choose to follow is irrelevant, as long as you believe in God."

"Thank you, Elisabeth; and thank you, Marlies, for baptizing Christa." She took the book and headed for home. Sadly, less than two months passed when a bomb destroyed their home, and both she and Christa perished. My heart sank, but Mama assured me, "God will find a nice place in heaven for them, now that they've finally recognized him." I was pleased to know that they'd finally made peace with God, and in some small way, I was part of their path to heaven. Occasionally, even the worst of times can bring out the best in us.

As Christa and her mother escaped to heaven, we were still stranded in Germany where we couldn't afford to make a fire during the day. We saved the heat for when Papa was home at night. He needed to have a warm meal, so that's the only time the stove was used. Otherwise, we layered our clothes—seemingly of little help, as I believed I'd never get warm again. Two to three inches of ice formed on our walls while we spent nights huddled around the kitchen stove with hot bricks at our feet and around our bodies trying to stay warm. That winter, we also lost our two rabbits, after feeding them weeds and vegetables that had been contaminated by phosphor bombs. Now we knew the garden was no longer suitable for consumption, further dwindling our food supply. Mama tended to that garden as if her life depended on it. I just didn't know how much more she could take.

13
Surviving on Faith

In spring of 1944, it was time for Peter and me to make our first Holy Communion. The priest had instructed us so solemnly that when the day arrived to receive it, Peter, overwhelmed, passed out like a sack of potatoes at the altar.

The priest, a wonderfully gentle, holy man, gave him his communion at the sacristy. The sacristy was behind the altar where the priest put on his vestments before mass. He taught us the true meaning of faith and gave us the ability to truly understand our religion. Many times, he came out into the streets as the safe alarm was sounding in the aftermath, to make sure that everyone was all right and had shelter. He rode his bicycle from person to person, lending assistance to any who required it and giving Last Rites to any who would soon take their last breath—no matter what religion they practiced, if any.

Shortly after receiving our first communion, we also received confirmation. We had to travel to Frankfurt, where we were confirmed by the bishop. We put on our Sunday finest, beginning our journey as we trudged through the damage and devastation, realizing every city of any importance in Germany had come under attack—most of them totally destroyed. Although the Frankfurt church had been damaged, as had all of the surrounding buildings, it didn't put a damper on our confirmation ceremony. As long as the structure was standing and safe, nothing would stand in our way.

Those were the days that made us feel proud. Our faith was of the utmost importance and to stand before God, the priest, and our family in that church made me glow. I couldn't have been happier or more thankful for days like that.

But the glory we felt that afternoon wasn't lasting. Thanks to Hitler and his henchman, we never knew what might lie ahead.

The Damage Circles In

Back in our apartment, the alarm began howling as we had become so accustomed to, but this time, Papa was home too. We were all in the cellar as he peered out from the small window opening, noticing a plane being shot down nearby. Engulfed in flames and heading directly our way, it looked as though it was going to slam into the side of our house. We sat with our heads in our laps. But it missed us, scraping so close it could have left landing-gear marks on the roof, before exploding within a mile amidst the sparse trees of the forest.

Before the explosion, Papa had seen parachutes. He made the mistake of saying out loud, "I hope those men from that plane make it safely to the ground." The next thing I knew, Peter got up, and in a trance-like state, walked away. Mama yelled, "Peter come back; the bombs haven't ended!" But he kept going. We couldn't believe it; the all-clear alarm hadn't sounded, but he had vanished, seemingly into thin air.

Papa realized, "Oh my God, he's left the house." Siegfried and I looked at each other without a word. We didn't want to cause Mama any more anxiety or anguish than we could see she was already enduring.

I couldn't be sure exactly how much time passed; the minutes dragged on. Finally, he stumbled back down the cellar steps. By that time, Mama was almost hysterical. She screamed at him, "Where have you been? Where did you go?" In the midst of her fury, she suddenly realized he was standing in front of her physically, but mentally, he was in shock. Papa hauled him aside and gave him the spanking of a lifetime, before trying to obtain some answers. He stared into the distance as he told them he had gone to find the soldiers.

When he neared the edge of the woods, close to the highway, he saw the remains of the two parachutes that hit the ground. They had been destroyed by fire and left to smolder, but were still attached to the bloody bodies of the men lying on the highway. "Papa, I saw a boot and realized that if I looked around, maybe I could find the other, and you would finally have a decent pair of boots to keep your feet warm!" He realized the soldiers no longer had use for them. Even used boots would be a wonderfully needed surprise. Scanning the area, he finally saw the other and ran over to it; only to find that a portion of the dead man's leg was still inside. Gagging, he quickly turned his head only to focus on a hand lying nearby, nothing but a hand.

He was only ten years old and frightened, running straight through the woods back to the house. His original intention was to find the soldiers before the Nazis did and keep them safely hidden in our house. Papa asked, "Where do you think we could have hidden them?"

"In the cellar, I just thought they could stay in the cellar."

"And keep them alive on what? We barely have enough food to keep ourselves alive. And the people upstairs are Nazis, and they'd surely notice men being harbored in our cellar. What a fruitless trip you took through those woods! Why would you attempt to do such a thing?"

"All I wanted to do was help them! I didn't want them to be captured by the Nazis!"

For months afterwards, Peter woke in the middle of the night screaming, and our parents would run to calm him. Seeing what he had seen did a tremendous job on his young mind, affecting him severely. From that moment on, it became difficult for him to see blood without feeling nauseous.

The next bombing we endured was the most hellacious for our family. It was a dreadful night when the reservoir, which was not far from where we lived, was bombarded with Spreng bombs and air mines. They blew the reservoir to oblivion, while proceeding to sprinkle the city with phosphor.

Papa again watched from the window opening in the cellar, observing the phosphor bombs falling like rain. The entire area where we lived was burning. In that surreal moment, he heard a strange thud from upstairs, and he rushed up to find the entire upstairs apartment engulfed in flames. A firebomb had fallen through the roof. He flew back downstairs, "Grab the suitcases, grab our things, and get out of the house now!"

He ran back up with a pail of water, because lying in our hall was a phosphor bomb that had not blown up. He believed the water was our only hope of keeping it from exploding. In a frenzy, he tried throwing the water through a window, but instead all he managed to do was cut his wrist open with knifelike shards of glass. Without skipping a beat, Mama put a tourniquet on the wound, enabling him to help us gather our things out of the cellar. Running on adrenaline, on a mission to save what little we had, he didn't have time to dwell on the pain. We grabbed our suitcases and trunks and pulled them outside, while the bombs continued to rain down.

I looked upward and wondered how the pilots felt, what their thoughts were as they dropped the steady stream of death upon us. We were innocent people, just like their sisters, brothers, parents, sons, and daughters. The irrevocable acts of destruction they set in motion were unfathomable to me. No matter how deep I searched, I couldn't make sense of the routine we had fallen into. I yearned for the simplicity of lying with my eyes closed in the shade of an old tree, cool, prickly grass beneath my body, and listening to the songbirds all around.

As I tried to remember better times, Peter and Papa worked as a team to drag the couch and Mama's sewing machine out of the burning house. They knew what their priorities were as she cried, "Please save my sewing machine! If that's gone, so is my opportunity to work and make money for food." As soon as the items hit the ground, Papa turned back for one more chance to run in and grab anything he could. Next to the bedroom door, he saw my little doll on the floor. She was already on fire, but he knew I'd need her, so he grabbed her by the arm, just as the ceiling crashed down, barely missing him as he made it to safety ... along with my burning doll. He smothered the flames and held onto her while she cooled; then he tenderly reached down with a warm smile and gave me back my baby.

There we were, with only those few items, as we frantically tried to cover ourselves with blankets to keep the phosphor off. I didn't want to burn like my doll, and I didn't want her to burn worse than she already had. We sat in the yard and literally watched our home burn to the ground. The last big crash we heard was our apartment falling into the cellar, knowing if we had stayed in there, we would have surely died that day. Surrounded by flames, we had somehow managed to survive once again.

Dark smoke billowed through the air like ugly clouds as dirt and soot accumulated beneath. It was difficult to breathe. When it was safe to come out from underneath our wet blankets, Mama took out a needle and thread and stitched Papa's wound to stop the bleeding. I knew many others had met their demise that day, and I wondered why we, for all intents and purposes, had been chosen to make it unscathed.

Our entire city was in flames; very few homes were left standing. Yet we needed to find some type of shelter. With time running out, Papa was able to contact a friend of Uncle Joseph's who was willing to pick up our belonging and take us to Aunt Hanna's. Her home was badly damaged, but it was still livable until we could find another place.

Once there, Mama sent a telegram to an old school friend who lived in Heimersheim, a town on the other side of the Rhine River from us. She had told us that if we ever needed anything, she had a large farmhouse with plenty of room and we were more than welcome, anytime.

She was the first person Mama thought of, since she lived in western Germany. The further west we could make it, the sooner we'd achieve our goal of being liberated. The reply arrived shortly, and Mama prayed the offer still stood as she slowly opened her girlfriend's return telegram. Her smile and sigh of relief gave the contents away: "You are all welcome to come. We are waiting for you."

Short and sweet, but to the point, it was exactly what we needed to hear. However, as so many times before, the good news was peppered with bad. Papa could not leave. He had to stay in Rüsselsheim with Aunt Hanna until further notice. Once again, Mama would travel alone with three young children. We traveled to the train station, found a train car to put our measly belongings on, and finally we were on our way to begin yet another chapter.

A "Peaceful" Farming Community

Heimersheim was a small town not far from the Ludendorff Bridge or more frequently called the Bridge at Remagen, where the Americans would eventually cross the Rhine River. Apparently, it was the last standing bridge on the Rhine. Mama's friend, Agnes, was a lovely lady who gladly took us in, and we were extremely grateful for that. Her husband was in the war, while she remained home with two sons a couple of years younger than I was. Her sons were forced to help out on the farm, and being so young, she was glad to have the extra hands available. We had little to bring with us—most of what we owned was lost in the fire—but we were happy to be there and delighted to be alive and well.

We were going to have to enroll in yet another school. Of course the schools usually met a similar fate as most buildings in Germany, skeletons of what they once were, good for nothing but demolition. The aftermath of bombing raids was usually so severe that the buildings, if standing at all, were not safe for occupancy. Finding teachers was nearly impossible as well, which allowed us a lot of free time when we otherwise should have been getting an education. I had lost count of exactly how many different schools I had attended, but we couldn't give up trying.

Maybe Heimersheim would be different, so we eagerly made ourselves at home. Maybe it would be a fresh start for Peter and me, and maybe we'd actually fit in somewhere and make friends. Being starry eyed, I still had faith in Utopia. Heimersheim, unfortunately was not going to be the place I dreamed of. Although the bombings were not as severe, there were different dreadful things, and it didn't take us long to figure that out.

Enemy airplanes dove down as low as possible and shot anything in sight. They shot at *everything,* including innocent folks meandering in the streets. The planes were primarily from England and the United States, and they destroyed small villages, barely scraping over the top of the telephone wires, which often hung loose.

One afternoon in broad daylight, a young, mentally handicapped boy walked down the street and waved at one of the planes as it flew overhead. In cold blood, they fired upon him, shooting him down with machine guns, leaving him for dead in the street. As his beautiful body, moments earlier filled with exuberance and zest for life, lay in an expanding puddle of blood, I realized a sad reality of living near the Remagen Bridge: the Allies used the townsfolk for target practice.

We however, *were* Americans, and Mama knew that if she prayed enough, they'd soon come and rescue us. They were murdering others in the streets, but for some reason, she believed we'd be different.

We heard reports that the Americans and the English were gaining on Germany, and that Russia and France had united and were driving the Germans back. As the Allies slowly encroached upon us, we sensed that the end of the war was nearing. We pondered our fate: Would we be gunned down in the street like the unsuspecting little boy? Would we be captured? Would we disappear like so many others, or could it be possible that Mama was right? Believing the latter was the only way I could carry on. Hopeful, I waited. As we all did.

Contact with Papa was solely through the mail. He was forbidden to leave Rüsselsheim, even though he had no home and his family had fled miles away. Missing his family, he requested permission to join us. The city of Rüsselsheim told him to stay exactly where he was.

I didn't understand why he couldn't be with us, but in his letters he wrote, "Please don't worry about me. Even though the bombings have not ceased, I still have my ration cards, and I'm doing all right. I do however miss you all very much." Hoping his letters would indicate his impending arrival, Mama was disappointed when they stated otherwise. She was lonely and often frightened, not having her husband by her side.

We would have preferred to stay at Oma's, but we couldn't since it would have been impossible for her to feed four more mouths. Living with Agnes, we weren't considered part of a family; we were refugees without a home. Therefore, we continued receiving our ration cards.

The people in our new town were cordial; they didn't know we were Americans, so they didn't taunt us like they did in the city. The children here were also required to be in the Hitler Youth, but no one questioned why we weren't. There were other refugees who had lost all of their clothing and belongings in the fires, and since the government couldn't replace the Hitler Youth uniforms, it was easily overlooked. So living there turned out to be more pleasurable than our previous residence. Peter and I called Mama's friend "Aunt Agnes," inasmuch as she seemed like family, which was a huge relief after my experience with Lena, my real aunt.

We had children to play with who actually played with us, and things were fairly peaceful. Still, we were busy, having assumed a lot of responsibility around the farm. It was the least we could do in exchange for a safe haven. Housing was at a premium by that point in the war. We helped with harvesting the fruit, picking apples, and putting them into baskets. We attached the baskets to the tree with a hook and, when it was full, lowered it down with a rope to put the apples into sacks.

We used our ingenuity to make our chores go as smoothly and quickly as possible, but sometimes things were out of our control. For instance one afternoon, while we were up in an apple tree, we heard a plane overhead. It was flying extremely low over the orchard, and Peter nervously whispered, "The pilot saw us, Marlies. I know the pilot saw us."

We had learned to fear the pilots who flew those planes. Knowing they had no sympathy for anyone, including women and children, we dodged for cover. It was safer to risk breaking a limb, than it would have been to act as sitting ducks in the tree. We no sooner jumped than the pilot turned around and started firing into the very tree we had been in. He passed through twice, blowing branches and chunks of the tree apart, but we had rolled far enough away that we avoided being hit.

We'd been hiding between two big trees with a thick brush covering, and he wasn't able to spot us. When we heard the sound of the engine diminish as the distance between us grew, we resumed our chores amongst the ammunition-riddled trees. We were that close, only feet away from being shot and killed, at the very point when we knew that the war was nearing its end.

The Yanks Are Coming, the Yanks Are Coming

In early March 1945, we heard reports that the Americans were preparing to cross the Rhine River. As far away as Rüsselsheim, Papa also heard the reports, and he knew that if there was any place he wanted to be, it was near the Rhine where the Americans would enter to liberate Germany. The area we were in was the most likely place for them to come through, so he decided he was going to ride his bicycle to Heimersheim.

We had been separated for more than a year, during which Papa had reached an important crossroads in his life. With the war ending, he feared that Hitler might order the Nazis to kill the men who worked in the underground ammunition factory—in order to keep his secrets. Papa was fifty-five years old and nearing starvation, yet he faced the hundred-mile trip with vigor. Six years of war had been enough. He wouldn't have it one more moment. So he hopped on his Englishmen's bicycle, under the cover of night, pedaling to exhaustion, with nothing but the clothes on his back and his passport strapped under his arm.

Meanwhile, back in Heimersheim, we had long noticed the German soldiers had grown weary of fighting, and after seeing the devastation of their homeland, I'm sure they began to wonder what they had left to fight for.

Behind Agnes's house was a mountain, and within the mountain was an area marked by a red cross that had been carved out and set up as a makeshift hospital. Inside were doctors and nurses who cared for the wounded, including French, Russian, English, and Germans. Soldiers were moved from army hospitals by Red Cross trains to our area. With so much destruction, it was amazing that the railroads were still in operation, but they were always the first to be repaired. Without the railway, it would have been impossible to transport food, fuel, prisoners, the injured, and—as I found out later—Jewish people.

Mama had made the acquaintance of one of the nurses in the hospital, and during one of their conversations, the nurse made a request. "If the Americans cross the Rhine and you meet them before I, please tell them that this is a Red Cross hospital, and that we have no ammunition, and we do not intend to fight anyone."

The farm where we lived was across from the school, and one day we watched a young Nazi officer no more than eighteen years old, pushing twelve, German soldiers along. The men were beaten down, as if they couldn't lift and point another gun. They were ragged and starving, while the Nazi ordered them around as if they were schoolboys.

One of the men had been shot in the leg, and another was helping him along. He had a large wound, his pants were torn, and blood was seeping out. He used a piece of wood as a crutch, with rags wrapped around the top to help sturdy him, while dragging his shrapnel-ridden leg behind. He clearly needed to go to a hospital—even I could see that—but the young Nazi wouldn't have any part of it.

After camping out for the night across from Agnes's, the officer ordered his men to do some sort of exercise. That was the last thing they needed, being exhausted and wanting only to rest. The soldier with the wounded leg pleaded with the Nazi: he couldn't do the exercises, and he needed medical attention. We watched as the young Nazi walked over to the wounded soldier and told him that he didn't need anything, and then he heartlessly kicked him in the leg.

The soldier fell to the ground in excruciating pain, and right there in the schoolyard, before all of us children, two of the other German soldiers pulled out their revolvers and shot the Nazi point blank, dead. The war and that Nazi officer had driven those poor young men to the point of no return. They were willing to murder one to end the suffering of another.

With their ruthless leader out of the picture, they asked if we knew where there was anyone that could help the soldier. We eagerly told them the mountain had a hospital inside and they could get help there. The soldiers picked up the man and carried him into the mountain. When they came out, they went into town, spoke to the mayor, and gave up their weapons, stating they could be found at the hospital where they were going to stay with their comrade. In the case that the Americans did cross the border, they were to be informed that the soldiers were there, that they were unarmed, and they had no intention of fighting any further.

Just days later, we heard an overwhelming explosion. The German air force was attempting to blow up the Remagen Bridge. They had previously rigged the bridge with explosives for just such an occasion. However, even though the bridge was damaged, it still stood. It was their last ditch effort to keep the Americans from proceeding forward. The bridge was more than one thousand feet long, the last intact bridge crossing the Rhine.

The German planes that tried to demolish the bridge were eventually shot down and destroyed, and shortly afterwards, the tanks began rolling into the village that provided us with our first sighting of the United States Army.

Hitler was desperate to destroy the railroad bridge before the Americans could cross, penetrating deep into enemy territory, but he didn't want to act prematurely. His hesitation cost him infinitely, as approximately forty thousand Americans did make their way across the structurally damaged bridge before it finally collapsed on March 17, 1945, due to an overload of men and equipment.

I was shocked when the tanks rolled into town, as the American soldiers looked like mountain men, much the way Vazil first appeared. They were dirty, with long, shaggy hair and beards, and looking weary from combat. Right away, they jumped off of their tanks and trucks and began corralling people into circles.

They ordered all weapons be turned over, but essentially the only people who had weapons were the Nazis. After six, long years of war, no one had the energy to fight them. There was no retaliatory shooting, and no one tried to prevent them from advancing. Everyone knew all was lost. It was over for us, but it seemed the American soldiers were still looking for a fight.

For my mother, however, seeing those men—whether or not they were spoiling for a fight—was the very moment she had been waiting for. She immediately went forward and, in broken English, begged to speak with them. She told them she was American, and that we were misplaced. They didn't believe her. They were only interested in whether or not she had food to offer. Desperately trying to reach them on any level, she told them the only food she had were the apples in her sack, but they were welcome to them.

When I first encountered the men, they looked like wild animals, and I was very confused. Mama had always promised that one day the Americans would come, and we'd become free individuals. She told us the Americans had food, and everything would be good again. But they crossed the bridge wearing jewelry, scarves, and things they had confiscated, while screaming, hollering, and shooting out windows and doorways and anything that moved. I was mortified.

Apparently, they didn't trust anyone, and afraid of what could be in or on the fruit, they ordered Mama, "Have your children eat the apples first." She told us to do it, to show them they weren't poisoned. Peter, Siegfried, myself, and Agnes's two sons bit into them. Immediately, they jumped off their tanks and stormed the apples, as they had the Remagen Bridge. They were devouring what little food we had. To Mama, however, it was a small price to pay in order to get them to understand the severity of our situation.

When they finished the last of our apples, one of the soldiers gave each of us a piece of gum. Peter and I took the gum and went behind the house and sat down. I told Peter, "How sad this is for Mama, all of the things she thought would happen when the Americans arrived are not holding true. In America, they don't have any more food than we have. Look how thin their candy is. If they had a lot of food, you'd think they'd have a thicker piece of candy."

Along with our apples, the soldiers disappeared, determined to take control of our broken-down town.

Later, Mama asked, "Who still has their gum?"

"Mama we haven't had candy in so long, did you expect us to make it last longer?"

"Oh, Marlies, you don't understand. What they gave you was gum—you chew it, and it lasts all day." I didn't know what gum was. We'd bit off small pieces and swallowed. She told us that information too late!

Thankfully Mama's pleading did not fall on deaf ears, as we found out later. The soldiers must have relayed her concerns to their superiors. One of the commanders came forward to talk to her. He wanted to know how she came about being in Germany, who we were, and so on. She told him all she could about us, including that they didn't have to worry about the townspeople either. They had given up their weapons, which had been placed in a pile in the center of town. We were completely vulnerable, yet he didn't believe her, "There must be more weapons."

"No, you're wrong. The Nazis had taken them away long ago." Not willing to risk their safety, and following orders, a number of the soldiers went from house to house searching to prove her wrong. Mama also told him about the Red Cross hospital in the mountain behind our house, and not to be concerned since they had no ammunition and no one intended to harm them. They didn't believe her regarding that issue either.

In order to help them trust her, she was willing to have us children walk in front of her to enter the hospital, as she took them in safely. She told them there were several German soldiers inside who had already given up their weapons, no longer having the energy or desire to fight. It didn't matter how compelling her arguments, their mistrust resulted in an atrocious act. They positioned a tank next to our house and proceeded to shell the entire mountain. Everyone in the hospital died that day. Mama stood, hyperventilating, with tears in her eyes, asking, "Why, Why?"

There was no reason for the senseless loss of life, leaving us more afflicted with sorrow with each passing moment. We believed they were there to liberate us, yet they killed droves of innocent people, including the bed-ridden who were desperately trying to recuperate. They killed doctors, nurses, surrendered German soldiers, and many innocent men who were prisoners of war. They were Polish, Russian, English, French, and probably could have made it home alive if the Americans would have had faith in what Mama desperately tried to convey.

As much as we hated what had happened, we began to understand that they didn't feel trust for anyone. The hatred had been so deep for so long resulting from losses they had suffered, that they simply followed orders and toppled the mountain hospital. Unfortunately, that was my first encounter with American soldiers, and it frightened me immeasurably.

Nothing was getting better as far as I could see. The atrocities of war continued with the "liberating" soldiers entering homes and confiscating anything they sought fit. They took what little food was left and accused people of crimes they hadn't committed. Some people deserved it—the Nazis—and the townspeople had no problem informing the American soldiers who the Nazis were. The Americans realized they were dealing with two different factions, and they were as disturbed by the Nazis as we were. The German people were happy they were no longer the only ones trampled on, and it was high time the Nazis got theirs.

The Family Reunited

Mama was plagued with concerns—things were changing so fast, and we'd had no word from Papa. She wondered what cards life had dealt him. She had no idea he had begun a journey where each night he rode as far as he could, while hiding in daylight, taking cover in ditches. He snuck up on areas after dark, looking for fruit or any kind of food he could live on, as he made his way across Germany. I don't know how many days he had been traveling, but one day without warning, there he was, simply standing in front of us.

He hadn't even told Mama of his plans, but he often had a propensity for surprising her, and this surprise was a much welcomed one. Her countless, sleepless nights wondering about her husband's whereabouts had ceased, and just as she had prayed day-in and day-out, Papa was safely home.

Our first instinct was to hide him, knowing that if they came looking and found him, we'd be in trouble, but fortunately, Germany had undergone such upheaval and destruction, that they didn't bother to investigate his whereabouts. They didn't know for sure if he was dead or alive, and they never expected anyone to travel across-country via bicycle.

He didn't tell Aunt Hanna he was leaving, nor did he tell anyone, leaving them to surmise that he had somehow died. He had never attempted anything similar in the past, so they trusted him and never suspected otherwise. The night he fled, they underwent a devastating bombing and many lives were lost, one of which, they most likely assumed was his.

The Americans had landed just a day or two before Papa's arrival from Rüsselsheim. Even though on his entire journey, he was concerned about the Nazis coming after him, once he arrived, he felt home free since the Americans had beaten him there. He couldn't have been more proud to be an American than at the moment when he realized he was about to cross paths with an American tank carrying American soldiers.

What came out of their mouths, however, surprised him. The men driving the tank vulgarly screamed at him in English, "Hey asshole, get your bike out of the street!" They were equally surprised and probably embarrassed when Papa replied in English, "Everyone has one! I never expected to meet the American Army and be called a name like that."

They jumped off the tank and grabbed his arms, "Who are you? Why did you answer us in English?"

"I'm an American citizen and have been trapped in this country throughout the entire war. I have waited a very long time for you to show up, and I am relieved to finally see you here."

They wanted to know why he was in Germany, so they took him and Mama to meet their commander. They explained what had happened, who we were, and why we were there. They still didn't seem to trust them, so Papa showed them on a map where we were from, he showed them our tickets, his passport, and our citizenship papers. Finally, they began to understand our situation. They still looked at us with skepticism, but not with quite as much contempt as they had before. Perhaps Papa had gotten through to them, unlike Mama who had already told them the exact same information, to no avail.

The American soldiers' supplies never caught up with them. They were hungry and tired and had seen things in Germany that we were not even aware of. Concentration camps were what they uncovered on their way into Germany. Witnessing the atrocities within the Nazi-controlled camps must have been why they were so cruel when they first settled upon us. The hatred for the German people continued to grow, and they became very suspicious of everyone.

Until the Americans arrived, I had never heard the words "concentration camp." It was as foreign to me as they were, but the pieces of the puzzle began to connect. The Steins, our good friends who supposedly moved to France, must have met their fate somewhere in a concentration camp. It was all making sense. They hadn't been allowed to leave the country any more than we had been allowed to leave. The only difference, they were Jewish, and the train they boarded surely did not take them to France.

14
Peace without Relief

Grateful that the war was over, I felt sad for my uncles who had been gone for years fighting for a country left virtually in ruins. We worried, wondering where they could be, and if they were still alive. One letter from Oma left us feeling pessimistic and depressed, as she explained how Vazil, the only "son" she had at home, had been forced to leave. The Americans arrived in Trier and proceeded on to Kell. Just a few days before the war ended, they made it clear that all prisoners must be returned to their homelands. They were being set free, meaning that Vazil had to leave and he had no choice in the matter. True freedom for Vazil meant living in Kell with the only family he had, but Oma's pleas went unheard. The rules of war were quite clear, and she had no input into them.

Just before his departure, Oma sewed him a coat with many pockets on the inside, filling them with food, hoping he would have a safe trip back to Russia. Vazil was extremely quiet while preparing to leave and didn't say much at all, until Oma put the sandwiches in his coat and found a revolver with two bullets. "Vazil, where on earth did you get this gun?"

"I found it."

Uncle Joseph had hidden the revolver behind some bricks in the house, and somehow Vazil came across it. He had kept it hidden for just such an occasion. Oma told him, "If they find you with a gun, they'll kill you Vazil."

"They're going to kill me anyway. If they return me to Russia, Stalin will have me executed."

"Why would they do such a thing?"

With tears streaming down, Vazil solemnly answered, "Stalin told us when we were drafted that anyone captured by the Germans and taken as prisoner, would be shot and killed, never to step foot on Russian soil again. He promised us, and I know that promise will be followed through. Now if the Nazis find this gun on me, they'll kill me, and if not, the first person who tries to kill me in Russia will get one bullet and the other will be for me."

Oma cried as she begged, "Vazil, please, you cannot take your life."

"I won't let Stalin kill me. I'd rather kill myself." He hugged her tightly, "If I live through this, I'm going to come back. I know my family is here. I'm sure by now my brothers are dead, and my mother couldn't have survived without me to help her. I have nothing to go back to, so I'll return to live with you."

"There will always be an open door for you Vazil, and I want you to come back to us. I'll be proud to be a mother to you as you have been like a son to me." Once more, he hugged her and, one by one, hugged everyone else, before turning away to head back to the camp. Heartbroken and not having even one son return from war, Oma prayed that God would watch over Vazil and bring him back to her. Her prayers went unanswered, however. That sorrowful day was the last time anyone ever saw or heard from Vazil.

But even that wasn't the end of Oma's suffering. Her letter went on to tell us that shortly after the Americans entered Kell, Uncle Johann was in the barn preparing food for the cows. The barn walls were not solid, as many of the boards had separated with age. One of the soldiers happened upon the property, and standing outside the barn, he could see my uncle's shadow moving back and forth in the barn. Calling to him two or three times, the American soldier ordered, "Get your hands up and come out. Surrender!" Uncle Johann had no idea what they were talking about and probably didn't care anyway.

He was going about his business of feeding the cows, not knowing he was in danger, when all of a sudden, the Americans pointed their weapons and shot a bazooka into the barn.

The big knife Uncle Johann was using to cut the food for the cattle was blown off the trough and pinned him onto the ground. When the grenade exploded, his legs were filled with shrapnel. When Oma heard the explosion, she ran outside and threw the barn doors open. There he was, Opa's poor, brain-injured brother Johann, lying there helplessly. She tried to communicate with the soldiers, "Oh my God, what have you done? He meant you no harm; he just didn't understand what you were saying … he just didn't understand!" The Americans seemed ashamed of what they had done, so they picked him up, placed him on a wagon, and rushed him to the hospital in Trier.

Oma was heartbroken to write and tell us that Uncle Johann was in the hospital, and they couldn't remove all of the shrapnel from his legs. He lay there for days, and slowly perished from the lead poisoning. There was no medication for the pain, and he suffered through every last hour of his life.

One of the only things he had the strength to tell Oma was, "Mother, I would gladly suffer all of this pain, if God would just let your boys come back home safely."

Oma knelt by his bedside, held his hand, and cried, "Johann, you have been such a good man, and you are suffering for no reason. You have never harmed anyone your whole life."

In all his pain, he tried to calm her, "Mother, don't cry for me, I'm going to be with my brother in Heaven, and may God take my suffering as a sacrifice and not take the lives of any of your sons. Oh, I'm not much of a loss … but I don't want you to lose your children." Seeing her share of tragedy, Oma watched as Uncle Johann died shortly after those last words. Oma made her way home and mourned, feeling as though she had lost two sons—first Vazil and then Opa's very special brother, Johann.

Since the war had officially ended, it was time for Papa to find employment again and housing for us. We could no longer stay with Agnes; we'd been guests at her home for more than a year, and it was due time to find a way to get back to the United States. While mapping our plan, Papa found a job in the small village of Winningen, which was about sixty miles south of us, near the city of Koblenz. Koblenz is a beautiful city located on the south bank of the Rhine River and the East bank of the Mosel River. It is located where both rivers meet and in Germany it's referred to as the "Deutche Eck", or the German corner. Winningen, bordering the Mosel River, was occupied by the Americans and we found a nice apartment, and Papa was eagerly and happily about to begin employment for a local winery. The Americans were kind enough to help move us and our meager belongings in one of their Army trucks.

After settling in our new apartment, we made contact with the American consulate, to make arrangements to return to the United States as our first priority. They told my parents they'd have to conduct an investigation to see what contact we'd had with the Nazi party during the war. Mama and Papa had absolutely no contact other than being persecuted by them, but the consulate needed to determine that for themselves. The Federal Bureau of Investigation started processing a background check on us from the first day we'd arrived in Germany until that very moment. Until their investigation was complete, we would still have no right to leave the country.

The Nazis had been defeated and the American soldiers had started befriending Peter and me. We felt special because some of them treated us like their own children. Those we had contact with had become kind and generous, occasionally giving us some of their rations, including crackers and chocolate. Other than the day my cousin Marlies teased us, I couldn't remember having chocolate in nearly seven years. Making us feel even more special, from time to time, while walking to school, they'd pick us up in their jeep and drive us over. It was like having our own personal chauffeur! We had forgotten most of our English, so we didn't understand when they spoke, but somehow we were able to communicate back and forth. Occasionally they let us tag along to the second floor of the hotel in Winningen and let us watch cartoon films in the ballroom where there was a stage and a large dance floor. We didn't understand the words, but the films were fun to watch.

Over the years, my parents had become scrawny, walking skeletons, their skin wrapped about them like paper. We didn't look much better, but it seemed as though our parents were dwindling away at a quicker rate. The year Papa was alone had taken a toll on him. Aunt Hanna was not known to be a good housewife, and she certainly couldn't prepare a decent meal. He did the best he could with the little bit he received in rations, but I suspect he wasn't eating much at all. He had gone without for so long that he had a tired look about him, and of course, he was no longer a young man. By that point, he was fifty-five years old. Fifty-five years old and the walking skeleton I called Papa rode his bicycle across an entire country to reunite with his family. He looked old and drawn, and I felt sad for him, knowing that life had not always shown him its kindest side.

War Is Over, but Not for Us

Winningen was a fine stopover. Even though there was massive destruction, the bombings had stopped. It seemed peaceful, and most of our fears had subsided. Then we found ourselves facing a new one, one we never imagined possible: the fear that we wouldn't be able to return to the United States and that they'd find some reason to keep us from going home. While we waited, we worried about finding enough food. We didn't have a garden like we had in Rüsselsheim. and it was tough to survive without it. The treats we received from the GIs were terrific, but few and far between.

Our apartment was located very close to the river, and we were able to spend a lot of time playing in the water. None of us had acquired a talent for swimming, so we had to be especially careful. Papa brought corks home from the winery, and Mama used her creativity to make me a life preserver. She sewed two bags together, filled them with corks, and put a strap in the middle. I was able to lie across the strap and wade into the water, spending my spare time splashing about on hot summer days, while continually watching Siegfried to ensure he didn't fall into the river. We played for hours, and for the first time since we left America, we actually felt like kids. Kids without the weight of the world upon our shoulders.

Peter hunted around and found an old gasoline tank that had been blown out of an airplane. He cut a huge hole in the top and bent the sides down with pliers to make himself a makeshift boat. He painted some stars on the side to make it look American, and somehow obtained a couple of paddles that he used to propel himself around the river. He was proud of his boat, and the mere fact that it floated was a miracle. It had become his main source of entertainment after we lost the Radio Flyer wagon when our house in Rüsselsheim was destroyed.

One afternoon while Peter was puttering around the river, I realized that I couldn't find my doll. She was my only toy, and aside from Peter and my cow, she had been my only friend since we stepped foot on German soil. I couldn't find her, and I became more upset by the minute. I looked under everything, and then I looked under everything a second time. I bellowed to Mama, thinking she must know where my baby was. But she didn't. Mama said that she hadn't seen her either. In fact, she hadn't seen her in quite some time. I ran to the door yelling to Peter, "Have you seen my doll?"

"Yes, I've seen her."

"Oh good, where is she?"

"I'm sorry, Marlies, but she was so badly burned from the fire, I couldn't stand to look at her anymore. She reminded me of when we lost our house, and she looked frightening, so I took her down to the river and threw her in."

"How could you do that to me?"

I was devastated to think that I had lost my doll. Her burned and disfigured face didn't bother me at all. She was the only toy I had, and it broke my heart to think that Peter would throw her into the cold, unforgiving river. It was like losing a member of my family. I cried and cried. I couldn't get over it, and then my sadness turned to anger. How could he destroy the only toy I had? I became so angry that I decided for the first time ever, to get even with my brother. I did something that I didn't think I'd ever be capable of doing, but I wanted him to feel the same pain I felt.

I formulated a plan, beginning with a large, steel screwdriver. Sneaking down the bank of the river while he was playing with friends, I took the screwdriver and drove holes deep into his boat and watched it sink. With the last of the air bubbles surfacing, as soon as it went under, I wished I could take my anger back and make it float again. Realizing my actions were going to hurt my brother and that now we were both without toys, it. didn't feel like I had gotten even. Revenge was certainly not as sweet as some may have you think.

I didn't dare tell him what I had done, and luckily, when he realized his boat was gone, he blamed it on the Nazis. The Nazis were bitter and harbored hatred for the Americans, so they were easy marks to blame. As many times as I tried, I didn't have the heart to tell him what I had done; that revenge had gotten the best of me. It wore heavily on my heart. Feeling guilty, I swore I would never do anything like that again. It made him feel better to blame it on the Nazis anyhow, and eventually he got over it.

The American soldiers often took us for rides to the pier. We'd soap ourselves up, jump in the river, and bubbles would bounce about the water. We thought it was great to be able to waste soap, something we hadn't had in at least six years. All of a sudden we were frivolously having fun and getting clean simultaneously by jumping into the river. They gave Mama soap for our baths too, which meant we didn't have to use vinegar or weeds any longer, freeing us from emanating tossed-salad scents.

While we romped and frolicked, as children should, something quite the opposite was happening to Papa. Apparently the hunger had taken too much of a hold on him. One morning, while sitting at the breakfast table, he keeled over and fell off the chair, lying unconscious on the floor. Mama called the American medic, who swiftly arrived and placed him on their army truck for transport to the hospital in Koblenz.

It was a difficult journey, as the truck maneuvered around the holes in the road and crossed a bridge that had been badly damaged. It held together with beams, but we could look straight down to the very point where the Mosel and Rhine Rivers intersected. Seemingly without hesitation, they walked with cat-like balance across the narrow boards where it had been torn apart, with Papa laid upon a stretcher. The concentration and fearlessness it took to cross those beams carrying a grown man on a stretcher was indescribable. As they approached the other side, another army truck waited to complete the journey to the hospital.

Upon arrival, the doctor examined Papa, determining that he was in critical condition. The level of iron in his blood had been depleted to virtually nothing, and he was losing ground quickly. He needed a blood transfusion immediately, or else he'd never gain consciousness. However, with the large number of wounded soldiers and civilians, there was no available blood in the hospital. Mama hurried to the American Red Cross and told them that she desperately needed blood for her husband. They told her she'd have to pay twenty-five dollars for that kind of blood, and it had to be in U.S. currency. Mama told them she didn't have U.S. dollars—all she had were German marks. The soldiers accompanying her even offered to give up their occupation money. It was all that they had, but the Red Cross said that wasn't acceptable either.

They told her the blood they had was for the GIs, and it made no difference that her husband was an American. They still wouldn't help her. Indignantly, she told them that if she ever had the good fortune to return to the United States, and the Red Cross came to her for a donation, she would be happy to reciprocate their kindness. Feeling deflated, she hurried back to the hospital and told the doctor that she couldn't find any blood. The doctor however, wasn't ready to give up. He asked the GIs to go to the city with a loudspeaker and ask anyone with Papa's blood type to report to the hospital immediately. Papa's life was a stake.

They took an orderly with them and traveled throughout the entire city trying to get the message out, looking for anyone with a matching blood type who was willing to donate. A German soldier came to the hospital to offer his blood. He looked like he needed it himself; he wasn't healthy looking, but he was willing to offer whatever he could to save someone's life.

A nineteen-year-old girl also came forward to donate. Those two people, who so willing volunteered, literally saved Papa's life. After the transfusion, he immediately looked healthier and began to improve, but they kept him in the hospital for a number of weeks to regain his strength.

When they brought him to the hospital, they never thought that he'd survive, but thankfully, God didn't fail us. While Papa was in the hospital, his rations were sent there, leaving only my brother's and my rations available for the three of us. Mama, not being a citizen, wasn't granted any of her own, so she walked to a neighboring village and found a miller whom she begged for anything he could spare. He generously gave her some flour, a couple of eggs, and a few potatoes. She had to carry the food home for miles, and it took a big toll, as she was skin-and-bones herself. Each day, I wondered if she'd suffer the same fate as Papa.

When desperate for food, I found you'll do anything, and we came up with an ingenious idea. If we clung to the sides of the ferryboat, without the captain finding out, it would pull us across the Mosel River where the water was shallow. In these shallow parts, we could see eels swimming, as clear as day. So we brought our kitchen forks with us, and if we sat very still in the water, we could stab them. We took a sack to put them in and attached it to our waists.

After we filled the sack, we'd grab onto the ferry and take our catch home. Mama skinned and boiled the eels before placing them on the table for dinner. Even though we had no butter or oil to season them with, we thought they tasted marvelous, and it became an occasional treat. But not something we could get away with doing very often.

One afternoon we were out playing by the river—just playing, not trying to hitch a ride on the ferry—when I saw German soldiers walking home with bandages on their legs, arms, and heads. They reminded me of my uncles, and I wondered if anyone would take pity on them. Would they even have a home when they reached their final destinations? Would their families have survived the bombs?

I was filled with questions, but there was really only one that mattered: were they hungry? One of them looked at me and replied, "Aren't we all?" The food from the miller would have kept us going for a while, but I felt so sorry for the three men, I answered. "Well yes, but we have some food, and if you want to come with me, my mother can give you something to eat."

One of them said, "You look like you could use the food yourself. Are you sure your mother has food?"

"Yes, she does. You can come with me, and I'll show you."

I took them with me to the house and ran upstairs and told Mama, "There are three German soldiers downstairs who asked me if we had any food, and I couldn't tell them no, so Mama, do you have anything for them to eat?"

"Oh my gosh, we have so little." She thought about what she had gone through to obtain the food, but nonetheless made me so proud when she offered, "I can't turn anyone away. This is all we have, but we'll share with them. Tell them to come up."

I went down and told them, "Mama's expecting you, so you can go on upstairs."

She asked them to sit down, while she made soup with water, parsley, and potato. She had a small chunk of bread, enough to give each one of them a piece. When they finished the meal, one of the soldiers wanted to convey his gratitude, "Mrs. Adams, this is the first warm meal we've eaten in three years. We appreciate what you have done, but let me ask you something. What you gave us today was all you had, wasn't it?"

"Now don't you worry about that. myself and my children will survive. We always manage to find something." One of the other soldiers approached, "God bless you for what you did here today. May he always bless you and your family, and may you find plentiful food and never go hungry again. You gave us all you had, and God should send his blessings to you for all you have done." He had tears in his eyes as he turned around and walked out. We never saw those three again.

From His Lips to God's Ears

Shortly afterwards, as Mama pondered what possibly could she fix for our next meal, an American soldier stopped by and told us of the UNRRA, the United Nations Relief and Rehabilitation

Administration. Located within the compounds of a German fort in the city of Koblenz, the operation was run by Americans providing relief to victims of war in the form of food, shelter, clothing, fuel—all the necessities. Additionally, and perhaps more important, they would aid refugees and prisoners of war in relocating back to their homelands. The UNRRA could possibly be the vehicle to put the brakes on our endless reign of misery!

The soldier told Mama, "If you can manage to get there, you are eligible to receive the rations."

I hadn't seen her so hopeful in such a long time; she was glowing, "Oh, we'll get there; we'll somehow manage to get there." She packed us children up, and we started the five-mile journey to the city. I thought to myself as we walked, *How nice it would be to have a warm meal.* Even the thought of such a thing made me run my hand up and down my belly. I know Mama and the boys were hungry too, but none of us said a word as we walked past the rubble of what once was a city.

"UNRRA?"

"It's at the top of the hill," said a war-torn older gentleman heading in the same direction, with the same look of excitement we must have had. Rushing to keep up, we arrived at the headquarters that overlooked the city.

Mama met the in-charge officer of the organization, and after they spoke, he gave us our rations, along with two, whole loaves of bread, some canned meat, rice, flour, eggs, and some miscellaneous items. They told us we could return once per month. We had to walk quite a distance, but we would have walked ten times that far. With all of our items in hand, we headed back home.

It was late by the time our house was in sight, but that didn't matter—we weren't going to bed hungry. Mama reflected, "You see, God has already listened to the blessings that soldier had bestowed upon us. Just think: this afternoon we had nothing, and now we have more than we ever dreamed." Straight from a stranger's lips to God's ears, we were provided for, and that became one of the most peaceful night's sleep we had since arriving in Germany. Our tummies didn't talk to us all night, and knowing we would receive more food in another month was truly a Godsend.

Because of overcrowding, it had become nearly impossible to travel by train, not to mention dangerous. Refugees and soldiers were trying to make their way home, but they didn't have the right to travel on the trains if either French or American soldiers ordered them to get off. People frequently clung to the outside of the cars and hung in the stairways, which became the main reason we always walked to Koblenz for our rations. It was much safer to walk than risk being thrown off of the train or separated by the crowds.

Mama did however risk taking the train to visit Papa in the hospital, since she usually went alone and didn't have to worry about us children. Papa was getting healthier each day, but he had a long way to go, and they continued monitoring him for quite sometime.

We had made a few friends in Winningen, but there were those who couldn't accept the fact that the Nazis no longer counted or had power. Even worse, there was extreme jealousy on the parts of some that the GIs showed us kindness. They saw us being transported to school, being taken for rides in the jeeps, and spending time with them on the Mosel River.

One day I walked home from school, and for some reason, Peter wasn't with me. I happened to be alone, and as I walked down the street, I heard two girls a couple of years older than me, taunting me. They were walking behind me calling me names, yelling, "Hitler should have won the war, and you should get out of Germany with the dirty Americans!" They kept it up, and I continued ignoring them, when suddenly one of them yelled, "Let's get her!" I knew I was in trouble, so I turned around just as one of the girls picked up a wine bottle from the ground. She smashed it against the wall and was holding the remains of the broken bottle by the neck as she lunged, pointing the jagged glass directly at my body. As she moved closer, I reached to grab the bottle and it cut into the skin on my hand. There was blood squirting everywhere, but with my good hand, I was able to grab hold of her other arm. I spun her around with every ounce of energy I had. She was still holding the bottle as she went hurling into a row of barbed wire. She started screaming, and at first, I felt sorry for what had happened. The barbed wire punched huge holes into her body. She was lying there on her back, and I knew she was hurting, but my arm was bleeding badly, so I ran for home.

The other girl stood there with her mouth open, and she didn't dare say a word. She was in shock witnessing the outcome of my reaction, but I needed help too, so I didn't look back. When I arrived home, Mama was frantic as she examined fifteen to twenty places where I had been cut deeply. She bandaged my hand as she tried to find out why I was bleeding. I told her as much as I could remember, and she replied, "My God, aren't they ever going to stop? You would think that now that the war is over, they'd just leave us alone."

"Mama, I'm sorry because I hurt her badly too."

Her reaction surprised me, "Marlies, sometimes if it has to be you or someone else that gets hurt, you have to fight back. I can't blame you for what you did; I just hope that this puts a stop to all of the nonsense."

The day's events had tired me out, so I decided to turn in early and get a good night's rest. The next day, I was nervous returning to school, and rightly so, as I was immediately called into the principal's office. My arm was throbbing as he scolded me, "The other girl's parents are going to get the authorities to press charges against you."

"I was defending myself, because she came at me with a broken bottle."

He was very abrupt, "You get out of here. Just go home and get your parents. I want to speak with them."

"My father's in the hospital, but I'll get my mother."

On the way back to school, Mama stopped at GI headquarters, and two of the soldiers decided they'd accompany us back to the school. The principal was surprised to see the Americans walk in. Mama explained, "During that incident, my daughter had been hurt badly as you can see from her bandaged arm. If she hadn't fought back, it could have been much worse. She shouldn't be charged with anything when *she* was attacked."

"Well, the other girl was hurt badly, and she has puncture marks all over her body."

Mama confidently replied, "That girl should have never done what she did. The war is over, and Hitler is done for. My children have been persecuted enough, and I'm not going to let anyone press charges against my daughter."

The principal threateningly erupted, and Mama translated to the Americans what he said to her. The GIs stood up, and again Mama translated what was said in reply to the principal.

"If we hear of one tiny incident concerning Marlies or her family, regarding this matter, then you will not only have to deal with her parents, but you will also have to deal with the United States Army. Now we don't want to hear another word about it."

They took Mama by the arm and walked out of the room, and another word about it was never spoken. I returned to class, and after that incident, no one attempted to attack Peter or me again in any way. It must have gotten out that we had protection from the Americans, or maybe my reputation as a fighter spread as quickly as it had in Rüsselsheim.

For the most part, we didn't venture outside of the small group of friends we had, but for some reason, one morning, a young girl came to our house and extended an invitation for me to attend her birthday party. I had never been to any kind of party before, and the mere idea was exciting. Even though she was part of a Nazi family, Mama gave me permission to attend since they no longer had the power to harm, leaving us no reason to fear them.

Mama found some scraps of material, making me a frilly apron with pockets to wear with my best dress. I was elated to go to my first party, as my brothers were asking, "Marlies, what's a party?"

"I don't know, but I'll let you know all about it when I got home."

Upon my arrival, there were seven or eight other girls in attendance. They welcomed me into the house that smelled of wonderful treats, and we ventured into the living room and started to play, when out of the corner of my eye I saw her mother come out of the kitchen with a huge platter of waffles. She placed them in the center of the beautifully decorated table, and they emitted the most delicious scent. I had vague memories of the sweet aroma, but I never thought

I'd be able to enjoy it again. I could hardly wait to find out if we were going to taste them. While I waited, we played games like pick-up sticks, but in between turns, I focused on those waffles. The young Nazi girl had a plethora of games and toys, which surprised me, as my brothers and I had virtually none—other than Siegfried's ball and one of our tops saved from the fire that Opa made years before.

My only purpose for being at the party soon became to taste one of those waffles. I didn't care about the girls, the games, or the toys, only the waffles mattered. Finally, when I thought I'd explode with anticipation, the lady came out and asked us to come into the dining room for a treat. She told us we could each have two waffles. She served them on paper napkins, and I was amazed. I had never seen paper napkins before. I didn't even know they made such a thing, but again, the Nazis had lots of things I had never seen.

The aroma filled my entire body, as I asked her, "Do your waffles have sugar in them?"

"Of course, you can't make waffles without sugar," she answered.

To eat something with sugar seemed like the greatest thing ever, but now I was thinking of my brothers, who were so excited for me to explain my experience with them. There was no way that I could eat the waffles and not share with them. Gushing with excitement, I wrapped the waffles in my napkin and placed them in my apron pocket. Quickly concealing that excitement as I conjured an excuse to get home. "Excuse me, ma'am, I really don't feel very well; could I please be excused?"

"Well, the party isn't over yet, but if you don't feel well, certainly you can leave."

I smiled at her and then her daughter, "Happy birthday, and thank you for inviting me."

As soon as I made it out the door, I ran as fast as I could, only slowing down to make sure the warm waffles were still in my apron. From a distance, I saw my brothers sitting on the corner waiting for me to return. When I met up with them, Siegfried and Peter immediately asked, "Marlies, please tell us what a party's like?"

Trying to catch my breath, I answered, "It was no big thing; there were games, and everyone was dressed up nice and having fun. But then the lady brought out something you'll never believe."

Peter's eyes filled with anticipation as he asked, "What, what did she bring out?"

"It was a monstrous platter of waffles, real waffles, there must have been a hundred waffles piled high. Nothing in your entire life has smelled so nice."

"Oh, you're lucky, you are so lucky! Real waffles, I wish I could have had one."

I reached into my apron and pulled out the paper napkins, and I teased, "Guess what's inside of this?"

"What, what do you have?"

"Waffles."

Siegfried's eyes were as big as saucers. Peter took one and Siegfried grabbed the other as Peter yelled with his mouth full, "Marlies, you are the best sister in the whole wide world."

"Wait a minute. Peter, you don't understand." As I was trying to explain, the waffles disappeared as quickly as the smile on my face. I stood with my mouth wide open and couldn't even talk. I ran behind the house, sat down, and cried. When I told them about the platter that had at least a hundred waffles, they must have thought I had my fill. I didn't have the heart to tell them that I hadn't had any. For months afterwards, I often smelled the scent of those waffles. I never told my brothers. I simply wondered what it would have been like to taste just one bite.

15

The Americans Prepare to Go Home

An announcement was made that the Americans would be leaving our area and would remain only in the city of Koblenz. They'd maintain the UNRRA, but the French army would occupy Winningen, along with our district. Anticipating the American soldiers leaving was a sad time for my family, leaving a pit in our stomachs. We had become very close to many of the soldiers. They had treated us with kindness and given us a sense of security. I felt safe with them, like at no other time in Germany, and they made me proud to be an American. They always tried to assist us, often giving Mama rides into the city to see Papa so she didn't have to take the train or walk the long distance. They took her as far as the river, waited until she came back, and then they'd bring her home again as well.

Jimmy, one of the GIs, had become close to Peter, in fact he was Peter's closest friend. Peter tried to teach him German, and Jimmy tried to teach Peter English. We learned *hello, good-bye, thank you*, and a few choice profanities, but other than that, we didn't pick up much of the language. Before leaving, Jimmy offered Peter his home address and told him if he ever made it back to America to write to him. He was curious to see if we ever made back home, and he wanted to keep in touch. They talked of the day when they'd continue their friendship on their own terms. After the announcement was made that the Americans were leaving, we cherished every moment with the GIs until their day of departure.

For ourselves, we continued to dream of a time when we'd be able to sit down at the dinner table and eat a real meal together. Even with our new-found rations, we still only received two loaves of bread per month. Mama kept promising how we'd have unlimited bread and food when we returned to America. Those were dreams that I eventually stopped believing in. The American soldiers were pulling out, and along with them went my hopes of ever making dreams come true.

Mama continued to wither away, living on the little bit of food we scavenged. Technically, she still didn't qualify for food rations: she was neither an American nor a German citizen. Plus, it was in her nature to put everyone else's needs before her own. But the consequences of that began to show in every aspect of her being. She had become a tattered woman. On top of that, her shoes were worn to the point that I couldn't determine what was holding them together. She owned one pair of stockings for special occasions and going into town. As a hole or a run started making its way through the material, I'd mend it before it became completely unmanageable. With my tiny crocheting needle and Mama's help, I learned how to make her stockings look nice again, even after all her years of wearing the same pair.

When we weren't doing chores, we tried to spend as much time with the GIs as was permitted, not knowing for sure when they'd be shipped out. Watching the films with them was always a thrill. But one afternoon when Peter and Siegfried went to watch one, I had woken up with a stomachache, so I didn't join them. The pain worsened as the day wore on. Still, Mama asked me to go to the hotel to get my brothers when it was time to come home. Slowly, I made my way over, and as I approached the bottom of the stairs in the lobby, I saw them coming out of the movie room and hollered, "Mama wants you to come home! She is waiting for you to eat supper."

Siegfried was excited about everything, like little kids are, and came down the stairs holding the railing and kicking his feet in the air. He accidentally clipped me in the stomach and I doubled over in pain. I did my best to hobble home, but the last thing on my mind was food.

"Mama, I don't want any supper."

"Marlies, you have to eat something." We were having oatmeal and she wanted me to have something in my stomach, but as soon as I swallowed the first bite, I began vomiting. I tried to go to bed, but couldn't sleep. I repeatedly woke during the night. "Mama, the pain's awful, and I can't sleep."

One of the GIs had given her a bottle of whiskey. "Marlies, you probably have a virus, drink a bit of this, and you should begin to feel better."

I took one sip and vomited again before going back to bed, but because of the pain, I couldn't sleep it off. In the morning, first thing, Mama came into my room, "Good morning Marlies, how are you feeling today?"

The sheer vibrations of her movements were causing the pain in my stomach to worsen. "Mama, please don't walk on the floor or touch me." She felt my forehead, realizing my temperature had risen, intensifying her concerns.

At the Brink Again

There were no doctors in the village, so she asked a GI to have a medic come take a look at me. As he walked into my room, he didn't even perform an examination. With one look, he ordered, "This girl needs to get to the hospital immediately."

"What about the bumpy ride? My daughter's already in so much pain."

He looked around the room and made a decision. Utilizing our stuffed, living room chair as a make-shift stretcher, they carried me down the stairs. I didn't want them to touch me at all; the pain intensified with every step. Somehow, they managed to lift me and the chair into their truck.

Mama hopped in the back and sat on a bench alongside my chair. Once they began moving on the war-torn road, the pain intensified so much I screamed, "Mama, please make them stop. Stop this truck and just let me die!"

"No Marlies, we're not going to stop, just hold on, we'll be there soon. Then everything will be fine."

A short time into the ride, the pain subsided. I couldn't feel anything. I reached over and touched Mama's hand, "They can stop and take me back home, the pain is gone."

Mama knocked on the window, "She says the pain has gone. I think it would be all right to bring her back home."

Just as quickly as the driver stopped the truck, the medic screamed, "Driver, get back in this truck and make tracks, now! Her appendix is ruptured."

The street was covered with ruts, boulders, and many obstacles, yet they were driving so fast I thought we'd be thrown clear out of the truck. When we made it to the damaged bridge, the medic picked me up and carefully carried me across to an awaiting truck on the other side. I didn't know it at the time, but later Mama told me what happened as I was swiftly whisked away. Terrified of the consuming holes in the bridge, Mama, without hesitation, began crawling across on her hands and knees. With fear that nearly paralyzed her, she crawled, in her dress, inch by inch for what she said seemed like a lifetime.

We made it to the other side, long before Mama could. The medic jumped into the truck, and without waiting for her, they rushed me into the hospital on a stretcher, as the GI tried to communicate with the Germans what had happened. They must have understood. I was rushed into an elevator, and a nurse began undressing me. They covered my face with a mask and told me to count to ten. I don't remember getting past three.

When I regained consciousness, I found myself in a ward with many children, and I was secured to the bed. My ankles were tied down; there was one strap across my knees, one across my stomach, one across my chest, and my hands—like my ankles—were tied to the sides of the bed. The nurse noticed I had regained consciousness and told me, "Please don't move; you have to lie there very quietly."

"All right, but I'm very thirsty, could I please have something to drink?"

"The doctor ordered that you only have two teaspoons of tea every hour." My stomach hurt badly, but all I cared about was getting something to drink.

Later that evening, the nurse came in to give me a sponge bath. She put the bowl down and started to untie the straps around my wrists and chest. As soon as she did, she was called over to another section of the room and when she turned her back, I reached for the bowl, tipped it, and drank every last drop of water. Still thirsty, I reached for a flower vase that was near me and just as I was taking the flowers out of the vase, she came back and caught me red-handed. She began yelling, "What on earth are you doing? Where is the bath water I prepared for you?"

"I told you I was thirsty, so I drank it."

"Oh dear lord, you should've never done that."

"My mouth was so dry. I just needed something."

"Well, now you very well may catch pneumonia, and you certainly can't deal with pneumonia on top of the operation you just had."

She was very upset and immediately contacted the doctor regarding my misconduct. He returned with her and explained, "There's nothing I can do about it now; I just hope that we'll be able to prevent pneumonia from setting in."

After she finished my sponge bath, she tied me back up. During the night, I developed a fever and the doctor came in, and shook his head, "This is exactly what I was afraid of."

I indeed had pneumonia with a severe fever that rendered me unconscious. I have no idea how long I was out, but as I slowly opened my eyes, Mama was sitting next to my bed praying.

I croaked her name, startling her. But she was overjoyed to hear me speak, "You've been unconscious for days!" she said, so sweetly. "And I doubted that you'd come out of it." I could see her fear on her face and hear it in her voice. Once again, I felt horrible for hurting her that way.

After performing the operation, the surgeon had placed a tube through an incision into my stomach, to rid any infection that may have developed. The tube should have been removed shortly afterwards. However, they left it in until I regained consciousness— seven days later. As I stirred in my bed, the nurse called the doctor. He immediately told me to lie still and remain quiet. Apparently, the tube had been in too long and needed to be removed immediately. The doctor gave me a piece of hard rubber that looked somewhat like a sponge and put it between my teeth, "Now you bite down on this if you need to."

"Why would I do that?" I asked

"There may be some pain, and we don't want you to bite through your tongue. Now don't worry, you'll be all right … it won't hurt much."

That doctor was a full-fledged liar. As he began removing the tube, I began screaming in agony. I bit down on the hard rubber between my teeth and squeezed the nurse's hand as hard as I could; but the pain was overwhelming, and I passed out again.

Everything was a blur as my eyes gradually opened. I realized that not only was I still in pain, but that I had been moved to another area of the hospital, with my hands again strapped to the bed. As I lay there yelling for the nurse, I could only imagine what it would be like to be home again. The hours passed, and my pleasant thoughts of being home with my family turned to anger. *How could that doctor have lied to me? And why can't I go home?* As time passed, I gave up wondering why … and dozed off.

Some time the next day, the doctor came in to remove the dressing from my stomach. He took hold of the large bandage that covered my wound and quickly tore it off. My eyes slammed shut. I thought an entire layer of skin had been ripped right off my body. Again, the pain was more than I wanted or needed. "I do believe that you're going to get well," he said, "I thought that we had lost you for sure." After examining the incision, he told me, "I'll be back in the morning." The nurse replaced the dressing and left the room.

The doctor's parting words gave me an idea. I decided he wasn't going to hurt me again. So, very slowly, throughout the course of the day, I removed the dressing myself. Once I was finished, I gently laid it on top of the incision and with an all-knowing grin on my face, quietly fell asleep.

That morning, the first thing the doctor did after entering my room was pull down the covers and attempt to remove the bandage. As he lifted it from the wound, he said in a stern voice, "You removed this dressing yourself, didn't you?"

"Yes."

"Promise me you won't do that again. Infection might set in, and you could become just as sick—if not worse than you were before." Again, he examined the wound and told the nurse to apply fresh dressing.

The next morning, as the doctor walked into my room to remove the bandages, he looked at me and said, "You did it again, didn't you?" Needless to say, he became very upset as I lowered my eyes admitting my guilt.

"You promised you wouldn't do this again. How could you break your promise to me, Marlies?"

"The same way you did. You promised me it wouldn't hurt when you removed the tube from my stomach, and you lied. If you can lie to me, then I don't feel bad about lying to you."

A little smirk crossed his face. "You're right. I told you it wouldn't hurt, and I shouldn't have done that. I should have been honest with you, so now I will be. The wound must remain clean. And in order to do that, we have to restrain your hands." That's exactly what they did. The nurse tied my hands to the sides of the bed and left the room.

Later that evening, I saw a little boy roaming around in the hospital. He was quite obviously a burn victim—the word was that he'd been abandoned when he was two and a half year's old. He was brought in with very little chance of survival, and his mother never came back to retrieve him. No one knows if she intentionally left him there to die or if she was killed during the war. The little guy tugged at the nurses' heartstrings, and they in turn adopted him as their own. Once he recuperated, he eagerly helped them with little chores they needed done.

He was around four years old when I met him, and I easily talked him into untying my hands. He was happy to help me, and during the night, I was once again able to undress my incision. The next day, when the doctor came in, he was infuriated. "I told you that you cannot continue doing this. You must leave the dressing alone. Why weren't your hands tied?"

"They were; but I found a way to get loose."

The doctor stormed out, ordering the nurses to make sure my hands remained tied until the following morning. They did their job, and double-checked to make sure I was still tied to the bed later in the day. But luckily, I saw the little boy again, and he untied one of my hands, and that was all I needed to undress my wound. The following day when they checked my incision, the same thing happened again and no one could figure out how I was getting loose. I continued receiving help from the little boy each day, and eventually the doctor gave up on it.

The Most Precious Gifts

While I was in the hospital, the GIs came to visit me. They often came by and brought me small pieces of hard candy or chocolate. They told me they were officially no longer stationed in Winningen, but they were still in Koblenz and they'd visit as often as possible.

Mama was usually there to translate for me, and one day, two of the GIs came by and brought me two precious gifts. One of them handed me a violin. "I want you to learn how to play this violin, and someday in America, when you are playing in one of the great orchestras, I will come to see you, and I'll know that I was instrumental in your becoming a great artist."

I looked at the violin and wondered if I could ever learn to play such a beautiful instrument. I had never had any interest in the violin, though I'd always wanted to play the piano. But there was no way I'd ever own a piano, so I accepted the gift as a wonderful gesture. He smiled and gave me a kiss on the cheek.

The other GI handed me a beautiful, gold ring with a blue semi-precious stone. It was blue topaz, and it was the most beautiful ring I had ever seen. When he placed it on my finger, it easily fell off. Mama promised she'd tie a string around the band, until I grew into it. I gave him a big hug and kiss, and thanked him for the beautiful present, placing my hand on top of my blanket to show off. I felt so wealthy lying there with such a gorgeous ring on my finger. It gave me courage and enthusiasm to get well and grow up, so I could wear my new ring properly. These were the two most precious gifts I had ever been given.

Many times the GIs visited me, and yet the nurses never understood why I was so important to the American soldiers. I told them it was probably because I was a child and reminded them of their own families that they'd left behind. Many of them had children of their own, and some had little sisters that I reminded them of. It was just nice to have become important to someone. We were no longer being mistreated, and that was a good feeling, a secure feeling. I loved the GIs. They made such a difference in my life—even though I didn't understand a single word they spoke!

I was in the hospital for about six weeks, before I recovered from the pneumonia and was well enough to be released. While I was there, another young girl about six years old had also undergone an appendix operation. The day after her surgery, the girl was up in her bed jumping around. With each bounce, she attempted to reach higher. The doctors and nurses were concerned, warning her of the dangers of not staying still. She had been placed in a crib with her hands and feet tied to the sides, but somehow, she was able to untie the restraints with her teeth! As soon as she was loose, she continued with her antics. I told her she shouldn't do it, for fear of what might happen to her, but she laughed, "I don't feel much pain, and I'm happy to be better again."

Just like me, she simply wouldn't listen. She continued jumping up and down, up and down. The next morning, her crib was empty. I didn't see her anywhere in the unit, so I asked if she'd been released. The nurse told me that she hadn't gone home. She died during the night from complications. The repeated jumping tore her insides, and the internal bleeding was too far gone. There was nothing the doctors could do.

I was filled with sadness when I heard she passed. She had made it through the entire war, only to die from just being a child. She didn't have a ruptured appendix like I did, she didn't have pneumonia like I did, and yet I survived and she didn't. Her mother wept bitter tears, while my mother didn't have to. She was a nice little girl, a good companion to me, making me laugh many times during our hospital stay. I was definitely going to miss that sweet, funny little girl.

The day had come for me to go home, so I said goodbye to the friends I'd made and eagerly headed out the door. When I arrived home, I was delighted to see Papa, who had returned home from the hospital after more than eight weeks himself. It seemed that Papa and I had a habit of getting sick together, and now Mama again had two sick people to tend to. He was still under the weather, and to top it off, he was home where food was still scarce. Being so thin and still weak from the operation, my doctor was worried about me too. He told Mama I would need a lot of milk, eggs, liver, and scads of other items to get me back on my feet. This added to Mama's worries—those products were luxuries and mostly unavailable to us.

Living on potato soup, oatmeal, and the few vegetables that Mama could gather, I often wondered what it would be like to gulp down a big glass of fresh milk or to taste those waffles that I could still smell from time to time. Pieces of meat with gravy or Oma's homemade kuchen were fantasies to me. Sometimes dreams kept us going—and sometimes, they actually came true. Simply being together again was a dream come true and the best remedy any doctor could have prescribed, for Papa and I continued to improve.

We were still waiting to get word from the American government regarding our return to the States, and it was taking a considerable amount of time. The FBI was thoroughly checking on us to make sure we had no connection to the Nazi party, and it seemed like we were never going to get back to America. Finally though, Mama was contacted and asked to go to the consulate in Koblenz regarding her papers. They had some questions that needed answering at the consulate, which was by that time occupied by the French. It was reminiscent of shades of the Gestapo, but we hoped not. How much more could our poor, beleaguered mother take?

Since it was a long walk to the UNRRA, she decided to go to a satellite office just outside of Winningen. As she entered the building, large lines had already formed by people trying to obtain rations. She realized it was going to take longer than expected. She thought she'd be in line forever, when she saw an American soldier standing in a corner near a small window. She decided to approach him and ask if he could expedite her visit. He turned his head, and she saw the entire side of his face was bruised. He wouldn't answer her questions, more or less ignoring her, but out of the corner of his eye, he made eye contact and snuck a small piece of paper into her hand before walking away.

Puzzled, Mama returned to the long line. While mixed amongst the others, she peered in his direction to see two French soldiers grab him by the arm and take him behind closed doors. She looked around to make sure no one was watching as she discretely read his words, "Please get help. Contact the American authorities immediately. There are four of us being held prisoner." Mama looked up from the paper, scanned the room, and left her place in line. She had decided that the best thing for her to do was to go to the American consulate at the UNRRA.

She walked to the fort as fast as her legs could carry her and gave the information to an American Officer named Major Faucett. He told her he'd look into it immediately, and although it didn't sound very optimistic, they'd find out what is going on. Two or three weeks later, when we went to the UNRRA for our rations, Major Faucett told Mama that he had indeed sent his men into French headquarters and they determined that there were actually six men being held against their will and tortured! The French were holding them as prisoners, trying to get them to join the Foreign Legion, while portraying them as deserters of the United States Army. In fact, many of our men who disappeared were reported as deserters. The question became how many were actually being held prisoner.

Those atrocities were part of war; things that don't come out in history books— things that few know about, but things that indeed happened. Mama was thankful to have had the opportunity to help the young men. The Americans had fought in Germany, and they were instrumental in ending the war, and yet the sad reality was sometimes their treatment—like everyone's—was less than desirable.

Every Blessing Mixed

Four months later, it seemed as though our prayers were answered when we received word that we were cleared by the American FBI to return home. To the United States! We were told to contact the American authorities in Frankfurt with regards to returning home. We did so immediately and in turn, they told us to go to Koblenz and report to the American authorities. It was a long, drawn out, yet extremely joyous occasion for us.

Mama said, "Maybe now that the war has truly come to an end, my children will return to America and a normal way of life." The downside was the arrangements were made quickly, and we suddenly had to leave Winningen for Bremen, where we spent two weeks in a camp. That meant we wouldn't have the opportunity for one last visit with Oma and to personally say our good-bye to the rest of our family.

We were heartbroken to think we might never see them again. We sent letters explaining our situation and also as a way to say our goodbyes, telling them we loved each of them immensely. We still had no idea of whether or not most of my uncles had returned home. The last we knew, Uncle Joseph was badly wounded and being held in a Russian hospital. Uncle Peter had been wounded and was being held prisoner in England. Uncles Bernard and Nicholas were also both prisoners in Russia. Uncle Matthew happened upon a group of Russian soldiers who were badly wounded in a field and barely alive. He was ordered to shoot the men by a Nazi officer, but he refused. Telling the Nazi he'd transport the men back to the hospitals, but would not shoot a man who couldn't shoot back, the young Nazi screamed, "This is a direct command, and I order you to shoot them!"

Again, he refused, "I won't shoot them."

"Be prepared, your stripes will be gone, and you'll be court-marshaled as soon as we return to Germany."

Uncle Matthew stood firm, "I'll take my chances," as the Nazi roughly ripped the stripes off his shirt.

The Nazi spun around with his revolver and tried to unload his weapon on the Russians who were lying on the ground. His gun misfired, and the men weren't harmed, so the remaining German soldiers agreed to pick them up and return them to the hospitals. However, while en route, the German platoon was taken captive and brought to a Russian prison camp.

The following day, they were pushed single file into an arena where they sat and watched in horror as German officers were sent alive through a saw. Because the Nazi officer had torn the stripes off of his arms, Uncle Matthew's life was spared. For whatever reason, they preferred only to butcher German officers, and because he had acted humanely, his life in turn was spared. For a short while, he was held in a prison camp, but soon released. He was the first to return home to Oma, that's how we learned of his fate, through the letters we continued to receive from her.

Knowing that Mama's brothers were held prisoners made it hard for her to leave Germany. She knew they were in prison camps somewhere, and wondered if they'd survive. Not being able to say good-bye to her dear, sweet family was difficult, but time would not permit. I was going on twelve years old; the last time I had seen them, I was nine. They had made a big part of my life ever so special, and not returning to the farm was disheartening. It was a lovely place, brimming with my beloved animals and all the love, attention, kindness, and gentleness that I had ever received. For my immediate family, however, leaving Germany was in the forefront of our minds. And we were not far from reaching our goal.

16
The Ends and the Means

Papa made the trip to Frankfurt, making the arrangements for us to enroll in camp in Bremen. The doctor told him that he wasn't well enough to make the trip up the Rhine, much less across the sea, but he wouldn't hear of it, "My family has waited too long to return to the United States, and I'm not going to miss the opportunity to relieve the suffering they've endured all of these years." The trip to Frankfurt, however, certainly took a toll. Having exerted most of his strength, he was once again needing Mama to care for him.

Since Papa couldn't make the trip to Koblenz, Mama took us with her, so we wouldn't bother him. We had been given small American flags to wear on our clothing, which indicated our citizenship and enabled us to board the train. We were told we had a compartment reserved for us, so we wouldn't have to stand on the platform or hang onto the side of the cars as they were moving.

We entered our compartment, only to find a few French soldiers had taken it over. They were nothing like the Americans. They were crude and abusive to German people, filled with hatred for everyone, including kids. There were times when small children stood starving in the streets, and French soldiers took fresh, warm bread, urinated on it, and threw it at the children exclaiming, "Eat this!" The French were bitter after Germany occupied their country, and they took it out on all of us. There may have been some decent French soldiers, but we certainly never encountered any.

In fact, another French soldier entered our compartment, and in very broken German ordered us to get out. Mama rationally explained to him that we were American citizens and the compartment had been assigned to us. Then as if she hadn't said a word, he muttered, "If you don't get out, I'll shoot you." Mama tried to re-explained our situation, telling him we had nowhere else to stand. He had clearly been drinking and easily became irate; he pulled out his revolver. Unfortunately for him, he had no idea that he had chosen the wrong family to terrorize.

Mama calmly responded, "After all we've been through, a gun no longer frightens us. If you're going to shoot us, do it now. And please shoot my children first, so I know where they are and that they're taken care of." Peter and I looked at each other, and it dawned on me how far we had come. We've fought the Nazis, survived the bombings, the starvation, and everything else that had happened to us. There was no way some stupid, drunken, French soldier was going to stand there and shoot us. At least not as long as I could breathe.

Without hesitation, I jumped on him, Peter jumped on him, and Siegfried—who was just a little guy—jumped on him and starting biting him on the leg! I was scratching his face; Peter was pummeling his back with his fists; and the soldier was trying to shake us off, when he screamed, "Stop it! Stop!" Panting heavily, and extremely surprised, he shook us off and yelled at Mama, while looking down at the three of us, "I can't believe the courage of your children. I guess they earned the right to be here, I'm done bothering you." The soldier offered up his seat and walked out.

We were fighting with all of our might to save ourselves. But especially to save Mama. After all, he was threatening to kill her, and we needed her. The soldier stayed outside our compartment the entire trip, and when we arrived in Koblenz, he actually helped escort us off the train. Mama thanked him, and that was the last we ever saw of him and the last we ever saw of Koblenz.

We prepared to leave for Bremen. While waiting for our departure date, we tied up loose ends, including relationships with good friends like Mrs. Krist, the woman who lived next door. She had been such a big help to Mama that I felt sad leaving her alone. She was a lovely lady, but devastated since not hearing from her husband in over three years. She could only imagine his fate, while praying daily for his safe return. Many times while visiting, her eyes filled with tears, "I just can't believe my husband is dead." But from the look on her face, I think she knew the answer, deep within her heart.

Dreams and Visions

One day before we left, Peter told Mama, "Last night I had a dream, and Mr. Krist told me he was coming home within the week. I think I should tell his wife."

"Peter, you've never even met Mr. Krist. You couldn't have had a dream about him."

Peter persisted that he had. After all, he had seen pictures of him, and in his dream, the man told Peter he was Mr. Krist and that he'd be home. Determined to ease her pain, he told Mrs. Krist about the dream. She hugged him and said, "You are such a good boy, and I know you want to try to make me feel better." Unfortunately, it only added to her sorrow and was soon forgotten.

Exactly one week later Peter, Siegfried, and I were down at the Mosel River playing when Peter stopped and yelled, "Marlies, there's Mr. Krist! There's the man I saw in my dream!" I turned around and saw three war-torn, tattered soldiers walking toward us. The man was limping and his leg was bandaged. He had long hair and a beard and looked nothing like the man I had seen in pictures. "That can't be him."

Peter assured me, "That's the man I saw. I'm going to talk to him."

"No, Peter, don't."

But he ran up the hill and stopped the soldier and asked, "Are you Mr. Krist?"

Puzzled, the soldier replied, "Yes I am, but do I know you?"

"No, but I've seen you in a dream, and I told your wife that you were coming home."

Mr. Krist smiled and rubbed Peter's head and said, "You told my wife that I was coming home?"

"Yes I did, and you look just like the soldier I saw in my dream."

Peter ran ahead of Mr. Krist, heading straight for their house. He was pounding on the door, yelling, "Mrs. Krist, he's home! I told you your husband was coming home."

She opened the door and looked at Peter. She then looked at the man coming down the street and sadly told him, "That isn't my husband."

Peter argued, "He told me his name was Mr. Krist."

She stared intensely at the man as he came closer, "Oh dear God, that is my husband! I would have never recognized him." She ran as fast as she could and they hugged, the way you'd hug someone that you never thought you'd see again. She was elated, with tears of joy streaming down her face. She picked Peter up and hugged him tightly. "Thank you, Peter, for giving me the courage to remember that there was hope somewhere in this world."

I didn't understand how Peter could have had such a vivid dream of someone that he had never seen before, and then I remembered the dream that Mama had when she so vividly saw me writing the letters with the horrible lice and the sore over my eye. I started believing in dreams. I really believed that they could come true, and that some were truly visions.

Finding Out the Beginning and the End

Ironically, a few days before our departure for Bremen, we heard from Mrs. Adams, the woman who cared for me when I was struck in the head by Joseph in Holtztum. Not believing that my parents were dead, she was finally able to contact Oma by mail asking if there was any way she could reach Papa. She had important information she wanted to share, but was having a terrible time locating him.

Oma followed through, giving her our address, and Mrs. Adams wrote to Papa telling him the reason she wouldn't help me was that she was desperately afraid of Aunt Lena. She wrote that "Many people in our village had disappeared due to statements she reported and my entire family feared what could happen to us." Her conscience was eating away at her, and she needed forgiveness for not helping me, merely a defenseless child. She told him she prayed for me and felt horrible for what I had been through, but she couldn't have helped any more than she did.

Mrs. Adams turned out to be the daughter-in-law of one of Papa's uncles, making her Papa's cousin through marriage. She wanted to tell us that Aunt Lena was alone. Her son lost his arm in the war, and upon returning home, found out his mother had been a Nazi informer. He wanted nothing to do with her, proclaiming he would never forgive her. She hadn't seen him since.

Her husband was walking across a bridge just as the Americans crossed into their village, and the bridge was shelled. Uncle Henry was killed, if not from a stray bullet, then surely from impact as his body lay in ruins beneath. With his death, she was rightfully left completely alone. Having been an informer, she no longer received favors or rations, forcing her to walk door-to-door begging for food. With long memories, the villagers hadn't forgotten and returned the favor by slamming their doors, and turning their backs on her. More important than Aunt Lena's perils, Mrs. Adams wanted to let us know the details of Joseph's attack on me.

She explained that I was hit in the head with a club, and that I probably didn't remember exactly what occurred. With torn emotions, not knowing whether he could continue reading, Papa took a deep breath and read on. She told how the miller entered the barn to pick up the grain, and found me lying unconscious with my clothes torn off. Joseph had molested me and left my cold, naked body in a bloody pool on the filth covered barn floor. I probably would have died before anyone noticed or cared that I was missing, if not for fate and the stranger who simply stopped by to do his job.

Her letter continued to say that the miller immediately came to my rescue before turning Joseph over to the authorities, who in turn arrested him. Having molested a helpless child, he was taken to prison where there was no sympathy for child molesters, no plan for rehabilitation, only just-desserts in the form of his own execution. She wanted to make sure that we knew that Joseph had been punished for the crimes he committed, and she and the doctor had taken care of me the best they could. It all began to make sense to my mother and father, and I finally understood why the pain was excruciating, why I continued bleeding, and why I kept fading in and out of consciousness.

My father couldn't hold a grudge against Mrs. Adams for not following the dictates of her conscience, because he understood her fear of the backlash that Aunt Lena could and surely would have inflicted upon her. Her guilt was of great significance in the end; otherwise, he would have never learned the fate of the despicable child molester and the sick woman who paved his way.

Papa read me a portion of the letter, and when I heard what happened to Aunt Lena, a slight smile came across my face showing my approval. I felt that she deserved everything she had gotten, and now with nothing left, she'd been reduced to begging for food from the very people whom she'd tormented and harmed year-upon-year. She was alone. I wondered what would happen to the old wretch, but feeling completely justified with my rancor, truthfully, I didn't care.

More Good News

As the number of days we had left in Germany were dwindling, it always made Mama smile when she'd receive any information from anyone in her family and luckily, prior to leaving, we received a letter from Aunt Mary. She was pleased to report that her husband had returned. At the end of the war, he was released from prison camp. She was also happy to tell us she was expecting another child. Carly, Marlies, and Yosefa would have another baby in their home. We were so happy for Aunt Mary! They were doing well in Kell, where the Americans still occupied the area. There were still so many uncertainties, but each letter helped to ease Mama's mind.

Refugees Encamped

It was time for us to leave Winningen. We said our good-byes and began our journey by train to the camp in Bremerhaven, where we'd be checked for illness and fed properly, so we could withstand the trip. Mama made arrangements to send the sewing machine she borrowed from Aunt Hanna back to Oma's farm, and our trunks were placed on the train.

Our future was very uncertain. We'd head across an ocean to a land I had little memory of, a land that was strange to me. I didn't know if I'd like it or if the people would like me. The future was frightening, but the past was even more frightening. I tried to remain optimistic, doubting that there could be anything worse than what I had already endured.

Mama was thrilled to think that possibly all of our suffering and worries might be over. It was what she longed for. As sad as she was to leave her family, she knew that it was something she had to do. If nothing else, her children had a right to be happy and free of oppression. She was looking forward to the trip, but not looking forward to crossing the ocean again. She was terrified of the deep water. Nonetheless, we were on our way.

As we traveled through Germany by train, we saw how truly devastated the country was. Everywhere we looked, there was destruction; not a single city, town, or village had been completely spared. The streets were rubble, the homes destroyed as if a huge whirlwind had gone through and torn everything to shreds. An impoverished, hunger-stricken, no-place-to-go-and-no-job look was on most of the faces we saw. No one knew what the future was going to hold. That's what war looked like.

When we arrived at camp, we saw a multitude of different types of people, many of which had been released from concentration camps. We began to realize the depths of the atrocities that had taken place, atrocities far beyond even what we had lived through. We heard of the horrible deaths and suffering that people in the concentration camps had endured. It was heart wrenching, listening to the stories. We had heard of the camps previously, but everyone was terrified to ask anything about them. Now, in Bremerhaven, people were openly talking.

We spoke to many people who survived the camps, and although we had previously heard that German people never died in concentration camps, that was just plain false. Many German people's lives were destroyed. It didn't matter who you were—Russian, German, Gypsy, Polish, Jewish, or whomever—if you went against Hitler in any way, you went to the camp; and most never got out.

We met a beautiful young girl. She was only sixteen when she showed Mama a tattoo with numbers, placed on her arm. She also had visible marks on her wrists and ankles from the shackles that had held her, and worst of all, she had lost her entire family; she had no one left to claim as her own. She was making the trip because the Americans had located a distant relative in the United States who was sponsoring her to go and stay with them, since she had no other living relatives in Germany.

There was also a young priest, who told how he'd been taken outside with other priests and stripped naked. They were forced to climb on top of each other until they formed a pyramid, resembling a Christmas tree. They were sprayed with water hoses and left literally to freeze to death. Was it some sort of sick entertainment for the camp? We couldn't fathom the sickening behavior.

He was one of the fortunate who hadn't been put onto the pyramid, and that's why he survived. He also told us how six nuns were brought into an arena and placed on a platform that was surrounded with wire fencing. The nuns were stripped naked and visibly ashamed as they huddled into a circle. They were told to dance, but they refused. The Nazis however, had their way of getting them to conform. They began heating the platform the nuns stood upon. As their feet burned, their movements resembled dancing, before they began climbing the fence for sanctuary. The fence, also heated, left them to burn to death in both mental and physical agony.

A Jewish man worked in the crematorium and was responsible for ridding the camp of dead bodies. Unbeknownst to him, his responsibility was to throw the deceased into the ovens for disposal, and after a certain number of months, he'd be thrown in himself.

That prevented any one person from keeping track of exactly how many people were cremated in the ovens. He happened to be the last person working the crematorium before the Americans came and released them from the camps. He was spared an unspeakable death and forever grateful.

Hearing those and other stories left us full of anguish. We'd known something horrible must have been happening, and yet we were all terrified to inquire. Mama knew how fortunate we had been, watching every word we spoke and obeying every command we were given, and yet we remained only one step away from being one of those families loaded onto trains that headed toward death. They were waiting for us to make just one mistake, but we didn't, and we thanked God for protecting us from that horrible fate.

The Saddest News Yet

At the end of the second week, just prior to boarding the train for Bremerhaven where we'd then board a ship named the *Ernie Pyle* to America, Mama gathered us together with tears in her eyes and she said, "Wait, I have some news to tell you."

I asked her, "What Mama, what do you want to tell us, what bad news could you possibly have to tell us now?" The words she uttered would become burned into my memory.

"I won't be going with you. There is something wrong with my papers, and they won't let me go along with you on this trip."

It felt like someone punched me in the stomach and pulled the world out from beneath me. As I was sinking into a deep black hole, I turned to her, "If you can't go with us, then I'm not going either."

"Yes, you children must go. This is your only opportunity. If you stay here, we may starve to death. You're all so thin now. You have to obey and go. My papers will be straightened out, and I might just be on the next ship behind you. It'll only take a short while to fix the misunderstanding, and I'll be back with you before you know it."

Mama and Papa knew there was something wrong with her papers, but they had decided not to tell us.

I cried, "Mama, what could possibly be the problem with your papers?"

The American government is paying for your trip, but they won't pay for mine. So we need to find another way."

"But we already have tickets. We've carried them with us for seven years."

"I'm afraid those tickets are no longer valid, the *Bremen*, the ship we traveled here on caught fire and was scrapped long ago."

"But, you're our mother! Can't they just understand and let you come with us!"

"No, they don't understand, and they won't permit me to leave. They told your father that once he arrives in the United States, he can sponsor me and pay for my trip, but he has to do it from there. He cannot do it from here."

"Mama, we'll all wait—until we write someone in the United States and have *them* sponsor you!"

"No, Marlies, it's too late; the wheels have been set in motion, and you're scheduled to go, and that is what you're going to do. You have to board this train today. There's no time to wait. The American army is trying to help me, and for all we know, my papers could be coming immediately, and I'll be on another ship right behind you. You never know, maybe my ship will be fast enough that I might arrive before you do!"

So focused on what she had just uttered, I stood in a daze, as she begged, "I need to be able to count on you to take care of your father and brothers. I need you to play the mother for me."

I couldn't refuse her, but I just didn't know how to leave her. I swore to myself when I saw her at Aunt Lena's that I would never let her get out of my sight again. I would never be without her again. Yet here I stood at this train station about to leave her one more time. It was breaking my heart. After all we had been through …We were so close to freedom and happiness … and yet I was supposed to leave her standing there alone.

Siegfried cried, "I'm not leaving without you! I'm not going anywhere without you!" He clung to her so tightly as he hugged her.

He continued crying desperately. Peter was of course heartbroken too, telling her that we simply couldn't leave her.

"Mama, we just can't."

"Peter, you have to be strong and obey." Mama looked at her devastated children and told Siegfried, "If you get on that train and travel to America, you'll be able to go into a store, buy a whole loaf of bread, sit down, and eat every single bit of it. You can have as much bread as you wish."

I asked, "Mama, how long have you known about this?"

"Since we first arrived at camp. We were notified that I wouldn't be traveling with you, but I couldn't tell you, knowing you'd find a way to keep me near you. Your father and I have discussed it, and we know this is the only chance we have. We won't let the opportunity pass us by. I have written to Oma, and they've invited me to go there and stay until I'm allowed to leave. I won't be alone; I'll be with family. And I need you children to understand. This is all we can do, and we must abide by their wishes."

After Mama told us that this was our only chance, I knew we couldn't find another way. Siegfried didn't take it too hard. He was still very young, and when he found out he could have an entire loaf of bread to himself, he turned around and said, "Bye Mama," and jumped on the train. Papa, however, stood with the greatest sadness I've ever seen.

As I looked at Mama, my fears surfaced. *What will happen to us now? What's going to happen to me? Am I going into another hell?* After all, life without Mama was like living in hell.

But, I had made her a promise, and I had to try to be optimistic. This time, at least, I was fortunate not to be alone. I had Papa and my brothers. I'd survive. But how would Mama? She looked so thin, frail, tired, and sick. I thought to myself, *What if I never see her again? Oh Lord, God, please don't let that happen.*

As thoughts raced through my mind, I gave her a big hug, while crying. I just knew that my heart was going to break, but Mama assured me, "Don't worry, going to America is like going to heaven. They have food, and people are kind and friendly. It's a beautiful country! There will be no more bombings, no more hunger, and no more fear. We'll have a new beginning, so please don't be afraid."

She made me promise her again that I'd take care of everyone. I made that promise and with one more hug, I got onto the train with Siegfried.

Peter was still standing there crying. I don't know what he said to Mama, or she to him, but I could see huge tears running down his face as they embraced. Reluctantly, Peter joined Siegfried and me on the train, and it was Papa's turn to say good-bye.

Until that moment, I had never seen him cry, and instantly I realized how deeply he was hurting. It looked as if he couldn't bring himself to leave his sweetheart standing there alone and I was praying that he wouldn't. But the window on the train was opened, and I overheard him say, "We were in this same position seven years ago, and we decided that if you had to stay, that we'd all stay together. But this time is different. The children are older, each one of us is slowly perishing, and we must go." Consumed with unbearable sadness and dismay, he didn't know how to say good-bye, he just held her tightly, before turning to board the train.

As we awaited our departure, none of us spoke a word. We didn't know what to do or what would become of us, as we each sat quietly with our own sorrow. As the train began rolling down the tracks, we could see Mama standing alone on the platform.

With my hands and face pressed against the window, I watched her until she was nothing more than a tiny speck. I can't remember crying as many tears or as hard as I did the day I left her alone at that train station. I was sure my heart was broken, as I helplessly and convulsively wept, heading for the harbor and a voyage filled with uncertainty.

I tried to make sense of why things had evolved as they had. After all, our first voyage was filled with wonderment and joy. I was the queen of the *Bremen* without a care in the world, and now the *Bremen* didn't even exist. Papa told me that an employee had torched her insides, leaving her in the harbor, good for nothing but scrap metal, never to sail again. All that we had left were some old photos and memories of days long gone. Perhaps if the *Bremen* continued to float with all her glory, Mama's ticket would have been honored, and she would have been by my side.

Separated Again, on the Troop Ship Ernie Pyle

My thoughts were interrupted by the shrill of the brakes slowing the train. We pulled up to the station, and it was only a matter of time before we boarded the ship for America. As soon as we got on, women were separated from the men, and we were taken to get vaccinations. We stood in long lines waiting our turn, and when I reached the front of the line, I could see a male doctor giving the vaccines. I remember him taking the needle, injecting the serum into the woman in front of me, and reusing the same needle on my arm. I had asked him to use a new needle, yet he grabbed my arm abruptly, stuck the needle in, and called for the next person in line. We were pushed through with as little dignity as cattle receive when they're prodded along to slaughter.

Afterwards, we were gathered in an area to receive instructions for what would happen next. While we stood there, not a word was whispered. The silence was frightening as we waited for directions. After what seemed like eternity, a man came forward explaining that the ship we would board was a troop ship called the *Ernie Pyle*.

"This ship traditionally had no accommodations upon it for women and men to share the same quarters, so again you'll be separated. The only time there will be contact between the two will be in the eating facilities or up on deck. Other than these two areas, there will be no contact between men and women throughout this trip. We expect everyone to abide by these rules, and we thank you for doing so."

That was especially difficult for me to endure because it meant that not only did I have to leave my mother, but I had to travel across the ocean without my father or my brothers. Fear started filling my insides all over again. Memories of the last time I went alone were all I could think of. The last time it took an entire year before I saw anyone who cared about me. *Could that happen again; would that happen again?* I was extremely frightened. In fact I felt paralyzed with fear as we were herded down below into a huge, dimly lit room stacked with bunk beds, three-high. People started milling about, claiming their space.

Since I had been separated from the others, Papa gave me a little suitcase of my own to carry my clothes and belongings in. As I searched for a place to call my own, I found a spot in the back corner. I climbed to the top bed with my suitcase, and that's where I lay, once again crying until my eyes were burning and surely bloodshot.

Just a couple of minutes passed when two young girls approached me. They must have been fifteen or sixteen years old, and they asked me if they could have the two upper bunks. It really didn't matter much to me which bed I had, so I agreed and climbed down to the bottom as they each climbed up and settled into their temporary quarters.

At last, an announcement was made that we'd begin embarking on our journey. Our first stop was a port in France, where we picked up more passengers. As we docked in in the French harbor, a major commotion was brewing. A woman had somehow managed to smuggle her little dog on board. Since the woman was sponsored by someone in America, she was one of the lucky few who actually had a cabin. Unfortunately, there was another woman sharing the room, and she discovered the dog and reported her.

The captain told everyone that there were no animals allowed on board and she was subsequently told that she'd have to let the dog go when we arrived in France. The woman began screaming and crying. She begged them not take her dog; it was the only living companion that she had left. Without her little dog, she had nothing, and no one.

Her entire family had been killed in the war. Her children, her husband, her parents, and all of her brothers and sisters were gone. They had all fallen victim to the war, yet she and her pet survived. "My little dog is such a good animal! He won't give anyone any trouble, please, please don't take my dog!"

With a total lack of compassion, they took him by the leash anyway and started walking him down the gangplank. The woman became hysterical; a nurse had to care for her the rest of her voyage.

I remember the woman's sadness as she pleaded to keep her pet, but no one heard her desperate pleas, and no one cared.

It was nearly time for our departure from France. All of the people had boarded, and I was consumed with a strange feeling as I felt the winds increasing, anticipating that it was going to be a difficult voyage. While I was in my sleeping quarters, someone came down inquiring if we'd like to go to the cafeteria. I went up, and I was elated to see that Papa and my brothers were there as well. Just seeing them for that short time meant the world to me. Papa told me not to worry, he'd see me at meal times and up on deck, and I'd always know that he was there with me on the same ship. I felt comforted as I hugged them all before going back down to my quarters.

Just as I had anticipated, a storm brewed during the night. The ship was tossed around, and it was like nothing I had ever experienced. The waves were so high that our ship seemed like nothing more than a cork in the water. Sometimes it stood up straight one way and just as quickly slammed back down in the other direction. One minute we'd feel the instant pain of our heads slamming into one end of the bunk, and the next minute we'd hang on tightly so we didn't slip off the other end. It was horribly frightening, and seasickness set in quickly—as if things weren't bad enough. If I wasn't consciously hanging on for dear life, I was undoubtedly going to be tossed out of my bunk and probably injured. I was exhausted, yet sleep had become an impossibility.

The girl in the bunk above me also became seasick. She leaned over the side of her bed and vomited. It hit the floor and just as quickly splashed back up onto my bunk. The odor made me nauseous, so I got up and struggled to make it into the hallway. I sat on a little step, about four or five inches tall where the doors closed. That's where I sat, holding on, thinking that my stomach was going to come out of my throat.

As I sat there, I realized that my arm had become extremely painful where I was given my vaccination. It had become so swollen that I couldn't even lift it, but at that moment, what I was really cared about was getting something to drink. I was suddenly very thirsty, feeling as though I had dust in my throat; I was desperate to find water. I headed down the hallway where I eventually found a sink. My eyes lit with excitement and for a moment, I forgot about my arm.

I ran over to the sink and placed my head under the faucet. I took one big gulp before realizing that the sink didn't have fresh water coming out. I didn't know that it was it was salt water used for cleaning the decks and the floors in the rooms. The taste of the water was sickening, like eating rotten eggs with a horrible stench. It made me vomit immediately before stumbling back to my little step.

While sitting there, a woman appeared in the hallway. She told me she was a nurse and asked, "Why on earth are you sitting out here? You should be in bed."

"I can't go back to bed; someone vomited, and I can't possibly stay there." She went to check it out and found that many people down below were sick. People were indeed vomiting everywhere she looked. "I agree, you can't stay there, but I'll try to find you some clean sheets and somewhere else to sleep. Where's your mother?"

"I'm here alone, I don't have anyone with me. My father and brothers are somewhere on the ship, but I don't know where, and I can't get in touch with them."

The nurse took hold of my hand to bring me with her, and she noticed I felt warm with fever. "You're burning up, what's wrong with you?"

"I don't know, but my arm hurts."

She pulled my sleeve up and saw how badly swollen it had become. It was filled with infection. I told her how the doctor had given me a vaccination with the same needle he had used on other people. She quickly took me to medical.

The doctor came over and looked at my arm and agreed that I had an infection. He told me they may need to lance my arm, and I wouldn't be permitted to leave medical until they lowered my temperature. Before it subsided, it had gotten very high, and I was falling in and out of consciousness. When I came to, the nurse forced me to take something to eat and drink. I didn't want it, but I took it, and then I wish I hadn't.

I couldn't keep anything in my stomach, so the nurse asked if there was someone else on this ship who'd take care of me. I remembered a lady in camp named Mrs. Stewart. Mama had asked her to keep an eye on me while I was on the ship. I knew she was onboard with her daughter, but I had no idea where.

The nurse took it upon herself to locate them. I think I was in the infirmary for two days, when Mrs. Stewart came walking through the door claiming she'd been worried sick. "I had searched the entire ship looking for you, and I couldn't find you anywhere. I've been deathly worried, until the nurse finally found me and told me where you were. As soon as they release you, I want you to come with me to our cabin. We have an extra bed, and that way you won't be alone." I quietly answered, "Oh, thank you Lord." I had prayed and prayed, and here God was answering my prayers again.

Everyday at mealtime, Mrs. Stewart and her daughter tried to bring me with them to the cafeteria, However, as soon as I stepped in the hall and smelled the food, I was instantly nauseous. I'd run back to the cabin in an attempt not to vomit again. That's where I spent all of my time. Now and then, I was able to drink a little bit, but that was the extent of it. The seasickness was really taking its toll, and I must have been withering away, because Mrs. Stewart seemed very concerned. She begged, "Marlies, please, is there anything you could eat and keep down?"

After thinking about it for a while, I realized, "Yes, there is. I think that I would like an apple."

"I don't know if I'll be able to find an apple aboard the ship, but I'll try."

Thankfully, the captain of the ship had taken an interest in Mrs. Stewart's daughter, Lisa. She was only seventeen years old but exceptionally beautiful. The captain had told her that if there was anything she would like, she should see him, and he would do his best to accommodate her.

When she found out I really wanted an apple, she went to the captain and asked him if there was any way that he could find one for her. She told him how she absolutely loved apples. Of course, he was willing to do anything for Lisa, so he went into his private quarters where he had a collection of fruit and told her he'd be happy to share. Lisa thanked the captain and hurried back to give it to me. That was the first time I had eaten anything since we left, and the first time I hadn't gotten sick. From then on, each day, the captain came by her room and offered her another apple. She always gave them to me, and I was thankful that Lisa was so beautiful.

The trip wasn't getting easier. In fact, the storm was growing more severe. Everything was tossed around, day and night. It seemed as though we'd never make it across that ocean alive. The trip should have taken six days. After all, it only took six the first time we crossed on the *Bremen*. I had been counting days, and I was so looking forward to that sixth, thinking the end was near. But the storm was unending. The waves constantly splashed over the edges of the ship, and we were continually being bounced around.

Just as it seemed we'd never get off the ocean, the sixth day arrived. I was ecstatic. Only to be deflated when the day came and went, as did the seventh, the eighth, and the ninth. Day in and day out, I thought for sure we were lost, and that I would never again see land. I had convinced myself that we were all going to die on that ocean.

One day, Mrs. Stewart came back to my room and told me the woman whose dog had been taken from her had died. Apparently, she had a heart attack, but the doctors said she had simply given up the will to live. She had lost all she had, and the only thing left that mattered was taken away.

The captain decided to have a funeral and bury her at sea. We all went up on deck to say farewell to the woman who had lost everything, including her will to live. As they buried her at sea, I filled with sorrow. I cried for the woman whom I had never met or had any contact with. She had made it through the entire war. Perhaps this was her opportunity to have a new life in the place that Mama had assured me was a taste of heaven. I watched as they dumped her in the ocean, and as far as I was concerned, that was the worst possible place she could have been buried.

As the sadness overtook me, I wondered if we'd all face a similar destiny: would I also be buried in the cold, unforgiving, and dreary ocean? This was an unimaginable fear that consumed my entire being. I never thought that anything could affect me as much as having lived through the hunger, the Nazis, the bombs, and the entire war, but the fear of dying on that ship and being buried at sea, topped everything I had previously feared.

Most of the voyage I cried. I began thanking God for not letting Mama board the ship. I knew in my heart that she'd never have survived. Any type of motion used to make her stomach tumble. The voyage would have surely killed her, and I was so thankful that she wasn't onboard. At least in Germany there was some sort of hope for her, but I wasn't sure that there was any hope for the rest of us who sought a new life by way of the *Ernie Pyle.*

After that first day on ship, I never again saw Papa or my brothers while we traveled. I became so lonely and my fears encompassed thoughts of what would we do if we made it to America? Where were we going to go? Where would we live? We didn't even have a house, or any place to call home. We didn't have family or any type of relations at all. There was no one to call our own, so I wondered what would possibly happen, and what was it that was going to make that place as wonderful as Mama promised. I thought maybe it was God's plan all along that we'd die there in the ocean. And why not? In reality, we had nothing and nowhere to go.

However, as we had always done, we kept going. Day by day, we forged on until finally, after eleven days on that ocean, just as dawn was breaking, I heard people screaming and hollering. Mrs. Stewart came into the cabin yelling, "The Statue of Liberty's in sight. We made it! Come on, you've got to get up on deck."

My greatest hope was that I'd get up on deck and find Papa and my brothers. I was very weak, and it had become difficult for me to walk, but I got up and went with Mrs. Stewart. We made it to the top and I went everywhere searching for Papa until finally, I found him. I hugged him tightly, practically squeezing the air right out of him. I was crying so hard, I began gasping for air. I shouted, "Papa, we're here, we're here, we finally made it!"

I looked around for Peter and Siegfried, and I was so happy to see them again. Siegfried had a hard time on the ship too. He often got sick, but he was young, and I don't think he really understood what was happening. I don't think they missed me one bit while we were separated!

Papa missed me though. He kept asking if I was all right. He said, "Mrs. Stewart told me that you were unable to eat and had become ill."

"Papa, don't worry, we've arrived and I found you and that's all that matters."

All of the people on board began lining up along the rails looking over the edge of the ship. They began singing, "Ade Du Mein Lieb Himatland." I began to cry as I realized the words meant, "Goodbye to my homeland." After all, Germany wasn't my homeland, but it was a place where I felt I had a home and a family. In America, I could only wonder what the future would hold.

As I continued crying, looking down at the waves, which had finally calmed, I began twisting my little ring. I was thinking about Mama, and as I twisted, it slipped off my finger and fell into the ocean. Just then, it hit me that I had left everything behind; even my precious ring was no longer. I think I must have been the saddest person on that ship as I pondered an uncertain future without Mama, in a land I had only vague memories of.

17

Back in America

As our ship pulled up to Ellis Island, there was an announcement that all United States citizens should depart first and make their way to speak to the authorities. Since we fell into that category, we were not detained long before being directed to return to the *Ernie Pyle*, which proceeded into New York Harbor. Many of the other passengers were detained on Ellis Island, remaining there as our ship pulled out.

I'm not sure of the particulars, but Siegfried had become a citizen on his second birthday, and Peter and I were born in New York, according citizenship by birth. It seemed as though everything was flowing smoothly, until we docked in New York, where Papa was detained by the FBI for interrogation.

Only to Wait in Fear Again

Our ship had docked in the harbor at approximately ten o'clock in the morning. Men in a taxi were waiting for Papa to exit the ship. They told him he needed to go with them for questioning regarding the seven years we spent in Germany. Papa asked, "What am I supposed to do with my children?"

"They should wait here for you; this shouldn't take too long."

He told us, "You stay right where you are with our trunks and suitcases and wait for me to return." He got into their car and drove away. The three of us sat there on the pier and waited the entire day. We had no food, no water, and we didn't speak the language. We were there alone, sitting and waiting.

The sun was setting, and it quickly became dark and cold. A couple of men approached us, they looked like some sort of port police, but I really don't know who they were. They began speaking to me, but I couldn't understand what they wanted. They began kicking our trunks saying, "Open, open." Peter told me he thought that they wanted us to open the trunk. We didn't have keys for security, but it simply popped open, and they began rifling through our belongings. They had taken out Mama's linens and sheets, throwing them onto the pier. We had great big bed pillows, tablecloths, clothing, and memorabilia that Mama had carried with her for years. Some of the items had never been unpacked the entire seven years we were gone.

The men found pictures that we had collected from our years in Germany, during the war. There were pictures of the bombings given to us by family, friends, and the American GIs. The two men took every single picture we had in that trunk, and they were gone forever.

After the men left, we did our best to repack our belongings into the trunk. Then Peter, Siegfried, and I sat on the old lid, pressing it down enough to secure the latch. By that time, it was getting late, and Siegfried started crying. He was tired, thirsty, and scared. Peter and I tried to keep him occupied and happy by whatever means we could think of.

Peter found a small pebble and he played soccer with him. We tried to tell him stories of how nice it would be now that we finally reached America, but sitting like this in New York City, my mind began to wander back to the time when we arrived in Germany and our entire family had come to greet and welcome us. I was remembering all the kisses, hugs, smiles, and happiness we shared. Now, coming here where Mama said Heaven would be was just the opposite. No one came to make us feel welcome and relieve our fears. We were three young children in New York, alone on a pier, with a trunk and three suitcases, no food, no water, no kind words, nothing but fear.

Siegfried continued crying, and I told Peter we had to be strong, that we had to show him there was no need to be frightened. After so many long hours, he had to piddle, but there wasn't a bathroom that I knew of, so I decided to tell him to go to the edge of the pier and pee in the ocean, and that's exactly what he did.

Afterwards, he came and sat beside me on the trunk. He laid his head on my lap and thankfully, he fell asleep. He was only seven years old and didn't know what to look forward to, and I was thankful to see him nod off.

We were beginning to wonder if Papa was ever coming back for us, and while Siegfried slept, I cried. Unfortunately, he didn't sleep for long, and when he woke up, he was hungrier than before. I asked him not to think about it. I told him we've been hungry before and he knew how to deal with it, but he reminded me that Mama said, "Once I got to America, I can have a whole loaf of bread for myself, so where do I get it?"

"Mama made us believe things were going to be different, but I don't really think they are. I think things are going to be just the same as before, and we'll always be hungry."

"But Marlies, I was looking forward to a loaf of bread."

"Siegfried, don't think about it. Please, just don't think about it. Look at the big ships that are coming in."

Peter took him for a little walk, and they looked at ships, which kept him occupied for a while as we continued to wait. People were coming and going; they uttered things about us, but we couldn't understand a word, not one single word. They asked us questions, and when we didn't answer them, they'd walk away. It was eleven o'clock in the evening. We had been on the pier for thirteen hours, and our fears had intensified beyond measure, when a taxi cab finally pulled up. Papa stepped out of it, looking like an angel to me. Not thinking I'd ever see him again, I ran over and hugged him, telling him how scared we'd been. He apologized for having taken so long and told us to help put our things in the taxi, because were going to a hotel. A real hotel—whatever that was.

Bread and Bananas, Taxis and Trains

We all climbed into the taxi, and we thought it was great to be in a beautiful, American car—until the taxi driver shut the door on Siegfried's hand. He was bleeding pretty good, and began crying hysterically. I took my slip out of the suitcase and wrapped his hand to stop the bleeding, as I tried to comfort him. The taxi driver was apologetic, but more concerned about getting us hastily to our hotel. It just seemed as though we could never catch a break. As soon as things seemed to look up, something would happen to drag us back down again.

Nevertheless, we finally did make it to the hotel. Once we entered our room, we saw two big beds, but as tired as we were, we were hungrier. And Papa knew it. He checked Siegfried's hand carefully, and then decided it was okay. saying "Come on, we're gonna take a walk and see if we can find you something to eat."

It wasn't too far down the street when we saw a small grocery store that was open. We went in and saw shelf after shelf with boxes of food. "They look nice, but they're probably empty like they are in Germany," I said.

Papa laughed, "Go ahead; shake one."

I shook a box, and it had something in it. I shook another, and it had something in it too. "I can't believe it—these boxes are full! There really *is* food here."

"Yes, and now that you see there is, what would you like to have?"

We wanted bread. He took us over to a counter where there were many loaves of bread. He bought us each our own loaf and a banana. We had smiles from ear to ear as we walked out of that grocery store.

We went back to our hotel room and sat on the bed, and we each ate an entire loaf of bread. And that was the first time I had ever eaten a banana. By the time we finished, we were completely exhausted.

I fell asleep beside Papa, and Peter and Siegfried passed out on the other bed. With the exception of missing Mama immensely, I slept pretty well for my first night back in America.

When we woke in the morning, Papa told us the first thing we were going to do was go to a restaurant and have breakfast. I couldn't imagine that. Where would we go, and where would we get ration cards to pay for our food? I asked Papa, "Did they give you our ration cards when you went with the men in the taxi yesterday?"

His answer was surprising, "America's different; you don't need ration cards here."

That was the first time I actually believed that maybe Mama was right; this could possibly be heaven.

We dressed quickly and found ourselves a restaurant nearby. The waitress spoke English, so Papa translated everything she said. First, she wanted to know what we'd like to drink. We all agreed that coffee was our drink of choice. She looked at us kind of strange, but Papa nodded in agreement, and she left to retrieve our coffee. A few moments later, she returned with our beverages. Still with the strange look on her face, she placed a cup of coffee in front of each of us, and I was the first to take a sip. It was dreadful, "Papa, this coffee is spoiled."

Laughing for the first time in weeks, he told us, "No, it's real coffee; it's not spoiled."

"I can't believe this is what Mama's talking about when she says, 'I can't wait to get back to America for a real cup of coffee.'" But he assured me this was indeed what she was longing for.

He waved the waitress over, "My children cannot drink the coffee. Would you please bring them each a glass of milk?"

The waitress answered, "I was wondering why children would order coffee."

He told her it was a long story, and he'd rather not get into it. She immediately brought three large glasses of milk, and I mean big glasses! When she put them on the table, I thought I'd pass out. I couldn't believe that it was milk, but I picked up the glass and took a big gulp and, sure enough, it was indeed real milk.

Now I knew I was definitely in the right place. Milk and bread were plentiful, and we could walk into a place, sit down, and order anything. And we didn't even need a ration card. It was real food, and surely the most amazing day of my life.

I was drinking my milk slowly. I wanted the moment—and the milk—to last forever.

"Marushka, go ahead and drink it, and when it's gone, I'll order you another glass."

I had two big glasses, and as my stomach filled, so did my heart, overflowing with love for America. After we finished our meal, and feeling full like I hadn't since before the war, I was positive that this was the greatest place on earth.

As we walked around New York City, people actually smiled and said hello! The city was a vision of loveliness. Nothing had been blown up or destroyed; buildings were still standing; and there was virtually no litter in the streets. There were no wounded soldiers wrapped in bandages and hobbling on crutches in search of homes that may no longer exist. There were no Nazis pacing the streets with machine guns. There were no jeeps or military vehicles, and everything seemed peaceful.

Most of all, I noticed people walking around wearing nice shoes and beautiful clothing. No one sported old, tattered, and dirty rags. They had purses and briefcases, all of which were nicely kept. It seemed to be too good to be true!

We were going to take a taxi to the train station, where the train would take us back to the city of Rochester, New York. A city I had vague memories of from seven years previous. Papa told us, "We have enough money for tickets that'll get us that far, and when we arrive, my old friend Mr. Boesel from Clinton Avenue will be waiting to pick us up."

"Who's Mr. Boesel?"

"A good friend, who happens to own Boesel's Bakery, and I know he and Mrs. Boesel will be happy to get a visit from us."

We had a good plan so we retreated back to the hotel, gathered our belongings, and hailed a taxicab. Our trunk was so big, it hung out the back of the car. Our suitcases were piled between us in the back seat. Siegfried had to sit on one of them; otherwise, we wouldn't have all fit in! Despite our overcrowding in the car, we made it to the train in plenty of time and headed for Rochester.

The train ride was wonderful—unlike the last one, when we left Mama in Germany. As I stared out the window, memories flooded back from the place I had been so many years before, and the entire way was just as I remembered. Nothing had been destroyed. Instead of bomb holes, there were streetlights and trees, everywhere still standing strong. It was truly beautiful; nothing like I had grown accustomed to in war-torn Germany. No one hung off the sides of the train, and no one threatened our safety. It was peaceful, and I was thankful for the calm that overtook me. I thoroughly enjoyed myself all the way from New York City to Rochester.

When our train arrived at the station, we gathered our belongings and, again, hailed a taxi. I had spent the past seven years walking miles to get anywhere, and in the last two days, I had taken three taxi rides, two train rides, and one troop ship. Things were certainly different in America!

Making Ourselves at Home Again

Papa told the driver our destination was Boesel's Bakery on Clinton Avenue, and I will never forget that day as we pulled up in front. Mr. and Mrs. Boesel ran out to welcome us. They hugged us and treated us with such graciousness, the kind that never leaves your heart. We weren't alone!

As I looked around, I couldn't believe what I saw. In America, people weren't thin; they had meat on their bones and looked nothing like the folks we had left behind in Germany. Absolutely no one looked as if they were starving. Quite the contrary, they looked healthy and happy—smiles were abundant!

The Boesels took us into their bakery and right away, Mrs. Boesel made us sit down while she made sandwiches and soup. The smell alone made my mouth water with anticipation. Eating bread without worrying where our next meal would come from was unheard of during my past seven years, but having bread with meat on it was absolutely unthinkable. I couldn't remember such specialties.

We finished our lunch, and she lead us out into the bakery and showed us the most appetizing baked goods. She had pastries, kuchen, and cookies; and let us pick all we could possibly want, before taking us back into the kitchen. The bakery and their home were all in the same building, and we could easily go back and forth between them.

As we ate our goodies, I looked over and saw a small statuette. It was a small monk, and she was able to turn it on and off with a switch. When she turned it on, it moved back-and-forth and sang a little song. I was amazed, because the words were in German and I was able to understand. He sang, "Bier hare, bier hare"—bring the beer, bring the beer—and continued, "or I will fall over." I found so much humor in that little statue. It was so good to laugh and relax.

After spending a wonderful afternoon, Mr. Boesel suggested we call Naples and try to make contact with Mr. Blier, our old neighbor. After all, Mr. Blier was an old friend, and maybe he would pick us up. Since the government had taken Papa's bankbook, we were each left with two dollars and a ticket to the nearest city we had previously lived, which of course was Rochester. Unless we figured out another way, Rochester would be the end of the line for us.

Seven years was a long time to be away. Who knew what could have happened to our old friends in Naples, but when Papa phoned John Blier, he was connected immediately, and thrilled with John's ecstatic reply, "Don't move! Stay right where you are; I am on my way to pick you up. I'll be there as soon as I can to bring you back to Naples, where you belong!"

Sure enough, around seven o'clock that evening, Mr. Blier showed up with his old station wagon. It was without a doubt, the biggest car I'd ever seen, and we easily piled all our stuff inside. Before leaving, we said our thank-yous and good-byes to the Boesels. They had been so generous, and I was thankful for having had the opportunity to know them, wondering if perhaps someday our paths would cross again.

We loaded ourselves into the car and headed out of the city and back to Naples. Mr. Blier had been our next-door neighbor, yet I had no recollection of him. A funny thing though, as soon as we saw him, he called me Dee-Dee and he called Peter Boobie. Of course, Mr. Blier had known us from the day we were born, and to him, that's who we were.

He told us how great it was to see us again, because they had thought for sure that we were dead and never coming back. He continued to chitchat, but all I focused on was what he called me, so we told him, "Mr. Blier, no one calls us Dee-Dee and Boobie anymore; now we're just Peter and Marlies."

"Well that is going to take me some time to get used to, but I'll do my best to remember." We also introduced Mr. Blier to Siegfried. After all, they had never met.

He commented, "Siegfried is a strange name for a little boy in this country. Why did you name him that?"

Papa explained, "Nazis forced us to choose the name—his full name is Siegfried John Adams. Mr. Blier told us we should start calling him Johnny as long as we were in the United States, and so we did.

I asked Papa if he could translate something for me, because I had a question to ask Mr. Blier, and he didn't speak German.

"Mr. Blier, do you know what happened to our dog, Moxy?" Sure enough, he knew. Apparently, Moxy had been staying with Mrs. Wrongy down the street, and he lived with her for many years. Every day, Moxy ran from her house to ours and sat on the porch whining and crying with sadness. He didn't understand where his family had gone, yet every single day, he loyally went back looking for us.

Eventually, Mrs. Wrongy had to start tying Moxy up, because the new people who lived in our house didn't appreciate his continuous crying outside their windows and doors. After being tied up for so long, he became nasty and tried to bite anyone who came near him. Moxy's spirit broke when he could no longer look for his family. Mr. Blier told me that it had been a long time since he'd seen Moxy. He didn't know what eventually happened to him, but upon our arrival in Naples, we'd be sure to find out.

It suddenly hit me: we're on our way to Naples! Everything thus far had been beyond my wildest imagination, but what will we do when we get to Naples? Where will we go? Where will we stay? My mind was filled with questions. It took nearly an hour before finally arriving, but when we pulled up to Mr. Blier's home, his wife ran out, welcoming us with open arms. She prepared a wonderful meal, and after we ate, she gave us a warm and cozy place to sleep. We were exhausted, both physically and mentally, so we retired for the evening.

After a comfortable night's sleep, we woke early and began making plans. While Papa and Mr. Blier tried to sort out what would happen next, Mrs. Blier made some phone calls to let our old friends know we were back in town without a place to call home. Immediately she started receiving offers.

The Hartmans down the street offered to let me stay with them. Mrs. Wiley also offered to take one of us in. And the Bliers insisted on keeping Peter with them. All that was left to do was find a place for Papa. Mr. Blier told us not to worry, because there were boarding houses where he could reside until we found a place of our own.

18
Parceled Out in Naples

It was a wonderful feeling knowing all of those people were willing to accommodate us by taking us into their homes and into their lives. Yet it was sad and scary knowing we weren't going to stay together. We weren't going to be a family, and I missed my mother terribly. I don't think there was a moment during the day that she didn't flash before my eyes. However, as we sat on the pier in New York City, I didn't even look for her. I knew she wouldn't be on the next ship; it was just something she told us, so we'd get on the train.

I knew in my heart she wasn't coming, because Papa never told us to watch for her. If she were truly coming on the next ship, we would have searched high and low until we found her, but there wasn't any mention of it. I was beginning to wonder how long it would be before she would come to Naples, and whether or not I'd ever see her beautiful face again.

The first thing we did was visit Mrs. Wrongy and inquire about Moxy. It was wonderful to see her. She spoke German and easily told us about our little dog. Sadly, she had kept Moxy until two months prior, when he had simply became too mean to handle. He was refusing to eat and she had to put him to sleep, not knowing if we'd ever return. She was so sorry she hadn't waited just two months longer, but she wondered if after all of those years he would have remembered us.

Little Moxy almost lived long enough to see his family again, but we had grown so much during the past seven years that he might not have accepted us anyhow. It was a sad day, the day that, in my mind, Moxy died. I knew the special place pets hold in our hearts, and I couldn't help but think back to my special cow Kushen, who saved my life by loving me when no one else would.

My sorrowful thoughts were interrupted as we reached our next destination. The second stop of our day was to a small ice cream store run by Mrs. Grove. Mr. Blier went inside and spoke with her, and soon after, we all went in.

She was introduced to us, and I immediately knew she was a wonderful lady. She said she knew exactly what we children needed, and she pointed to all of the different ice-cream flavors in her case. My eyes grew large, as I told her, "My God, Mama was so right, this place, America, really is heaven!"

She asked which flavor we preferred, and as we each told her, she made us cones filled with three of the largest scoops of ice cream I'd ever seen. As she handed each of us our cones, I looked at Papa, "We don't have money to pay for such a treat."

She shook her head sympathetically, "Don't you even think about it! No one is going to pay for this ice cream. It's my gift to welcome you back to America, and it's the least that I can do!"

I had no recollection of ever eating ice cream before, and as far as I was concerned, it was the best-tasting stuff on earth. I imagined it being better than the waffles I had yearned for years before. As our treat came to an end with the last bites of our cones, we knew we must be leaving.

The third stop of our day was to a boarding house on Main Street right in town. Mr. Blier thought it would be a good start for Papa. The home was just a few houses down from the main intersection, so he wouldn't be too far removed from my brothers or me. The woman must have been an angel, as she told us she'd allow Papa to occupy one of her rooms, and she'd provide him with meals, and he could pay her when he obtained employment.

Her words were a blessing, "Until you find something, you are welcome to stay here." I just couldn't get over how kind the people of this small town were. With Papa's accommodations taken care of, we moved on.

The fourth stop of our day was visiting the people who agreed to take me into their home. They seemed like a nice couple. They never had children of their own, but Mrs. Hartman had always wanted them. In fact, seven years earlier, when our family prepared to go to Germany, she offered to take me in and let me stay with them for the duration of the vacation. She desperately wanted to have a little girl in her life, and seven years later, she still felt the same way.

I would've hated being away from my family all those years, but this was a different time, and I was grateful to have a place to live—even though it wouldn't be easy living with strangers. My mind wondered how long it would be until we were a family in the true sense of the word. When would there be any sense of normalcy? After all, we had only been in America for two days, and I was already being told to live with strangers again. Luckily, the Hartmans spoke German, and that was a major benefit of staying with them.

Our fifth stop of the day was the Wamp's house. They were willing to take Siegfried—now Johnny—in and give him a place to stay, while turning out to be the two nicest people in the world. As soon as we arrived, she opened her arms, and he liked them right away. They were friendly, warm, and wonderful people, and Johnny was thrilled to be staying with them. They had children of their own who were all grown up, but they still had many toys in the house. He knew he'd have lots of fun there.

In addition to the toys, they had a piano, and more important, they had food! Lots of food, and that's exactly what Johnny was looking for. To a seven-year-old who had spent his entire life nearing starvation, that was the dream come true.

The four of us had been placed into different homes, and Papa immediately began looking for work. He finally obtained employment at the potato factory in Naples. It didn't pay a lot of money, but at least it was a job, and he began working that weekend. The house where I stayed was located directly across from the Catholic Church, and Papa promised that each Sunday, we'd all meet at the church and go to mass together. He reminded us, "We need to go and give thanks for all that we've been given," and that's exactly what we did.

Mrs. Hartman came by the Blier's and gathered me and my belongings. We drove to her home, and she took me upstairs to show me where my bedroom was. There were two rooms, and one was decorated for a princess. It was a bedroom that she had planned for the daughter she had expected to have someday. Adorned with beautiful furniture, gorgeous bedding and curtains, and a great big canopy bed. With carpeting on the floor, everything in the room was magical. I was so sure that was going to be my room, and for the first time in my life, I'd live like a little princess.

It wasn't meant to be however. She closed that door and showed me to the other room. It was clean, with a nice-sized bed, but it was drab compared to the first room she had shown me. Ultimately, the room I ended up with really didn't matter. More important to me was that the house was clean, the people were clean, and they spoke to me.

The following Monday, Papa took the three of us, and we registered for school. Once I registered, Mrs. Hartman told me there would be certain rules she expected me to abide by. First, she wanted me to take a bath and be in bed every night by eight o'clock in the evening. She told me there wouldn't be much for me to do around the house, because she took care of everything. She was meticulous about her housekeeping, and she didn't need any help. Even if I wanted to listen to the radio, she wanted to turn it on and off herself, because she didn't want fingerprints on the dial.

Second, she had a piano, but if I wanted to play, it was mandatory to put on white gloves, again to avoid fingerprints. She wouldn't even let me help wipe the dishes, because she was afraid I wouldn't do the job properly. That was going to take a long time to get used to, being accustomed to pitching in and doing my share, especially while living with my grandparents in Kell.

Perhaps her most important rule was that I was never to bring friends or my brothers over to the house to play. Even Papa wouldn't be allowed to come and visit me unless he was specifically invited to do so by her.

I wondered what I would do to keep busy, until finally, Mr. Hartman spoke up. He told me I could help him in the garden. They had a beautiful flower garden that needed tending to, and I could help by pulling weeds. He had a strong accent, and when he spoke English, he always made me giggle. He'd say funny things like, "De squirrels have been in de backyards dropping nuts on mine head." Of course, at first, I didn't understand any of the things he said, but each week after church, they helped me learn English.

The Hartmans were kind and generous and they asked me many questions about my years in Germany. I told them only what I wanted them to know, never telling them the whole story. All of our conversations always led back to Mama and how terribly I missed her. I immediately started writing letters to send to Germany. Papa had given me the Hartmans address, and I wrote to her on a daily basis. In my heart, I was hoping she'd arrive in America long before the letters had a chance to get to Germany. Unfortunately, things did not happen that way.

School Dazed

On our first day of school, Papa took us in and the nurse wanted to do a physical on each of us. The first thing she did was put us on a scale to weigh us. While I was on the scale, she looked at my father with disillusionment and asked him again, "How old is your daughter?"

"She's twelve years old."

The nurse was stunned when she read what the scale reported. "Your daughter is twelve years old, and she only weighs forty-three pounds. She's nothing but skin and bones."

Papa replied, "That's not bad considering what she's been through. I'm just happy she's alive." That was all that mattered to him, and after all, he was five-foot-eleven inches and weighed only ninety pounds himself. We were certainly a far cry from all of our new American friends. The nurse was truly shocked with how little we each weighed.

When it was time for us to be placed in our classrooms, they told us that Peter and I would both be placed in the fourth grade, since we couldn't speak English. We were upset, because in Germany, chronologically, I had already completed the sixth grade, and Peter had completed the seventh. They told Johnny that he had to repeat first grade and he began crying. "I won't go back to first grade!"

It was hard for us to accept, but it didn't last long. After only one week, I was moved to a six-grade class and Peter went on to seventh. Our math skills were superior, and because of that, we were moved ahead. We still couldn't speak the language, but I had learned a couple of words including *mudder, fadder, tank you,* and *I am from Naples, U Nork*. I knew that everything else would come in time.

When I was in the classroom, things were difficult, to say the least. I watched the other students to see what they did. If they took out a certain book, I took out the same book. The problem was that the words inside and everything the teacher said was completely foreign to me. I still couldn't read, write, or speak English, and I didn't see how I was ever going to learn.

In an effort to accomplish the impossible, Papa asked the Hartmans to speak to me only in English. "First, say something in English, then translate what you said in German." He knew that this was the only way I'd learn, so he began doing the same thing. He would speak, tell us what he said in German, and then make us repeat it. He also warned us that he did not want to hear any German being spoken until we had mastered the English language, and that was a tough order to fill.

When I was born, Mama taught me German. Then school was about to begin, so they began teaching me English. We moved to Germany and Hitler ordered us to speak German. Now back in Naples, Papa was ordering me to speak English. It had been a confusing journey, at only twelve years of age.

Saving Everything for Mama

That was my beginning in America, and as far as I was concerned, it was the most glorious time of my life. There were no more bombs, no more destruction, no more hunger, and no more fears. We had left *hell* behind, and my life with the Hartmans was warm, safe, and secure.

Their house was called a Cape Cod. Upon entering the front door, there was a small vestibule, and off of the vestibule was a good-sized, heated porch. The porch had a sofa and a couple of nice chairs, and the room was entirely surrounded with windows. There was a small table in front of one window, and beautiful mahogany table with a radio on top, in front of another.

The porch led into a dining room, and off of the dining room was a huge—to me—living room where the piano was situated. To the left of the dining room was a hallway that led to their bedroom and a bathroom, and further down the hallway was the kitchen. The kitchen had two doors; one led outside and the other, to the basement.

The basement in their home was nothing like any of the others I remembered. This one was "finished"—big and clean, quite comfortable, and containing another small kitchen. The second kitchen had everything you could ever need: a sink, a stove, a refrigerator, as well as a washing machine, and a large tub. There was another door off of the basement, which led to a gigantic wine cellar where hundreds of bottles of wine were stored. The wine cellar always remained cool. The temperature never fluctuated, and the wine was kept in great condition.

The stairway that led upstairs was also in the kitchen, and in addition to the two bedrooms, there was a massive cedar closet off of the room that I was using. The items in the closet included all of their winter clothes and Mrs. Hartman's fur coats. One look at Mrs. Hartman's furs left me feeling melancholy, as memories of Vazil popped into my head—from that first day we met, as he walked into the courtyard with his thick fur coat and shoes.

Luckily, my focus changed when she showed me there was another closet where I would be able to keep my clothes and belongings.

I diligently worked on learning English, and since I was so lonely, there was little else to do. I was constantly working on it. One of the things I had the most difficulty with was the word "the." In

Germany, we used a hard "Da." I had to practice over and over, and it was tough to change, but Mrs. Hartman was always willing to help me learn to speak properly. She started me off with the smallest words and worked her way up. She also taught me how to write the words, so I could recognize them when I saw them in school. She was incredibly helpful, and I don't know how I would have gotten through without her.

Still, I missed my brothers. I missed the boys and all of the noise that came with having them around. Fortunately on Saturday's, I was invited to go to either the Blier's or the Wamp's, and my brothers and I hung out together. We played all day long, and we'd laugh until we cried, especially when we tried to communicate in English. We knew we weren't speaking properly, but it was nice to be able to laugh at each other while trying.

Mr. Hartman spent most of his time reading the newspaper and listening to the radio. Other than that, there really wasn't much going on in their house. It was so quiet you could hear a pin drop. In fact, the Hartmans rarely spoke to each other. If something had to be said, it would be; otherwise, there wasn't any laughter, any nice stories, or anything amusing going on.

I looked forward to the weekends when I'd be allowed to see my family. Spending time with them was so important. I'd go to school during the week, just waiting for the weekend; school was so difficult. It was difficult to hear the other children talking, but not understanding them. Most communicating was done through sign language, until little by little I began to understand.

The school we attended was a central school that all of the children in town attended. It didn't matter if you were in kindergarten or in your senior year, we were all in the same building. I rarely saw my brothers in school, but now and then, I'd pass them in the halls on my way to the next class.

The students were great, nothing like most of the kids we encountered in Germany. Peter had it especially good, since his teacher also spoke German. She was able to help him get through many problems, unlike *my t*eacher, who only spoke English and really wasn't much help when I was stuck on something.

One Monday morning, we were called in for an all-school assembly. It was my first one ever, and I was so excited when the children began singing "My Country 'Tis of Thee." I immediately looked at Peter with excitement. "We know this song Peter!" We began chiming in, unfortunately, the version Papa had taught us was quite different from that which the other children sang. We sang, "My country 'tis of thee, I came from Germany ...." I looked around and noticed that all of the children were laughing at us. I told Peter we were singing the wrong words. We immediately stopped; however, one of the other girls kept saying "Sing, Marlies, Sing." Looking at Peter, I shrugged my shoulders, and finally, I finished the song as Papa had taught us.

My country 'tis of thee
I came from Germany
My name is John
Give me some sauerkraut
Don't leave the wieners out
Plenty of lager beer
And I will stay here

The next time I saw Papa, I told him what happened in assembly, and he laughed profusely as he told me, "I knew that would pay off someday." I didn't understand what he meant, but he told me that someday I'd laugh too. He was right, when I finally understood English and the words that I had sung, it made me chuckle.

Time was passing so slowly, and every week I waited for Mama. I missed her terribly. Each night I had to be in bed by eight o'clock, but many nights I couldn't sleep. I thought of her continuously when I was awake, and I dreamt of her while I slept. I prayed to God daily, asking him to please bring Mama home. I couldn't understand what was taking so long. That weekend, I asked Papa. He finally told me the truth: the reason it was taking so long was that he hadn't been able to save enough money for her trip.

After paying for his room and board and his meals, he was left with little at the end of the week. He saved as much as he could, but it was going to be some time before he was able to come up with the entire amount for the trip.

Additionally, it was required to have three letters of recommendation from prominent people within the community. These people had to vouch for Mama's character, in order for her to be granted permission to enter the United States.

Considering the Widmer's were my parents' best friends prior to our leaving for Germany, Papa asked them to write a letter. To his utter shock and disbelief, they refused. How could they have been so cold hearted? Mrs. Widmer had been Mama's best friend. How could she help keep a mother away from her children? They justified their refusal by saying that writing a letter could jeopardize their wine business, and they weren't about to do that. I had no idea what they meant by that.

Papa tried to explain it me by telling me that after the war, Germans were looked down upon, and they didn't want to have any association with Germany. Mr. Widmer did, however, tell Papa that although he wouldn't write the letter, he would allow him to return to work at the winery. Papa had to think about that for a good long time before responding.

Thankfully, there were people willing to write letters and sign the forms. The Wamps, the Bliers and the Whileys all did so. I thought for sure that she'd be on her way within the week, but things did not turn out that way. The weeks turned into months, and yet still, she hadn't arrived. In fact, Thanksgiving was just around the corner. I couldn't believe we had been in America so long that the holidays were approaching. The holidays, the meaning of which was bound by family for us, would be meaningless without Mama to share them.

With or without her, however, time did not stand still. We carried on with our lives. Naples was having a Thanksgiving raffle, where people could buy tickets with the hopes of winning a turkey. Mr. Hartman took me with him to the festivities. It was Friday night, and Papa told me he'd also be attending. Peter and Johnny were there with the Wamps and the Bliers, and it was good to be with family.

Mr. Hartman gave me fifty cents to spend at the raffle. I knew it was fifty cents only after he told me it was. I was having a difficult time understanding money. I learned there was one cent, five cents, ten cents, twenty-five cents, fifty cents, and a dollar, but then someone would ask me for a quarter, and I'd be confused, having no idea what they were talking about. They were speaking about dimes and nickels and pennies, and none of that sounded right to me. Nothing made sense, with so many different ways to describe the same thing, but little by little, I was learning.

With the fifty cents Mr. Hartman gave me, I bought two tickets for the turkey raffle. When the man calling the numbers finished, I realized I had the winning number. I walked forward through the crowd to claim my prize. This was not your average, frozen turkey. This turkey was very big and very much alive! The farmer was holding it upside down by the legs. The wings were flapping and I had no idea what to do with the scary, squawking bird. I had never seen a turkey before, and this one practically weighed as much as I did. When I couldn't hold it much longer, Mr. Hartman came forward and took it from me. "Here, Marlies, I'm going to give the turkey back to the farmer and have it butchered for Thanksgiving dinner." He was quite pleased that I had won our turkey dinner!

I was proud to be a winner and shared my excitement with Papa. He decided to give me a quarter to buy another raffle ticket, thinking that I could be his good-luck charm. I eagerly gave the man my money, and he gave me another ticket. The wheel was spun and when it stopped, it once again landed on my number. How could I have been so lucky? I won again! Two turkeys in one day, I couldn't believe it.

I was thrilled, "Papa, I won! I won again!" Until Mr. Hartman came up and grabbed my second turkey too. "No, Mr. Hartman, you don't understand. I won the second turkey with my father's quarter."

Hr. Hartman argued, "Oh no, I gave you fifty cents, that's our turkey."

I told him how I had gotten two tickets with his fifty cents and won a turkey, but the second ticket was from Papa and that turkey belonged to him. "We should give the second turkey to Papa. We couldn't possibly eat two turkeys for Thanksgiving anyway."

Mr. Hartman refused, and while holding the bird up high he exclaimed "Oh no, we'll take both and eat one for Christmas, and your father can come to Thanksgiving dinner at our house and share in this one."

My elation was quickly deflated. I didn't understand how a rich man could take food away from someone as poor as Papa, but he did, and I never looked at him the same again. Why couldn't everyone share? Why were some so greedy? I knew they took good care of me; they gave me shelter and food and clothing, but I felt bad for my father. I wanted him to have more. Even though Mr.Hartman told Papa he would be invited to have Thanksgiving dinner with us, Papa was never formally invited.

I asked Mr. Hartman when my father would be coming and he said that Papa most likely had plenty of invitations to have dinner with the other families in town. I even called Papa to tell him what Mr. Hartman said and to make sure he had a place to go. Papa told me that he indeed had a place to go and not to worry. I later learned that was not the case. My father sat alone. He spent the day at the boarding house with no family, no friends, and no turkey dinner with all of the trimmings. I knew deep down that Papa must have been hurting that day but I also knew he would never have let us, or anyone else know it.

Thanksgiving came and went, and I remained distant from Mr. Hartman, but Mrs. Hartman and I were still all right. Every week, she gave me fifteen cents allowance. I knew I'd have to share my money with God, so each Sunday, I put some in the collection basket at church. I still didn't understand the value of the coins, because in Germany, the larger the coin, the greater the value. In the United States, I found that didn't hold true. Each week, I put the dime in the collection, thinking the nickel was worth more because it was bigger. After weeks of giving away two-thirds of my income, I finally realized what I was doing, and I began giving my nickels instead of dimes.

It's not that I didn't want to give more to God, but each week I saved my dime, wanting to buy Mama a pair of shoes. I knew winter was coming and wondered if she'd gotten a new pair. I thought about her shoes often and remembered what they looked like the last time I saw her. They were barely held together with cardboard and thread, and I was hoping they hadn't fallen apart.

I worried since she didn't belong to a country and received no rations that her shoes would not be replaced. I hoped Oma had an old pair she could give her to keep her feet from freezing in the upcoming months. In case she didn't, I wanted to do my part, so for every bit of money I earned, I put five cents a week in the collection, and saved the rest for Mama's shoes.

Mrs. Hartman had a catalog delivered from Sears and Roebuck. I was in awe as I thumbed through the pages. There were things in that catalog I'd never seen before. Things I couldn't have imagined. But my heart skipped a beat when I saw the shoes, the shoes I needed to buy for Mama. Mrs. Hartman told me they only cost five dollars. At that time, five dollars might as well have been a million, but I had already begun saving, and I was determined. I saved and continued to do so, until I could finally afford to purchase those beautiful, warm shoes.

Each day after school, the girls I made friends with went across the street to Millers, the neighborhood store that sold everything from gas and snacks to sandwiches and ice cream. They invited me to join them, as they had made a game out of running across to the store to buy themselves an ice cream cone. The ice cream cost exactly five cents, and each day we stood in front of the counter displaying all the flavors, and the clerk asked me what kind I wanted. As they stood there, licking their cones up and down, I could only shake my head and say none, thank you. I wanted the ice cream so bad my mouth watered, but each day, I told myself tomorrow I'll get ice cream with my friends. Yet morning would come, and I couldn't bring myself to take even five cents out of the little box where I kept my savings.

I thought to myself, *What if she comes home and I don't have a gift for her?* I couldn't spend the money; no matter how desperately I wanted that ice cream. When I learned to speak better English, I told my friends I didn't like ice cream, and finally they stopped pestering me to join them. It was hard to watch them eat it in front of me, but those shoes were much too important, and ice cream doesn't last long at all.

Johnny and Peter lived a mere two blocks from each other so they were able to play together quite often. Peter was happy living with the Bliers, and they were equally happy to have him. Mr. Blier took him for rides in his car and hiking in the woods, and they often brought Johnny along. They had many friends that lived nearby, and they learned how to play baseball and other American games. Papa had been a huge baseball fan. He could easily rattle off the stats of any player in the league, passing on his love of the sport to my brothers.

They were really having a great time, and their rules were not as strict as mine, giving them much more freedom. Even though they were enjoying childhood more than me, I didn't begrudge them anything. They'd been through so much and deserved to reach out and grab every bit of happiness they could.

Johnny fit in like he was meant to be at the Wamp's. He practically ran the house; those Wamps treated him like a little king. Since he was a bright boy, it didn't take him long to figure out he could get anything he wanted if he begged and pleaded long enough. The Wamps spoke German, and it was easy for his needs to be known. Their daughter, Molly, was living there too and she spent a lot of time with Johnny, teaching him. I was amazed at how quickly he adapted to reading, writing, and speaking English. I was grateful they were happy, yet I felt sorry for myself, filled to the brim with loneliness.

When it seemed that my loneliness couldn't get worse, Christmas was upon us, and I would spend most of the holiday alone with the Hartmans. It certainly wasn't the kind of loneliness I felt with Aunt Lena, but nonetheless it was real. For whatever reason, the Hartmans weren't interested in entertaining others, so the three of us spent an extremely quiet and lonely day together. They gave me a nice, warm coat and a pair of boots for Christmas gifts, and I was grateful for their generosity, but they didn't invite Papa to join us for dinner, leaving me preoccupied. I know they sensed my sadness, so later that afternoon Mr. Hartman offered to drive me to the Wamps where the rest of my family had been enjoying the holiday spirit.

Thankfully, I was able to spend a bit of time with them as we shared cookies and candy and I played with my brothers. As the afternoon wore away, I called Mr. Hartman to come and get me. It was time for Papa to return to the boarding house anyway, so I thought it was proper for me to return home as well.

The Christmas season came and went, and still no sign of Mama. Just before our school vacation came to a close, Mrs. Baader asked if I could come over on Sunday to visit them. She said they'd pick me up after church, and I could spend some time at their house on Rhine Street. I was in my glory because they had six children. They were all younger than me, but I didn't care; anytime I could be with children of any age, I wanted to do so. The Baader children understood German, and I spent a glorious afternoon with them, laughing and playing all day long. Spending time with their family was a breath of fresh air. There was excitement and happiness like I hadn't been a part of in such a long time, and it left me feeling rejuvenated. I'm sure that my being there also helped out Mrs. Baader tremendously. It couldn't have been easy for her to entertain six children at once. I hoped she would ask me back again soon.

Winter was cold and long. The days ran into each other, and it seemed as though spring would never arrive. Yet it did, and still no sign of Mama. I had however, saved enough money to buy her shoes from the Sears and Roebuck catalog. Knowing she wore the same size I did, I traced my foot on a piece of cardboard and Mrs. Hartman sent it with my order. I waited each day for the mailman to deliver my package, and the day the shoes arrived, I was beaming. I knew when Mama arrived in America, I'd have a gift for her, a gift she desperately needed and, more importantly, deserved.

I took the shoes up to my room and each morning and night, I took them out and dusted them off. I wanted them to be perfect when she arrived. Many times, I'd stare down at the shiny leather, and like so many times before, my reflection became clouded as my eyes filled with tears and my mind filled with questions. I wondered if she was ever coming home. *Would she ever wear the shoes I had saved so diligently for? Would I ever see her again? Would I ever be able to hug her and tell her how much I loved her?*

Every night, I wiped the tears from my eyes and then off the shoes. I placed them under the bed, and while still kneeling down, I'd say a special prayer, hoping God would know how much I loved and missed her. I prayed each and every day—just like she taught me.

I had freedom, a nice home to live in, and no bombings—everything I could ask for—but I didn't have the people that I loved most around me, leaving me feeling as though I had nothing but loneliness and loss. They were hard days to get through, with nothing to look forward to except the hope that someday soon she'd return.

Carrying on, one afternoon, spring was in full bloom as I walked home from school. I was staring down at the ground and as I looked up, and down the road, I saw a little lady walking toward me. She looked exactly like I remembered my mother! Tears ran down my face as I ran down the street toward her. "She's back, she's back! She's here! She came home!" I cried. As I got closer, I realized that it was Mrs. Widmer. She looked so much like Mama. Most of the time she drove her car, but that day she had decided to take a walk. When I realized it wasn't her, my heart nearly exploded. As we neared each other, she saw my disappointment and asked, "You thought I was your mother didn't you, Marlies?"

"Yes, Mrs. Widmer, I did."

"I am sorry to disappoint you, but I really wonder if your mother's ever coming home."

She continued walking and never said another word. That was just about the last thing I wanted or needed to hear. *Didn't she have any feelings? Didn't she at least care about mine?* I continued the rest of the way home in tears and ran upstairs and cried the remainder of the day.

Still Making Trouble Standing Up for Others

As spring began, so did religious education instructions. Each Saturday morning we met at church and attended class. One particular day, Peter wasn't feeling well and didn't attend, but Johnny made his way alone. During class, the skies turned black, and I could smell the rain coming. By the time we were dismissed, the skies had opened up, and the raindrops pounded the streets below. I told Johnny we could make a break for it and run across the street to the Hartman's. On the count of three, we bolted across, but within those few moments, the rain hit us hard and we were instantly soaked through.

As we entered the vestibule, Mrs. Hartman ran out, "Marlies, hurry up, get upstairs and out of those wet clothes."

"Johnny has to come with me. I don't want him to get sick either."

She refused, "No, no Johnny, you just stay put in the vestibule and when Mr. Hartman returns, he'll drive you home."

I became agitated. "Johnny can't stay out here. There is no heat and he's soaking wet. Mrs. Hartman, please let him come in to put dry clothes on!"

She continued to refuse, saying, "He'll be fine."

"Mrs. Hartman, if you don't have room in your house for my little brother, then you don't have room for me. Come on Johnny, I'll walk you home. We're already wet, what can it hurt?"

On our way back to the Wamp's, we stopped at the potato factory to see Papa. He was very upset. "What are you doing walking around in these heavy rains?"

"Mrs. Hartman refused to help Johnny, so I had to help him. He's my brother, and it's my job to take care of him. Please don't make me go back to the Hartman's. Papa, I don't want to stay there any longer."

"You have to return," Papa said. "There is no other place for you to go."

Shortly thereafter, Mrs. Hartman showed up with the car. "Get in the car so you can go home and change out of those soaking clothes."

"I'll only get in if you're willing to take Johnny." It was raining so hard, the windshield wipers could barely keep up, but she agreed and drove him home. The Wamp's were relieved, as we pulled up in her big car. They had been worried about Johnny, and Mr. Wamp had been driving around in circles looking for him. He had been to the church, to the Hartman's, and all around town searching for us. I was so thankful that someone cared so much about my little brother. They were genuinely concerned, and he was so fortunate to have become part of their loving family.

Mrs. Hartman and I returned home and I took a hot bath, put on warm clothes, and the day's events were never mentioned again. But I think she was embarrassed by her behavior. She learned a valuable lesson, realizing people need to take care of all children, not just the ones under their roof. I was proud to stand up for Johnny, and there wasn't anything I wouldn't have done to protect my family.

A couple of days later, Mrs. Hartman asked me, "Marlies, do you enjoy staying in our home?"

"Yes, of course; it's very nice, and I appreciate all of your kindness."

She wanted to know what it was I missed most, and I immediately told her, "I miss my family and the animals on my grandparents' farm." It had been so long since I'd spent time with my beloved animals.

"Well, I go to Mr. Schenk's farm every morning to buy milk, and Mr. Schenk has lots of cows. Marlies, would you like to come with me to see the cows?"

"Yes, that would be fine!" and we agreed to make plans to do so.

The following Saturday, we headed off to the farm, and I was brimming with excitement to see cows again. When we arrived, I asked Mr. Schenk—who also spoke German—where they were. He told me they were up in the big barn, and I was welcome to go visit them. He didn't have to tell me twice, I ran as fast as I could, but when I stepped into the barn, I stopped dead in my tracks. I was in shock; there were at least twelve cows, and they were all standing in manure over their knees. They were chewing while so many flies swarmed around them I could actually hear buzzing. I couldn't believe what I was seeing. I turned around, ran out, and shouted at Mr. Schenk. "You should be ashamed of yourself! How can you let your cattle stand in all of that manure?" I proceeded on, "If my grandmother ever came and saw this, she'd beat you to death with her broom. She would never allow this. What a shame!" I barked at

Mrs. Hartman, "You shouldn't buy your milk here. Those cows can't be healthy. This is a disgrace."

Mr. Schenk was not happy with my display, but I didn't care. I simply told him to clean out that manure and put down fresh straw for those poor animals.

He told Mrs. Hartman, "I would appreciate it if you didn't bring her back again."

I piped up, "Don't worry, I don't want to come back to see your abused animals."

When we got back into the car, Mrs. Hartman yelled at me, "You were very disrespectful to Mr. Schenk."

I already knew that, and I felt bad about it, but I told her, "The animals are helpless and depend on us for their care, so people who abuse them don't deserve respect." It was a quiet ride home.

Easter was right around the calendar and the Hartmans decided that they were going to take a trip to Switzerland. Mr. Hartman's parents were getting up in years; his mother was ailing, and he needed to visit her, but the kicker was they wanted me to go with them.

A trip to Switzerland meant a trip across the ocean, and there was no way I was ever going to do that again. Other than going back to get Mama, I never ever wanted to step foot in Germany or any other part of Europe again. Besides, I told her, Papa would never allow me to go. With that being the case, they needed to find another place for me to stay while they were gone.

One Surprise and then the Best One Yet

Like a dream come true, one afternoon after church, Mr. Baader told us his parents had offered to let me stay with them on Rhine Street. I was thrilled! They lived next door to their son and their six grandchildren. Also living in their home was Mr. Baader's aunt Mary, whom I liked from the first moment we met. The thought that I was going to be living with that family, a family where there was life and energy, filled me with joy and excitement. I wouldn't be able to visit my brothers as often, since the walk was much farther, but I didn't mind. After all, it wouldn't be the first time I had to walk six miles to get somewhere.

It was a number of weeks later when the Hartmans left, and I began residing on Rhine Street. It was almost as nice as being in Germany with my grandparents. Things were wonderful as I got to know all of the neighbors, most of whom spoke German and welcomed me. I finally had good friends! For the first time in my life, I even had a best friend—Joanie—who lived just up the street. We did everything together. A couple of teenagers taking in all life had to offer.

At the Baader's house, I didn't have all of the strict rules like at the Hartman's. I didn't have a specific curfew, and many times I'd come home at nine or ten o'clock, and that was fine. I was always able to keep up with my studies, and it never became a problem. The house was buzzing with activity; friends were abundant, and I was in a home where I was loved and happy. If I couldn't be with my real family, I couldn't have asked for a better substitute.

I had finally fallen into a comfortable way of life. Considering my circumstances, things were as good as I could have hoped for, and when I least expected it, things suddenly changed. Early one morning in July, I was in the kitchen washing dishes when the phone rang. Mrs. Baader yelled for me to answer it.

"Hello."

"Hello, who is this?"

"This is Marlies."

"Marlies, do you know who this is?"

"No."

"Have you forgotten me already?"

"I'm sorry; I just don't know who I am talking to."

"Marlies, it's Mama!"

I had never heard Mama's voice over the telephone before, and I had no idea it could possibly be her. I never expected it to be, and when I heard those words, I was dumbfounded. As the phone receiver hung dangling from the wall, I furiously ran into the bedroom and grabbed the box with the shoes inside. I yelled to Aunt Mary, "My mother's here, my mother's here!" I ran out the door and headed down Rhine Street. I doubt that two little feet have ever run so fast, but I was running to Papa's, where I was sure she'd be. I was on a mission; I was finally going to see Mama. As I ran, I cried. The tears streamed down my face, and I continued to repeat, "She's here, my Mama's here, she's here, Mama's here!"

One of our neighbors, Mr. Reisenberger was driving by. I knew him very well, and as he rolled up with his truck, he asked me where I was going in such a hurry. "I'm sorry, Mr. Reisenberger, I can't talk right now, I have to get to Papa's house. Mama's finally arrived. She's here!" He continued slowly following me, trying to make me understand he was offering to give me a ride over.

"Marlies, don't you think it would be a lot easier if you got into the truck? I can drive you over, and you'll get there much faster."

It finally dawned on me. Of course, of course it would be faster. I jumped in exclaiming, "Can't this truck go any faster? Please, make it go faster!"

He answered, "Well yes, it could go faster, but I want to make sure we get you there safely."

As we drove through town, I wanted to scream out the window and let the whole world know my mother was back. The greatest woman on earth was actually in Naples, New York.

As we pulled up in front of the house, I jumped out of his truck while it was still moving. I never closed the door, and I never thanked Mr. Reisenberger. I barged into the house, down the hall, and into Papa's bedroom. There she was, standing right there in front of me, just like an angel. She looked like God had sent her straight from heaven, and all I could do was stand and stare.

Finally, I remembered the present, the present I had saved for this very moment. "Mama, I brought you a present," but I dropped the box on the floor and wrapped my arms around her. I hugged her so tight, "Mama, I am so glad to see you. I thought we'd never see you again. Thank God, you're here. Thank God, you're finally here. Everything is going to be perfect again, and we'll finally be a family!"

Johnny was already there, and Peter came running in the door. Our reunion was glorious and words couldn't describe the feelings that rushed through my body, my mind, and my heart. We all tried to tell her, "Mama, you were right; it is just like you said it would be. There's food, and everything you need is here, just like you promised us. You're going to be so happy here." All of a sudden, it struck me how frail she was. She looked more tired and worn than when we left her. Her clothes and shoes were still tattered and ragged. I ran over to get my box, "Mama, look what I have for you."

She took the shoes out of the box, and as she looked at me, the tears ran down her face. "Oh, I hope they fit!" She tried them on, and they did. They fit perfectly. She walked around the room like a queen, and at that moment, she *was* a queen. She was the most beautiful thing that God had ever given me.

There was no way anyone was going to get me out of that room. I wasn't going to let her out of my sight. The lady who owned the boarding house was kind enough to give us blankets and we all spent the night lying on the floor, just to be close to her. Aside from the day they rescued me at Aunt Lena's, it was the most glorious day I ever spent.

Thankfully, the next day was Sunday, and we could stay together as a family. We went to church, and after all of the years she'd been gone, people still remembered her. They welcomed her home, and everyone was happy that our family was finally together and complete. Friends wrapped their arms around her and told her how long we children had waited for her arrival.

The task at hand was to find somewhere we could all be together. We yearned to be a family, all five of us under one roof. What a miracle that would be. With the grace of God, the miracle came true.

Mr. Parsons Brings Us Together Again

There was an old man in town who was terminally ill, but he didn't want to go into a nursing home. He offered to let our entire family move in, rent free, if we'd only watch out and care for him. He knew Mama would give him the care he needed, and she agreed right away. We each gathered our belongings after thanking all of the people who'd been so kind to us, and within a couple of days, we were all together living in Mr. Parsons' home.

It was a magnificent, old Victorian home with a large table, and at that table, we sat together beaming with joy. For the first time in over a year, we had a true family meal, a meal with good, nutritious food. But it wasn't the food that mattered; it was the fact that we were all together. Saying grace at that meal was truly meaningful; so many blessings had been bestowed upon us.

Mr. Parsons' bed and belongings had been moved into the vestibule downstairs, near the kitchen where Mama could easily tend to him. She needed to keep him clean and comfortable, and that was a big job, yet she never complained even once. She was so thankful to be in that beautiful home, she would have done anything for Mr. Parsons.

The house had a huge, front porch that led to a room surrounded completely with windows. Glass doors separated it from another, which we called the piano room. It had a gigantic grand piano, and I loved sitting at it, dreaming of becoming an accomplished pianist. I still had my violin from the GI in Germany, but with no idea how to play it, I doubted I'd become accomplished at either instrument. But it was great fun pretending. On the other side of the piano room, was Mr. Parsons' vestibule, which was not far from the dining room, kitchen, washroom, and a second porch that led to the side yard. Upstairs were four huge rooms and one bathroom.

Mr. Parsons condition seemed to worsen by the day. He had cancer, and tending to him was quite a job. Each morning, Mama came downstairs to clean him up, and she had to wash him and replace the dirty sheets with fresh ones. Without a washer or dryer in the house, Mama had to scrub them by hand each day.

She hadn't really had time to recover and gain her own strength back, before we found out she was pregnant again. Carrying a baby and caring for Mr. Parsons was exhausting, and even though she never complained, I could see the difficulty in her eyes. She was changing the sheets two or three times a day; keeping up with it was nearly impossible, so she asked the priest at church to ask his parishioners if they could find it in their heart to donate any old sheets they may have to Mr. Parsons.

The priest refused, claiming that since we had been in Germany during the war, then we must have been Nazis and his parishioners would not want to help any former Nazi. She explained to him that we were never Nazis, and if we had been it would have been impossible for us to return to the United States. He continued refusing, which deeply troubled her. America was supposed to be the land of religious freedom, a place where people were good Christians, yet when she asked for help, she was not heard. She didn't want the parishioners to do it for her. She wanted them to donate to Mr. Parsons. "This man has been a member of your community his entire life, and you won't help him because of me? Well, thank you very much, Father. I will manage without your help." Mama decided that since she didn't have enough sheets, she'd put newspapers underneath and use the sheets to cover him.

Soon after Mama's first fallout with the priest, another followed. She wanted Peter and Johnny to become altar boys, so they could assist with Sunday mass. Again, Father told her that because of the animosity the townspeople felt toward Nazis, he didn't want her boys to step foot on the altar. Of course, we were all upset, but Mama said we shouldn't think that way. "It doesn't matter; it just doesn't matter, and we should pray for the priest." The priest's prejudices didn't sway her one tiny bit. He wasn't going to discourage her, as she remained as dedicated to her religion, her faith, and her church as she had ever been.

My brothers never did become altar servers in this country, yet in Germany, a country where Hitler didn't want anyone to have any association with God, Peter was an altar boy. Here, where there was supposed to be religious freedom, they were denied—for supposedly being something they weren't—thanks to the priest who wrongly assumed they were.

The prejudice came from people not understanding the truth. Mama always told us we shouldn't dislike people for what we think they might be. Preconceived notions regarding others can be detrimental to all involved, while she adamantly believed everyone should be given a chance. We however, had become used to it. In Germany, we were discriminated against for having lived in America, yet in America, we were discriminated against for having lived in Germany. It seemed to be a vicious cycle, which after eight years we were still caught in, especially as the stories regarding crimes against humanity committed by the Nazis began to unfold.

19
Together for the Duration

It was summer; school was out, and life was grand. One hot afternoon, my brothers were playing baseball, and I hollered, "Hey, you guys, can I play?" For whatever reason, they wouldn't let me join, so I decided to sit on the porch and watch. All of a sudden, smash! I watched as the chards of glass fell to the ground from our neighbor Mrs. Blake's window. We were all shocked as to how something like that could happen, but deep down it was good to know that it wasn't my fault. When Papa came home, he wanted to know who was involved. Since I was sitting on the porch watching, he blamed all of us and told us we'd each be responsible for paying for a new window. I hardly thought that was fair—I wasn't playing—but there was never any arguing with Papa.

In order to pay for the window, Peter and I began looking for work. There was a huge, berry patch in town so we decided to give it a try. Mrs. Bowles was the owner and after asking her for jobs, she said, "No, I never hire children to work in my berry patches. It's a waste of time and money."

We pleaded, "Please, Mrs. Bowles, we really need a job, and we promise to work hard."

Against her better judgment, she replied, "All right, I'll let you work for one day, and if you do well, you can have a job. If not, you will understand why I let you go."

To say the least, we were thrilled and immediately began picking berries. Little did she know that Peter and I would be the best berry pickers she ever hired. The first day, we each picked one hundred quarts. Mrs. Bowles was amazed. She told us no one had ever picked one hundred quarts for her. Our baskets were nice and full, the bushes were picked clean, and we left none on the ground. She said she'd be proud to have us, and we were thankful to have jobs.

When we received our first paychecks, we thought we were millionaires. We were both so proud. The pay rate was usually nine cents a quart, but we did such an extraordinary job, she paid us thirteen cents. All of our money went toward helping our parents—except of course what was subtracted for the broken window, which by the way, was not my fault.

Papa had been working at the potato factory, but the income was minimal, so he decided to take Mr. Widmer up on his offer for employment. He was extremely knowledgeable regarding all aspects of the wine business, and Will Widmer knew it. When Papa started out at Widmer's again, he earned forty dollars per week. The pay was more than he earned at the potato factory, but it still wasn't a lot of money, so we all pitched in.

Mama began sewing for the townspeople, even though she was forty-two years old and very pregnant. She had taken on a great deal between taking care of us, Mr. Parsons, and his huge house. Having children so late in life was dangerous in those days, and it was a big concern for Mama, who'd weighed a mere seventy pounds when she returned from Germany.

Almost exactly nine months from the day she returned, one morning while lying in bed, I heard a baby crying. Days before, Mama had told us that we'd be getting a new baby, but I never thought it would be that soon. I ran down the stairs and found her lying in a bed in the small room near the grand piano, and I whispered, "Where is he?"

Papa pointed and said, "He's right over there."

Later, he asked me how I knew the baby was a he. "Papa, I wanted a sister so badly, and I knew you wanted another little girl as well, so if it had been a girl, you would have come running up the stairs to tell me already." He smiled in agreement.

Mrs. Whiley, Mama's close friend, was holding the baby, and they were all concerned about Mama. She had lost a huge amount of blood and needed a transfusion. She almost didn't survive the birth, but she hung on, and God let us keep our mother. They handed me the baby, who had been named Joseph William, and I thought he was the most beautiful little guy I had ever seen.

A New Baby and a New House

Things were different with my brother Joe. I was fourteen years old and looking at the world through different eyes. When Siegfried came along, I was an insecure five-year-old. This baby didn't frighten me in the least.

As the circle of life goes on, sadly, not long after Joe was born, Mr. Parsons died. That meant we were again going to have to seek a new place to live. My parents had saved one hundred dollars and went looking for a home of our very own. At the far end of Naples, we found a little, old house. It had at one time been the first church in Naples, and it was right next door to the animal hospital.

The veterinarian had lived in the house, but for some reason, he left town and wished to sell. It was in poor condition and needed a lot of work, but it was a house—and we needed a home. In order to obtain it, however, we needed to get a mortgage. Oddly enough, the man who graciously agreed to give us the mortgage was Mr. Schenk, the very farmer I had been so nasty to. The only problem was that he wanted two hundred dollars down and we only had one hundred.

Some things are meant to be though, and this was one of them. Mrs. Whiley came over to tell us she was willing to lend us the additional hundred dollars. She told Mama she could pay her back if and when she ever obtained an extra hundred dollars. If not, she need not worry about it; it was her gift to us. For the first time ever, we were going to be homeowners, the proud new family of One Main Street, Naples, New York.

After having the baby, we were in debt to Doctor Lyons too. He told Mama if she'd bake him a kuchen once in a while, then he'd call it even. Mama was so grateful, she baked him a fresh kuchen every Saturday and delivered it to him hot and fresh right away. At one point, he told her she had more than paid for having the baby and she needn't continue bringing him kuchen each week, but she wouldn't hear of that nonsense and continued to bring Dr. Lyons his Saturday treat until the week he died, many years later.

Although we finally had a home, initially, we had nothing to put in it. We didn't have furniture, and we certainly didn't have money to purchase any. As luck would have it, there was an old mattress in one of the rooms upstairs. We covered it with Mama's beautiful linens and pillows, and that became my parent's bed. A neighbor had given us a crib for Joey, leaving Peter, Johnny, and me sleeping on the floor. We had been used to sleeping on the floor in Germany just to keep warm in the winter, so to us this was kind of like camping out. We piled the blankets high and made an excursion of it.

In the kitchen, we used a piece of plywood over two sawhorses as our table, and we had orange crates for chairs. We didn't have any dishes of our own, but in the cupboards, we found a few discarded items. There was one pot, three plates, a kettle, a coffee pot, and some silverware. All of Mama's meals were creations made in that one pot. I remember so many times, standing in the kitchen waiting my turn to eat, with only three plates it seemed like forever until the last bit of food was scooped up so I could grab a plate, wash it up and fill it with one of Mama's delicious meals. It worked out fine for us, but others were talking.

People said we had to be the poorest people in Naples, yet even though we shared plates, we never saw it that way. We may not have had a lot of impressive material belongings, but we sure did have everything else. Our home was filled with warmth, joy, happiness, singing, jokes, and the most beautiful stories. We owned our home, planted a garden, and Papa earned an honest living. It wasn't a lot of money, but enough to pay our debts. We had clean clothes, a warm place to sleep, and there were no more bombings, no hunger, no Nazis, and no fear.

Our *new,* little house had become our castle, and we were extremely proud. I had the love of two wonderfully kind parents, my faith, respect for myself and others, and I knew somehow, we'd make it. In time, my uncles had each made it home safely from the war—including Uncle Bernard, who was imprisoned in Siberia for another four years after the war ended. Mama felt better, knowing Uncle Johann had not died in vain. Leaving all of that behind us, we forged on, believing that there's no shame in being poor, when you're truly rich at heart. And we were.

I was truly blessed to have grown up at One Main Street in the small village I called home. It was one of the oldest houses in Naples; It was also the only home our family ever owned and we loved every inch of it. The old house is now designated a landmark and is appropriately called the Adams house in the town registry.

My brothers and I worked hard, studied hard and did our best to make Mama and Papa proud. I couldn't even imagine letting them down, we loved them too much to do that. We all graduated from Naples Central High School and as the years passed, my brothers and I all left to start our own lives and families.

Peter graduated with academic honors and received scholarships in sports. He was drafted into the U.S. Army where he served for four years. Peter was stationed in Germany for three of those years where he worked in the intelligence unit, as a translator for the military. After being discharged, he attended Cortland College in New York, graduated with a degree in education, and became an American history teacher. During his thirty-four years at Cortland High, he was named teacher of the year three times. Peter, now retired, resides in Cortland, N.Y. with his wife Shirley.

My brother Johnny received a scholarship to Hobart College in Geneva, New York where he was elected into the Hobart Hall of Fame for his achievements in basketball, baseball, and soccer. After graduation, he entered the United States Air Force and was stationed in Colorado Springs. He was with the Air Force Space Defense Command and worked in the Cheyenne Mountain underground complex. He stayed in the Air Force Reserve and retired as a Lt. Colonel in 1983. Johnny then became part owner of a Rochester,

New York company that operated Job Corps centers around the U.S. and he managed all the company centers west of the Mississippi River. Johnny retired in 2006 and now lives in Carson City, Nevada with his long time partner June.

My brother Joe graduated from high school and moved to Rochester where he lived with me while attending a semester at the Rochester Institute of Technology. Joe then joined the Air Force and following his service, attended college in Colorado Springs, Colorado where he graduated with a degree in Construction Engineering. Joe and his wife Carolyn now live in Maryland. They have two children, Aaron and Marlies and three grandchildren.

As for me, I loved my high school years and made plenty of friends. I especially enjoyed watching my brother Peter play ball and put my heart and soul into cheering him on for every game. In fact, I was chosen by the student body to cheer on the varsity team all four of my high school years. Naples High School had never before chosen a student to cheer varsity in their freshman year so as you can imagine, it was not only an honor but a privilege to say the least. I also loved to play soccer and was surprisingly good at it too. I guess in a way, I just loved being a kid and having good friends.

Following graduation, I never went on to college. It's not that I didn't think about going it's just that I felt it was more important to start working right out of high school so I could help my parents financially. But it could have also been the fact that I never wanted to be more than just a short ride away from Mama and Papa. I found a job in the electronics department at Taylor Instruments Co. in Rochester, N.Y., where I met Dominick DiFante. Dominick became a Police Officer with the Rochester Police Department and we married in 1958. We settled down and purchased a home on Clay Avenue in the city and later moved to the suburbs. Dominick and I have four children together, Kathy, Tony, David and Tommy. When the kids were young they loved traveling to see their grandparents in Naples and spent plenty of summer days fishing or walking in the hills with Mama. As time passed my children also moved on with their own lives and blessed us with ten wonderful grandchildren that

I love so very much. Dominick and I are still married and have been together now for 53 years.

Mama and Papa lovingly remained together in their tiny castle for 27 years until Papa passed away on December 15th, 1973 at the age of 83. Buried in a cemetery high in the hills of Naples, Papa will forever be overlooking the vineyards of the small town he loved so much.

After his passing, we sold our little house at One Main Street that meant so much; it was no longer the same for Mama. Without Papa's helping hand, it was just too much for her, and she was all too lonely without him. At the time Peter and I lived in New York but Johnny and Joe resided in California. Mama made the decision to move to California and live with my younger brothers, where the weather was warm, and the winters were much kinder to her. I was only fortunate enough to visit her three times during the fifteen years she lived in California. On my third trip, January 9, 1988, God took her to live with him. She was 83 years old. I brought her home for final resting alongside Papa. Shortly after as I went through her belongings, I found a letter in her Bible. It must have meant a lot to her because she kept it safe for so long. I still can't bring myself to read the words I had written so many years ago, without shedding tears.

Letter to Mama

October 17, 1977
Dear Mama,

I just got home from taking the kids to school, so this is a good time to send you a letter and tell you a few things that I may have forgotten to tell you before.

I know you must have had a good trip, because I called on all the help in heaven to go with you. I'm sure they did, because I also asked them to help me when it came time to see you go. It was something I did not think I could do. I think it was the hardest thing I have ever had to do. I remember telling you when you came back from Germany so many years ago, that I would never let you go away from me again. But I guess we never know what life has waiting for us. It's just something I will have to learn to get used to.

Mama, I know there are so many things I did not thank you for. So I will try and remember them. Thanks for all the little gifts, like the pictures, the clock, and your sewing machine that you spent so much time working on for all of us. Thanks for all the clothes that you made for me on that machine. Thanks for the beds and the plastic bags. Thanks for the kuchen you baked and all of those apple pies. Thanks for always having a chair at your table ready anytime we came home. Thanks for the fruit and vegetables from your garden. Thanks for giving me Papa as a father. Thanks for my grandparents and my chance to have gone to see and know them all. Thanks for your brothers and sisters. Thanks for making all of us walk a straight line all the time. Thanks for all the things you told me about God. Thanks for every prayer you ever said for me. Thanks for all the good times as there were so many of them. Thanks for my brothers. Thanks for all the songs we have sung together. Thanks for all the times we have laughed. Thanks for all the beautiful Christmases. Thanks for the old house. Thanks for the many jars of jelly. Thanks for all the socks and pants you fixed for the kids. Thanks for the way you made spinach. Thanks for all the words of encouragement. Thanks for being a nurse when I didn't feel good. Thanks for all those trips to the hospital in Germany. Thanks for saving my arm. Thanks for taking me home when I lived with Papa's sister. Thanks for making my children love you so very much. Thanks for all the times you took care of my kids for me. Thanks for always having faith in me. Thanks for teaching me to have courage. Thanks for teaching me how to work. Thanks for teaching me how to get along with others. Thanks for teaching us about love for each other and the people around us. Thanks for the constant peace in our house. I don't know of anyone who has ever done so much for so many so often with so little. You gave us all the good things in life. We never had much money, but I think we were the richest kids that ever walked the face of the earth. It's because we have you. God gave us the very best when he gave you to us. For this, I will always thank him. May he always keep you in his very special care.

Mama these are a few things I wanted to thank you for. They are all the things I feel in my heart. I wanted to tell you all this when you were here, but words like these could not make it past the pain in my chest. When they talk about people with broken hearts, I know just how they feel. Mine broke yesterday; I wonder if I can ever get used to the thought of you not being just a short ride away from me. Today is not any easier than yesterday, but I hope that tomorrow will be a little better. I know I will make it; it just takes time, and I know it's going to be so very hard.

I hope this letter does not make you feel sad. It is not meant to do that. I only wanted to let you know how much I love you, and that all I want for you is happiness and all the good things in the world. I am so very proud of you and to be one of a family who had the honor of being loved by a great lady like you. Thanks, Mama, for being my beautiful mother, and thank-you most of all for your constant and unselfish love. For this, I will always be so grateful and satisfied. I will thank God everyday for giving me the greatest gift he ever gave to anyone. That gift was you, and I only hope that I can be just half the mother to my children that you have been to me. I should have no problems, because I have had the best teacher.

Mama, when you step out into the sunshine in California, think about me, because it is a smile that God is sending to you from me. Each time you see a star, think about me. It is a sign of a thank-you and a kiss just for you, just from me. Don't worry about the rain, a raindrop is not a tear, I am not going to cry anymore. Best of luck to you, Mama; I am going to be alright. I am only going to miss you on the days that end in Y.

Give all my love to Johnny and Joe. I hope they will make you very happy, but if they do not, then come back home to me. If I can't give you anything else, I will give you a home and all the love in my heart. Better days are coming, Mama; I just know they are, and they will all be just for you.

I love you very much,
Marlies

Angels that Graced My Life

I walked through hell, that's undeniable—but not without the help of angels. I'd like to honor all of the angels who made it possible for me to find the strength to make it through each day. I may not have recognized them as angels then, but I surely do today. They made life for me a small piece of heaven.

Oma

Opa

Uncle Matthew

Uncle Bernard

Uncle Peter

Uncle Nicholas

Uncle Joseph

Aunt Clara

Aunt Mary

Aunt Ann

Aunt Rose

Aunt Ida

Uncle Johann, for his suffering, which brought all of my uncles safely home from the war.

Vazil, who helped Oma after Opa passed, before disappearing, never to be heard from again.

Mrs. Adams and the doctor who took care of me in Holtztum when I had no one else.

Especially my cow, Kushen that became my best friend! She gave me comfort when no one else did.

Agnes and her family, who helped us after our home was burned in the bombing.

The three German soldiers who gave us blessings to prevent starvation.

The American soldiers who were so kind to us in Germany.

Mrs. Stewart and her daughter, who took care of me on my journey across the ocean.

Mr. and Mrs. Boesel, who took us in our first day in America.

Mr. and Mrs. Blier, who took us in our first day in Naples.

Mr. and Mrs. Hartman, who gave me a home.

Mr. and Mrs. Wamp, who gave Johnny a home.

Mr. and Mrs. Blier, who gave Peter a home.

The landlady who gave Papa a place to live when he had no money.

The Baaders, who gave me a home on Rhine Street when I was so lonely.

Mr. Parsons, who gave our entire family a home when Mama returned.

Mrs. Whiley, who gave us the money for our mortgage down payment.

My friend Joanie, who was there for me.

My brothers, Peter, Johnny, and Joe—I would give my life for them.

My father, whom I loved so very much.

Most important, Mama, who was the greatest angel. She was a gift from God, never angry or upset with anything. She always trusted in God. She made a promise that if she made it back to our family safely then she would go to mass every single day, and she did. She never missed a day, until the day she died at the age of 83. She was gentle, kind, and always wore a smile on her face. She gave us hope and the courage to believe that tomorrow would be a better day. She was hardworking and talented. She was the best cook, baker, seamstress, and housekeeper. She was filled with laughter, and gentle with the animals, and she always had a kind word to say about everyone. She gave us everything we needed to grow up and become responsible, decent human beings. Our home was peaceful, and she kept it that way. Mama never once gave up hope, and she based her entire life on the belief that you have to trust in God. She was truly my angel. And even with all of the horrific things that I have lived through, I still believe I am more blessed than anyone, because God chose me to be her daughter.

Afterword

This is my family; my life, and for all of this I thank God. I thank America for all of the wonderful things that have been bestowed upon me, as this is where my dreams became reality. I thank the Hitler regime for only one thing; calling me a dirty Ammie. I once hated that name because I did not understand what it meant. But, I understand now and I am proud to be an Ammie.

I have learned from my experiences that no matter what happens in life there is always a way. If you have love and an understanding that out of all the bad, there will always be an abundance of good as long as you have faith in God.

I have also learned that you need to forgive those that have offended you. Anger will never grant you peace. I know the anger I carried inside for all the things that happened to me when I lived with Aunt Lena would never end unless I found it in my heart to forgive her. It took me more than sixty years, but somewhere, deep inside, I found the strength to do just that. I am now finally at peace with what happened to me so many years ago and I pray for her soul every day.

I want to thank my daughter-in-law Ann Marie for taking the relentless time and effort to put my life down on paper. She is very special to me.

I would also like to thank all of the service men and women who put their lives in harms way for our country and especially those who risked and gave their lives to free us from the evils of the Hitler regime.

Marlies DiFante

Afterword

To those who suffer hardships each and every day, it is possible to face adversity, and in the end emerge a stronger, merciful, generous, kindhearted, loving, hardworking, spiritual, and humane human being. I know this to be true. I have witnessed it first hand. Having been given the privilege of writing my mother-in-law Marlies Adams DiFante's memoir, I have come to understand the sheer scope of magnificence that surrounds her.

She was a child who experienced and witnessed some of life's most atrocious acts, and still managed to evolve into a beautiful human being, both inside and out, while fighting each of life's challenges. Surviving seven years of Nazi rule, war, starvation, prejudice, abuse, battery, molestation, fire, and homelessness, she emerged with unwavering integrity.

During the time it took to complete her story, I have learned, through *her* experiences, to believe in dreams, to believe in miracles, and most important, to believe in God. It has been an honor for me to write her story. I only hope I told it well.

To my wonderful husband, Tony, thank you for giving me the opportunity to finish what I started. Your love and support make everything possible. To our children, Nicholas and Gianna, I love you more each day! May God bless you always.

Ann Marie DiFante

Made in the USA
Middletown, DE
21 August 2018